Pat MacLean

Pat MacLean's writing career has spanned 35 years during which time she won numerous journalism awards. In 1998 she was honoured with the coveted Harvey Southam Editorial Career Award. In this book she shares her personal experiences selling homes, both with and without the aid of real estate agents. She is unwavering in her conviction that every homeowner selling a house can save thousands of dollars with the for-sale-by-owner concept using the steps she so clearly defines in this book. Pat's keen observations (sometimes brutal, sometimes humorous) of the process and the real estate industry coupled with her easy, narrative writing style create a compelling read as well as a valuable tool.

4SBO INC.
Mount Albert, Ontario

The information contained in this book is not legal advice and should not be treated as a substitute for legal advice. 4SBO recommends seeking the advice of a lawyer qualified in the relevant jurisdiction in cooperation with utilizing information contained in these materials.

Printed in Canada

Contents

Chapter 1

Why you need this book

Twenty years ago, I listed my home with a real estate agent working on the team of a well-known brokerage firm. Over the first couple of weeks, there was a spattering of open houses; business cards from competing real estate offices piled up in a small basket on the kitchen counter. A few couples were shown through the house, but during the 90-day listing, we did not receive a single offer.

I knew it would not be an easy home to sell. First, it was expensive - $280,000 in 1982 was an upmarket price. It was an extraordinary home - almost 6,000 square feet overlooking three acres of ravine property including a serene pond and a gurgling waterfall. One day I was in the house while it was being shown. To my surprise and dismay, the agent never mentioned the features that made my home a pleasure to live in.

Stranger at the door

Then something happened that triggered the idea of selling the house myself. The doorbell rang; I wasn't expecting company so peered out to see a meticulous black Mercedes parked in the driveway. Standing on the welcome mat was a middle-aged, well-dressed couple. I assumed they were lost and needed directions.

"Hello, we're the Crispins," smiled the woman, extending a hand. I shook her hand but could not conceal my confusion. I didn't know any Crispins. "We were supposed to meet the real estate agent here at 3:00 p.m.," offered the husband. "I'm sorry we're a bit early."

Ah ha! They were here to see the house. The agent had not advised me of a booking. I regained my composure, hastily invited them in and cordially took their coats.

What should I do next? Two polite strangers were awkwardly standing in my home awaiting my next move. What was the protocol? Should I walk them through the house myself? Should I stand and chat with them in the large foyer? Should I usher them to comfortable seats in the living room and leave them alone? Should I casually invite them into the kitchen for a cup of coffee? I was flummoxed!

Chicken Little to the rescue

Just then, the door burst open and a young agent from the listing broker flung himself into the foyer, apologizing for being late. Herding the potential buyers like a mother hen guiding her clutch of chicks, he started down the large atrium clucking, "I haven't had time to walk through this house myself yet. Shall we go and discover it together?"

From flummoxed to flabbergasted! I couldn't believe it. This agent's brokerage firm stood to collect $16,800 on the sale. He would pocket half of that. Yet for the opportunity of earning $8,400, he couldn't motivate himself to preview the home, or get organized enough to advise me of the booking. If that seems like a lot of money today, reflect on what you could have bought with that much jingle in your pockets in 1982. For $8,000 you could drive a new, imported compact car off the lot.

As much as I liked the Crispins, I prayed they wouldn't buy our home. That agent simply didn't deserve to earn the money. Either God listened to me, or our house didn't suit their needs; they did not present an offer.

The listing contract expired and our agent returned to re-list the home for another three months. She suggested we reduce the price - even though it was listed at the price she had originally said it would sell for.

"If price is the problem," I mused aloud, "why haven't we seen even one offer at below the asking price in the last three months?" She had no answers. I had no confidence that this realtor or any other could sell our unique home. It was time to be brave, to take a stand.

Goodbye agent, hello 4SBO

"We would like to try selling the house ourselves for one month," I ventured. "Of course, if anyone buys it that you or any other agent introduced to the property, we will pay the full commission." As she left, I asked her to please take her sign along. I didn't want potential buyers to wonder why we had planted a real estate sign on the lawn if our home was for sale by owner (4SBO).

In retrospect, I did a lot of things wrong. I didn't run a photo of our house with the ad. I didn't put any signs on the property. But I did write a good ad. It was not high pressure. It simply and clearly detailed all the special features about our home that had appealed to us in the first place. It was written to intrigue that special person who could appreciate the lifestyle it afforded. You'll find more about the ad in Chapter 8.

We tested the ad for one Saturday in Toronto's Globe And Mail. To give ourselves a bit of wriggle room for negotiating, we priced our home at $285,000. That was another mistake, as you'll see in a later chapter, but I didn't have the advantage of reading a book like this in those days!

Six nibbles, three bites

Six people responded to the ad by telephone. Four made appointments to see the house, all within two days. Two of the four couples came back two days later, inspected the house again and drew up their offers using forms we had picked up at a bookstore. A third couple returned with an offer their lawyer had drawn up.

One offer was for exactly what we were asking – $285,000, but it had a number of messy clauses and was conditional on the sale of their home. They argued and bickered constantly as we showed them through the house. This raised concerns that they would be difficult to deal with in future negotiations, so we agreed to pass on that one. The second was a low-ball offer of $270,000. We ignored it. The third offer was for $280,000 with no conditions. Bingo!

You can do it too

Selling your home yourself isn't difficult. Who knows its key features better than you? An agent can point out the gleaming hardwood floors and the recently remodelled kitchen. You can add more personal details such as how cozy it is with the family gathered around the fireplace during a fierce winter storm, how solid and safe it is and how good the neighbourhood is for raising children. You can convey the quality of life a buyer will experience when he holds the keys to this home.

Buying a home is not based solely on filling people's needs; it's also about satisfying their wants. Yes, location is important and the price has to fit into their budget. But I have observed that many individuals will drive further or push their financing to the limit if features of a house spark their desire. In their minds, it rises to a "must have" status.

Where do you start?

What are the prerequisites to selling your own home? What should you be prepared to do yourself and what can you find professional help with? You will have to bring your home up to a gleaming, market-ready condition. But you should do that even if a realtor is listing it. Here are the extra steps you will have to handle that an agent would normally do for you at an excessive fee:

- Determine a market price
- Put up for sale signs
- Advertise
- Book appointments
- Show strangers through your home
- Negotiate with a prospective buyer
- Fill out the offer-to-purchase form
- Close the deal

Expert help is available at reasonable rates for anything on that list that requires specialized knowledge or skill. From making the signs to pounding them into the lawn to pricing your home to closing the sale, help is as close as your telephone book. In this book you will find out how to select the best real estate lawyer. He will be invaluable to a 4SBO

Let's be realistic – selling real estate is not brain surgery. You've seen those real estate ads with rows of beaming agents. Don't they look as average as your aunt? And in all likelihood, most probably have no more formal education than you. It is not difficult to become a registered sales person. You can even sign up for courses on the Internet and as long as you successfully complete three phases with a 75% average within 18 months, you're deemed ready to join a real estate brokerage firm.

In the chapters that follow, you will find the information you need to confidently handle each step you need to sell your home by yourself. You will learn how to become more professional and more trusted than those realtors who provide sloppy work to their clients.

Best of all, you can improve the odds of selling your home quickly and saving thousands of dollars in commissions, just as I did.

That's why you need this book!

Chapter 2

Save money, sell quickly

By cutting out the middleman, you save the commissions the real estate agent would siphon off the proceeds. You can either keep this money, or apply some of it to reduce the price of your home. Buyers recognize and respond to a legitimate bargain.

Just how much money can you save by selling your home without an agent? While real estate commissions have been known to soar as high as ten per cent in remote areas such as Ontario's cottage country, six per cent is traditionally the standard in Canada. The following table tracks what you would hand over to a real estate broker who charges six per cent, depending on the value of your property.

Owners of lower-priced homes often carry more debt in relation to the value of their home, than those with expensive homes. It is not unheard of for a person to sell a home and end up deeper in arrears by the time she pays closing costs and real estate fees. She can't afford that $6,000 real estate fee, but a real estate broker doesn't care about her financial difficulties, nor should she. The homeowner will logically assume the agent is working for her, but in reality, she's working for herself. You'll read more about that in Chapter 4.

What can You Save?

House value	Commission
$100,000	$6,000
120,000	7,200
140,000	8,400
160,000	9,600
180,000	10,800
200,000	12,000
220,000	13,200
250,000	15,000
275,000	16,500
300,000	18,000
320,000	19,200
350,000	21,000
375,000	22,500
400,000	24,000
425,000	25,500
450,000	27,000
475,000	28,500
500,000	30,000
525,000	31,500
550,000	33,000
575,000	34,500
600,000	36,000
650,000	39,000
700,000	42,000
750,000	45,000
800,000	48,000
850,000	51,000
900,000	54,000
950,000	57,000
1,000,000	60,000
1,300,000	78,000

Appraisal fees collected by realtors working on a 6% commission

It's a generally accepted rule of thumb that the average Canadian moves every three to five years. If you are one of those average Canadians and you sold six homes over a 30-year period, at an average price of $175,000, you would have banked $63,000 by not going through a realtor. Tax free dollars! In most instances, the capital gains tax is not applied to profits from the sale of your principal residence.

A quick look at the table showing the commissions earned explains the appeal of selling homes as a way to earn a living. Some agents specialize in carriage trade homes. Wouldn't you, if you could earn $120,000 in commissions by closing a sale on a two million dollar home? Even if you had to split the fee with a broker, one sale a year would bring an income that exceeds the annual wages of an average worker toiling for 40 hours a week. Few small towns in Canada boast million dollar homes, but in large urban areas, such a bonanza is there for the taking.

Time or money?

Before you start making a list of how you'll spend all the money you can save by using the 4SBO method, consider your primary goal. Is it to make money or is it to sell the house as quickly as possible?

If time is the critical factor, you can speed up the sale by applying some of or the entire windfall to reduce the asking price of your home. By offering your residence at a lower price than its true market value, you will attract more potential buyers, which should logically translate into a faster sale.

House hunters have a well-honed sense of house prices. Many have put in weeks of comparison-shopping before they arrive to view your home.

They are savvy enough to recognize a good deal when they find it - and everyone loves a bargain. By not having to pay the agent's commission, you can give the buyer a discount and still come out dollars ahead.

Chapter 3

Big pay for little service

You list with a real estate agent on the assumption she will work for you, right? Well, maybe yes and maybe no. A close friend of mine, Pat Gibb of Uxbridge, Ontario, learned the truth the hard way.

She approached three major real estate firms to evaluate her property and suggest a listing price. They came back to her with prices ranging from $699,000 to $799,000. For an appalling example of how an agent might not work for you, read Pat's story:

"The house was built in 1886. After buying it, we completely gutted and remodelled it. The property was unique comprising over 10 acres of professionally landscaped land and a one-acre pond. I insisted they were undervaluing the property and told the agents I would not sell the house for less than $999,000. They all told me I was being greedy and that it simply wouldn't sell at that price.

"One of the firms agreed to list it at my price. The agent promised they would feature our home in a deluxe, four-colour brochure and would place ads in all the major newspapers. In the first 45 days, they ran one small ad in the local paper. It produced no showings.

"I contacted the agent who reminded me that the listing price was too high. In her mind, the fact there had been no showings was proof the asking price was not realistic. The firm said it would not run any more ads until I reduced the price. You can imagine my frustration, and I was stuck with a 90-day contract. All the real estate company had done for me was to stick a large sign on the front lawn. That probably cost them no more than a couple of hundred dollars.

Just wait, the price will drop

"One Sunday afternoon, the doorbell rang. I opened the door to find a couple and their two adult children. They had been driving by, liked the look of the house and wondered of they could view the property.

"I pointed out that they would have to contact the listing agent to set up an appointment. They replied that they had tried this and were advised that the property was overpriced. "Wait a couple of weeks," they were told, "the price will be adjusted." This infuriated me. Who did this agent and company think they were working for? Obviously, it was not for me.

"Upon hearing that, I decided to invite the people in and show them the house myself. I proudly pointed out its unique features and the quality of all the upgrades that we had poured into the renovation. Then we went outside and walked the property. They were visibly impressed. "Can we come back tomorrow?" they asked. We set up an appointment for the following morning.

"When they left, I immediately called the real estate agent and told her about the people who had just seen the house and let her know what time they were coming back the next morning. She was at her cottage and would not be available for the showing. "You know the house better than I do," she suggested. "Go ahead and show it to them and if they want to make an offer, have them call me."

Easy money, hard lesson

"During the second visit, the family expressed their interest in buying the house. I confirmed that I would not take less than $990,000. They wanted to deal directly with me, hoping to shave more off the price by saving on the real estate commission. I explained that I had signed a contract and unfortunately had no alternative but to pay the commission. We shook hands on the price of $990,000.

"For a commission of nearly $60,000, the real estate agent figured it was worth scurrying back from her cottage to write up and present the offer. The deal closed and I ended up handing over to the agent precisely $59,940 for the service of posting a $200 sign on my lawn. That was an expensive lesson, in how not to sell your home. Trust me, I learned!"

It is not fair to assume that one agent and a single episode are representative of the whole real estate industry. There are thousands, of honest, hard working, people in the business. But in pursuit of a listing or a closing, some turn a blind eye to what they were taught about ethics in their real estate class.

Just as for a sales person in any other line of work, closing a deal is paramount to a real estate agent. That message is repeatedly confirmed in courses, books, audiotapes and seminars. Are you ready for another true story? This one illustrates a tactic used by an agent to secure a signature on an offer.

Closing under duress

We had bought a new home, and sold the house we were living in before closing, but we had not been able to sell the adjoining lot. We were counting on money from that lot to cover the massive mortgage we required for the new house. In order to close, bridge financing filled the gap.

Because of the financial constraints, we opted to forego the luxury of a moving van, relying instead on a rented truck and a lot of help from our friends. All of the furniture was carried out to the lawn while we figured out how best to load it into the truck.

In the midst of the commotion, the listing agent telephoned, insisting we come to the office immediately so she could present an offer. The skies were growing blacker by the minute and thunder was rumbling in the distance. We were torn between risking water damage to our furniture or losing a possible buyer.

Suspicious minds

The agent knew it was our moving day, and she also realized we were desperate to sell. After much wringing of hands and apologies, we left our friends to continue filling the truck while we drove to the agent's office. There sat a couple we recognized – they had measured off the lot more than once. They had their offer in hand, an offer so low they should have been embarrassed to sign it. To make matters worse, we both harboured a nagging suspicion that the agent had explained our financial crunch to them and had suggested they sit on the fence until moving day when we just might be desperate enough to accept anything.

We quickly scanned the offer. Then, in what I still consider one of my finer moments, I threw an evil eye in the direction of the agent and dramatically tore the offer to shreds. The horrified agent cried, "What are you doing? That is a legal document!" It was too late. As the pieces floated to the table, we strode out tight-lipped and returned to the furniture waiting on the lawn.

Agent versus broker

I'll take a minute at this point to explain in simple terms how the real estate agent and the broker divvy up responsibilities and the commission from a sale. The broker is a licensed agent who heads up the office and may own the business. He hires or appoints the agents and provides them with office space, support staff, promotional material, supplies and an advertising budget. In exchange, agents hand over as much as half of their commissions.

For purposes here, I'll use a fictitious agent named Susan. Her goal is to sign up as many listings as possible for her broker's agency and to find buyers for homes listed not only with her broker but also with competing real estate companies. For those listed with her broker, the full 6% commission flows into her firm and she keeps half of it. If an agent for another broker nabs the sale, Susan's broker receives 3% of the sale; Susan earns half of that, or 1½ %. Once you realize how the system works, you can understand the effort agents expend finding homes to list. The broker with the listing is guaranteed half of the commission, no matter who sells the home. A multitude of listings is money in the bank.

Statistics Canada reports that in 2001, there were almost 12 million households in Canada, of which 65% owned their dwelling. This translates into a pool of

7,800,000 homes that could be in and out of the resale market at any time. There is no shortage of real estate agents because it's relatively simple to qualify for a licence; there's abundant business and in good economic times, there's serious money to be made.

If the most important feature for a home is location, location, location, for a real estate agent, it should be service, service, service. If by the end of this book you decide you aren't cut out for the 4SBO system, you will need to list with a realtor. Tips on how to select an agent who will give you the service you deserve are in Chapter 15.

Chapter 4

Build trust, give value

The majority of real estate agents are honest and reputable, but unfortunately, those who do not deliver what is expected of them have tainted the industry's image. Your goal, is to convince potential buyers that you are above realtor ploys they may have experienced or heard about.

When you make the commitment to sell your house by yourself you will be more successful in finding a buyer and realizing the price you want by doing three things:

- Establish your integrity
- Provide qualified, unbiased information about the condition of your home so they are assured you are not trying to unload a lemon
- Build in added value give them free bonuses they will seldom receive from a realtor

Before I explore these points, let's consider the types of people who will be ringing your doorbell once you have prepared your house for sale, advertised it and opened it to public inspection.

Just looking, thank you

You surely realize that not everyone viewing your home is seriously interested in buying it. Some will be "Sunday drivers" – your home is their destination of choice for a casual day's outing. They might be hunting for decorating ideas for their own home. Or they just might enjoy seeing how other people live. You have no way of knowing their intentions when they make the appointment. Even if you pre-screen every caller, no one will be naive enough to blurt out that they aren't really on the market for a new house, they just want something to do that's more interesting than schlepping through the shopping mall.

Assume that at least 80% of the people who come through will not be potential buyers, but don't let that discourage you. They may spread the word about your home to a friend who is seriously looking and there's always the chance that your home will tug at the heartstrings of a casual visitor who decides on the spot she simply has to have it. That does happen! Two years ago, my husband and I went to look at a cottage that was advertised in the newspaper, mainly out of curiosity because it was on a lake we had never heard of in an area we knew quite well. We drove in, fell in love with the lake and bought the cottage!

The price choppers

Then there's that other category of shoppers – those who never pay full price for anything and are always sniffing for a deal. You know the kind. They will haggle with the cashier at Sears, or try to wrangle a discount at Loblaws on a carton of milk three days before its expiry date. In their world, everything is negotiable.

They flock to 4SBO signs because they smell a bargain. You are saving significant money by bypassing the real estate agent, and it seems entirely logical to them that you should hand over the full benefit of that to them. Your home may not be perfect for them, but if it's a big enough bargain, they'll buy it.

How do you prove to potential buyers that you are a decent, upright person they can trust? If you try to verbally convince them that your integrity is beyond approach, you will only add to their scepticism. Three major steps that will derail the bargain hunter and accomplish the three goals listed at the beginning of this chapter are:

- Pay for an unbiased home appraisal (See Chapter 4)
- Pay for a home inspection, and
- Offer a home warranty

Check out the Inspector

Be careful who you hire to inspect your home. Do not call your buddy who turns to home inspections when he's laid off from his regular job in a brick factory, or that friend of your son-in-law, or a small outfit with no reputation that might give you a cheaper price.

If you live in the wired world, you can search www.cahi.com, the Web site for The Canadian Association of Home and Property Inspectors (CAHPI). Here you'll find listings of registered home and property inspectors for every province. You can also reach the head office in Brighton, Ont. through a toll-free number 1-888-748-2244.

If no one is listed in your area, look in your local yellow pages or ask friends or your real estate lawyer for referrals. Always insist on checking qualifications before you authorize anyone to start poking about in your house.

This industry is not regulated - many practising home inspectors are not licensed. To ensure the inspector you hire has performed an acceptable number of inspections plus written exams, you'll want to know if he belongs to CAHPI. An inspector, who is a member of one of its provincial chapters, has had to pass specific set standards to be registered.

You'll want to conduct an interview with whomever you plan to hire as a home inspector. If he doesn't have the right credentials, you could end up paying for a worthless inspection or worse, having damage done to your home. This is a serious undertaking. Don't hand it to an incompetent person.

On the following page are the questions to ask. Please photocopy and use for your interviews.

Home Inspector Interview

1. Are you a member in good standing of CAHPI?
2. Which of the following registrations do you hold that are recognized in this province? Check all that apply.

   ☐ Professional Engineer
   ☐ Certified Engineering Technologist/Technician
   ☐ Registered Architect
   ☐ Certified Architectural Technologist/Technician
   ☐ Provincial Certificate of Qualification as:
      ☐ Electrician
      ☐ Plumber
      ☐ Carpenter
      ☐ Gas Fitter
      ☐ Other Certified construction trade. Specify ________
   ☐ Certified Building Code Official
   ☐ Ontario New Home Warranty Builder, for how long? _____

3. How many additional courses have you completed beyond those required for the above certification? What were they?
4. Please indicate your level of practical experience:

   ☐ Have completed 200 home inspections during your career.
   ☐ Have worked as a home inspector for at least two years and have completed 150 home inspections.
   ☐ Have worked in the home inspection field for at least two years and have completed 100 home inspections.
   ☐ Other. Specify. ______________________________

5. Do you do this full-time or do you have another job? Specify.
6. How many homes have you inspected in the last six weeks?
7. Do you have a list I can call for references? ☐ Yes ☐ No
8. Have you had legal action brought against you for damage you caused to a house during an inspection? ☐ Yes ☐ No
9. Do you have liability insurance? If yes, for how much? _______
10. Do you provide a written report and certificate?
11. What do you charge for a full inspection? $__________

When you have selected the most capable home inspector in your area, contract him to probe the inner workings and outer structure of your home from top to bottom. On his list will be your plumbing, your electrical, your heating and air conditioning, the rafters the insulation, the roof, the basement, the foundation, the windows, the doors and the garage.

The home inspection fee is set by the independent contractor and in Canada ranges from $250 to $600, depending where you live and the complexity of your property.

What - me pay?

You might be scratching your head at this point. Why should you, the seller, pay for a home inspection, when everyone knows that the buyer traditionally shoulders this cost? Here are three good reasons:

- First, you want to be proactive. Aren't you at an advantage if you discover problems with your home **before** the buyer presents an offer conditional on a home inspection? You can fix up any deficiencies that the inspector finds as part of the exercise in getting your house ready for the market. Defects that show up after a conditional offer to purchase has been signed can lead to acrimonious discussions about who should pay for the repairs and how they should be done. You risk having to lower your price or potentially losing the sale.
- Second, when a buyer comes to view your home, you hand him the home inspection report, along with copies of work orders and receipts proving

you have fixed everything. Imagine the impact! This one act establishes you as an honest person selling a reliable home.

- And third, the inspection is part of your arsenal to quell a potential buyer's appeal for a deep discount. If a bargain hunter starts whinging about the price, you firmly point out that you have saved him the expense of the home inspection, you have paid for an appraisal, which proves the house is priced at fair market value, and you are offering a home warranty. By adding value, the buyer wins some bonuses and you hold firm control of the negotiations.

Guarantee the goods

Providing a free Home Warranty is another measure that adds value for your buyer and boosts your credibility, but won't cost you a penny until you have a firm sale. For about $230, you can insure the inside plumbing, electrical, and heating systems as well as most of your appliances and the garage door opener for one year. Excluded items include central air conditioning, the refrigerator, washer and dryer. Unirisc provides this coverage in Canada. Learn more through its Web site www.unirisc.ca or by the following toll-free number 1-800-461-5048.

Some Canadian real estate agents have started to offer home warranties in recent years as a reward for the buyer. It's actually more than that. It protects the real estate firm from legal action if the seller fails to disclose a known problem with the home and the disgruntled buyer goes after the realty firm.

In many of the states in the USA, full disclosure is law. The law in Canada, at the time of writing, is caveat emptor

– buyer beware. Despite that, wisdom dictates that you put everything on the table that you know is wrong with your home. If the inspector did not find a problem with the water heater, but you have noticed it's erratic, mention it. If the basement flooded once, a few years ago during a severe storm with wild winds blowing from the west, but you have never been able to pinpoint the problem and it has never recurred, tell him. Just when you least expect it, those conditions might be repeated. Imagine the buyer's reaction if, during the final inspection before closing, there's an inch of water in the basement. There is less risk of this disrupting the smooth path to closing if you entrust him with the information in advance.

Chapter 5

How to price your home

It's human nature for owners to harbour an overblown opinion about the value of their possessions, be it a child's outgrown bicycle or a used automobile. Nowhere is this more apparent than in what the homeowner thinks his property is worth.

If you have decided to join the rapidly expanding 4SBO ranks, you have probably kept track of homes selling on your street or in your area. Those that have sold at close to or higher than what you believe yours is worth are the ones you will pay heed to. You will dismiss any that sold for less. You can always find a reason why yours deserves to fetch a higher price. And you are probably also guilty of overlooking the extra features of a home that sold at top price – things like a swimming pool that yours doesn't have or a lot with twice as much frontage.

You might also be guilty of overestimating the value of the upgrades you put in your house. Top-of-the-line carpet will not return what you invested in it. Kitchens and bathrooms are usually worth upgrading; they add considerable value to your home, but only within reason. If you install a $50,000 kitchen in a $200,000 home, you will not have a $250,000 home. Your home may sell faster and you will net more for it than if you did nothing in the kitchen, but don't expect it to automatically jump the price by the equivalent value.

Setting market value

How can you realistically calculate what your home will sell for? Something that will have an impact and over which you have no control is the market. If interest rates have leapt to restrictive heights and people can't afford to remortgage at the higher rate, the market will be swamped with homes and prices will be low. You'll be caught in the disparity of a buyer's market.

Barring that, there are three ways to evaluate your home. One is to call in three local real estate agents. Tell them you plan to list your home as a 4SBO, and ask if they will help you determine a listing price. Why would they want to do this when they won't be earning a commission on the sale? Most agents believe that individual homeowners have a remote chance of selling their own home. They assume that after a few months have passed and you haven't been successful, you'll be knocking on their door to list.

By asking three to give you a quote, you keep them honest. It is not beyond credibility that an agent would bring you an unrealistically high number knowing if you price it for that, you'll never get an offer, your house won't sell, and you will come back to them with the listing. There is less chance of this happening if you approach three from different agencies to do the appraisal.

Compare other homes

An alternative system requires immense effort on your part and may end up being a total waste of time. I'm talking about a comparative market analysis. That sounds very official and definitive, but to my mind, it's about as accurate as putting 10 prices in a hat, tossing them up in the air and picking the first one that hits the floor. However, since it's a process often used by the real estate industry, I'll tell you how to go about it. Then I'll explain why I don't think it's worth the work.

As its name suggests, it's a system to compare homes similar to yours that are currently on the market or that were sold in the past six months. You don't want to consider anything that sold outside that time frame because the price may not reflect current market conditions.

To do the analysis, you visit a minimum of three and as many as five homes that are for sale or sold recently in your area, or in an area similar to yours. Take notepad and pen with you and record attributes of each home that yours doesn't have and features yours has that they lack. It is important to write this down – don't rely on your memory. After you have been through a few homes, it's easy to be confused about which house had what when you return to your domain.

Record the listing price. For homes that sold within six months, contact the listing realtor and find out what they sold for and what their features were.

Once you have the information on all eligible properties, draw up a master chart on graph paper. Down the side you list all the basic information such as age of house, location, square footage, lot size, number of bedrooms, number of bathrooms, type of floor covering, finished basement, size of garage, and as many other features such as central vacuum, built-in dishwasher, fenced yard as are applicable. Your bottom three rows will read *Price*, *Value Added* and *Value Subtracted*.

Across the top, mark off one column per home and insert the addresses of the houses you are comparing. Then for each home, go down the list and check off what it offers and record the asking or sold price. The last two rows are the tricky ones because you have to “guesstimate” how much more or less that home is worth than yours based on its features, condition and location. If it’s less than yours, you fill in the Value Subtracted row. It it’s more, you fill in the Added Value row. How much more or less? That’s up to your discretion.

When you have completed this chart, you are ready to calculate that magic number – the price tag you should supposedly affix to your home. Start with a separate piece of paper. As on your master chart, allocate one column per house across the top. Down the sides you insert the information from the last three rows on your chart: *Price*, *Value Added* and *Value Subtracted*. For each property, there will be two numbers, the price and either a plus number for homes that have more features than yours or a minus number for those that offer fewer features or are in worse shape than yours. Your last row is labelled *Comparative Value*.

Fill in the appropriate numbers and do the math, either adding or subtracting to determine the comparative value of each house. Then add up all of the sold or listed prices and divide by the number of homes in the study to arrive at the average sales price. Next add up the figures in the Comparative Value column, and divide by the number of homes to reach the average comparative value.

According to experts who believe in the system, this is an accurate reflection of what your home is worth. But is it?

Tedious and flawed

Much of the information is not reliable. For example, shouldn't you consider the difference in listing price over actual sales price for the homes you are comparing? No one can predict with any certainty what that home four blocks away will sell for. And how unbiased can you, the owner, be when estimating how much more or less a stranger's home is compared to yours?

The system is not a straightforward process of evaluating two homes built in the same year with identical floor plans on the same street on comparable size lots, finished with the same quality of materials. Only under those conditions would I put much stock in a comparative value done by a home owner extracting an accurate price. Under any other circumstances, it is simply too unscientific. As well, it's an extraordinary amount of work for such dubious results.

Had I even a modicum of faith in this system, I would have provided sample work sheets to guide you through the comparison process. You won't find them here: I am that reluctant to encourage you to take the comparative analysis route. Conserve your energy for more productive projects such as fertilizing the lawn or painting the window boxes.

The better way

There is a more accurate method – the one adopted by financial institutions to establish the amount of money they will lend to a purchaser. Plus it's simpler. All you do is hire an impartial, professional appraiser to assess the value of your home and write a cheque when he's finished

He will take two approaches when determining the market value of your home, the cost approach and the direct comparison approach. For the cost approach, he analyzes the value of your land as if it were vacant then adds in the cost of erecting a new house at current building costs. To this new value, depreciation is subtracted and extras are added – things like a garage. The direct comparison approach is similar to the comparative market analysis in which other properties similar to yours that have sold are compared to your home and a value determined. If all things are equal, the results of the two approaches should be very close. If there is a discrepancy, the appraiser will apply his professional expertise to arrive at the most realistic value for your home.

Ouch, more money out of your pocket. I can just hear all the husbands complaining at this point! But we're not talking thousands of dollars. An appraisal fee can range from $200 to $400 and is money wisely spent. As a 4SBO seller, having a certified appraiser value your home ranks up there with providing a home inspection. You erase a potential buyer's worry that he's paying too much and you cement his confidence in your integrity.

There is another more tangible benefit to having your home appraised professionally before you settle on an asking price. Consider this scenario. You advertise your home at what you believe it is worth and find a buyer who writes up an offer. Then he tries to arrange financing and discovers that the mortgage company will only lend him money based on a price below what he has offered – the price set by its appraiser. Now an ugly scene unfolds. He will either walk away from the deal because his offer was conditional on being able to get the financing or he will angrily demand a lower price – accusing you of duping him. Isn't the appraisal fee a paltry price to pay to ensure you are not caught in this situation?

The low-ball appraisal

You'll want to be aware of an appraisal pitfall and how to deal with it. Appraisers often deliver a price below what the homeowner believes, or even knows, her home is worth. They have to be cautious to avoid a potential legal suit by quoting an unrealistically high figure. The lender could hold the appraiser liable if the mortgagee defaults and the lender can't sell the house for enough to recoup the mortgage money still owing.

There are two things you can do to ensure the appraiser comes in at a realistic price for your home. First, join him as he walks through your home and point out unique features and upgrades that you believe make your property special. Don't be shy. The more you can tell him, the more he'll know about your property and the more accurate he can be.

Second, if he still comes in with what you honestly feel is an unacceptable number, ask him to review his findings with you. How did he price your home, compared to others on the market? Tour those houses yourself to confirm he rated your home accurately. If he missed something significant, let him know.

This exercise is worth doing because if your home is going to be appraised at a lower price than what you intend to list it for, it's better to find out now when you have an opportunity to do something about it rather than later when the potential buyer applies for a mortgage and it's out of your hands. The banks will lend money based on the lower of the sale price or the appraisal.

The lender will not accept a professional appraisal done on behalf of a homeowner. It will use one of its authorized appraisers to repeat the process when the buyer applies for the mortgage.

Once you know the market value of your home, you should consider something else before you flash big price stickers on your ads. How fast do you want to sell? If you have lots of time and are prepared to live with maintaining your house in pristine condition for months and months, go ahead and list it at fair market value.

You will quickly discover that today's sophisticated buyer has figured out how much you are saving on the real estate commission and fully expects you to share the booty with him. Most will recognize the validity of your keeping at least half of the commission an agent would receive because you have taken on the agent's responsibilities. On top of that, you have invested money on the buyer's behalf with the inspection, the home appraisal and the home warranty.

If you are desperate to sell, you may end up passing on to the buyer most of what you saved in commissions. Don't beat yourself up over this. You sold the house quickly. Wasn't that your primary goal? If you had listed with an agent, it may have taken months longer, the price probably would have been reduced and you would have ended up pocketing even less money, as well as paying the commission.

Chapter 6

Make space and add sizzle

If you want to wring every possible dollar out of the buyer for your home, you have to work hard. Your home must look better than you've ever seen it in years.

Preparing a home for the market is best done methodically over a period of at least two months, whether you are selling it yourself or through a broker. You can do it faster in an emergency situation, but to capture the maximum price you must mobilize all the energy you can muster. It takes planning and close attention to details.

In a perfect world, you would first consider when you want to start advertising and showing your house. Timing is important. Your home should be on the market when the greatest number of people are house hunting. Families with children choose to move during the summer holidays so the offspring have an opportunity to adjust to their new surroundings and hopefully meet some new friends before they have to register for school in September. Even people without children prefer to move during spring, summer or fall when Canadian weather is most likely to co-operate. It's certainly not by coincidence that the Canadian house market traditionally opens up in the spring.

But the world is not perfect and there are many events in a lifetime that will dictate your not being able to move at a time that is most convenient or practical. Maybe your job has been transferred. Or you are going through a divorce (See Chapter 16) and assets must be sold. Or a house you have had your eye on suddenly becomes available and if you hope to buy it, you have to sell yours as quickly as possible.

Whenever you sell, here are a few basic rules you must follow to move your home quickly and profitably. The more time you have to get ready, the better the end result will be.

Chuck the clutter

First, build in space. Everyone collects clutter over the years. The longer you live in a home, the more belongings you hoard. If you are a certifiable pack rat, there are probably boxes upon boxes in the basement and in the garage. Every shelf in every closet and every drawer and cupboard is so tightly packed with items that you would never be able to find anything if you wanted to.

The day of reckoning arrives the moment you decide you would like to move. By weeding out the stuff you can live without, not only will you reduce your moving costs when you take over your new home, you will make your home more attractive to a future buyer.

When people see a home stuffed to the rafters with boxes, when they open a closet door and find clothes jammed so tightly together there isn't room for one more hanger, they react in a totally irrational manner. Psychologically they decide there is no room for their belongings in the house. "Did you see that closet, Ethel? Where would you put all your slacks and tops?" Common sense dictates that the clutter will walk out of the door when the present owners move, but the human brain doesn't work that way.

My husband and I once went through a home for sale that had a basement workshop. The man of the house refinished antique furniture in his leisure hours. Dismembered chairs, sagging sofas, three-legged tables, dressers with yawning holes where drawers used to be and countless other rickety items were piled up from floor to ceiling in that basement. Alongside this mess were boxes overflowing with woodworking tools. The real estate agent assured us the man would be taking the stuff (referred to as junk by my husband) with him. In our minds the nagging thought remained, "And what if he doesn't take it all? We will be left to deal with it." This chaos cast a pall over what was otherwise an appealing home. We walked away without making an offer.

You want visitors in your home to open a closet and find roomy shelves with only a shoebox or two on them, one neatly marked "scarves" and the other "gloves." They see space they can use and they also note that the homeowner is organized, tidy, and clean. If your home matches their needs and desires, would they want to move in? In a heartbeat!

Make a plan

Like any major project, the daunting task of downsizing should be tackled systematically, room by room. Allow at least one month to do it properly and if possible, start two months before you plan to take your home to the marketplace.

Go to the grocery store and lug home three boxes, a small, a large and a medium size one. On the largest, print with a dark marker, Rejects. The midsize one will be marked, Maybes, the smallest one, Keepers. Once again, psychology comes into play. The largest box will encourage you and other family members to toss a lot of products into it. If it were the smallest, you would be encouraged to keep too much.

The whole family should get involved in this project. Get them on side by calling a meeting during which you discuss, as a family, what your final goal is and why each member has an obligation to make tough decisions. For young children, add an incentive. Give them a dime for every item they discard. Or tell them they can keep all the proceeds from their toys and books sold at the garage sale to buy new toys for the new house.

Yes? No? Maybe?

Open every box and bag that you have stashed away and start sorting stuff into the appropriate box. Keepers will live to see another day in your home. Rejects will be turfed out, ending up at either a charity, your garage sale or in the garbage. The Maybes are in a sort of Purgatory for a time – some will join the Keepers, others the Rejects.

Once you have sorted the contents of everything in the room into those three temporary boxes, your task is to assign the Reject goods into items you can sell and items you will give away or throw out. The Maybe box is next; it will be the most difficult to address. You have to decide life or death for items you may have hung on to for many years. Unless you are planning to have them buried with you, brace yourself to be really tough. How often have you used the vase that has been out of reach on a top shelf in the kitchen for five years? Would you miss it if you never saw it again?

Room to breathe

By now, you and your family should be able to step back and appreciate the difference you have made by working together. Already your efforts have unlocked space you didn't know you had. By the time you are finished, your house could look 30% larger. You might even start developing second thoughts about moving!

Before you deposit the Keepers back into storage, go through one more time with deeper resolve. What else can you toss into the Reject box?

Repeat this process in each area of your house, moving methodically from kitchen to dining room to family room with videos, tapes and CDs, to bathrooms (how many hair dryers does one family need?) to bedroom closets and dresser drawers and finally to the basement and the attic. Nothing escapes the culling process.

Once you have conscientiously cleaned out the useless items, replace what is left in an orderly fashion and enjoy the space you have opened up. A word of caution - resist going shopping to fill those empty shelves! Learn to live and enjoy your new-found elbowroom. Assign at least one empty drawer and a large shelf in the kitchen, a shelf or drawer in each bedroom and one close to each bathroom, if not in it. Later in this chapter, you'll find out why you need these empty drawers and shelves.

Hold your garage sale at the earliest possible date, at least one month ahead of the day you plan to put your home on the market. A couple of weeks before your garage sale, call the Salvation Army or other charity that will recycle used items, and arrange a pick-up for leftover items after the sale. In major cities, these organizations schedule their collection routes in advance.

Suddenly your home and your life open up. No longer are you hostage to surplus products infringing on your living space. As well, you have helped others by either selling at bargain prices or donating things you do not use

Banish the boxes

The needless clutter has been eliminated, but you aren't done yet! Now that you are down to the absolute minimum number of boxes, evict them from your house. Why? You have a basement for storage. Can't you use it? Not until after the sale. Find a place to store boxes, toys, clothes on hangers and small pieces of furniture. Does a relative or a friend have room for them for two or three months while your home is on the market? If not, rent a room or a storage unit. The minimal cost will be well justified. With all your storage and excess goods out of the way, your home will look spacious and tidy. Your garage and your basement will be absolutely cavernous with nothing blocking the view.

You'll do this two months ahead of listing your home because once there's no mess to obstruct your view, you have a better idea of what areas need to be repaired or repainted and you'll have the opportunity to fix them.

Now it's time to pull out the ten-times magnifier and critically inspect every room. When you live in a home, you don't see it the way visitors do. Your eyes take in the big picture, accepting things that might startle a stranger. For example, you keep the toaster on top of your counter because you use it every morning. It's a shiny old chrome toaster with scratches and an ugly patch of melted plastic on the side where a bread bag drooped against it one morning. You don't notice these small details. To a stranger, that toaster makes your kitchen look shabby. But it's a good toaster. There is no need to get rid of it. Now that you have made room in your cupboards, you can stash it away after breakfast every day - at least until you move!

Train yourself to look beyond the items in the rooms and absorb the overall impact. If you are not confident you can be totally brutal in your assessment, invite a friend to walk through the house with you and to be blunt about its shortcomings. Everyone has at least one friend who thrives on the opportunity to be blunt!

Is the paint in good shape? If not, touch it up or completely repaint. How is the grout around the tiles in the kitchen and bathrooms? Are the windowsills in good repair or has condensation left mould and wood damage? When did you last have the rugs cleaned? If it's been longer than six months, send them out or have a service in. Do the hardwood floors need refinishing or polishing? Are the window coverings dirty or just plan dowdy? What do they say about your home? Invest in new bed and window coverings for each bedroom. They do not need to be expensive. They do need to look inviting and reflect the personality of the home.

This is the time to call in the home inspector. He will let you know what other projects you should tackle before listing your home.

Call in the gremlins

Now that you have freshened up the paint, cleaned carpets and draperies and done minor repairs, it's time to chase away all the grunge and dust that has collected in areas we don't usually observe too closely.

Realistically, count on needing at least two people to help you for a full day in order to cover every square inch of your home from attic to basement to garage.

Book a two- or three-person team from a professional cleaning service and before they arrive, prepare a checklist of what must be done in each room. If you are wired to the Internet, I suggest you visit two sites that will give you lots of ideas for your checklists of essential cleaning chores. They are: www.doityourself.com and www.allabouthome.com. With a list, there is less chance your team will overlook anything important. On both sites you'll pick up cleaning tips you can pass along. Not everyone from a cleaning company knows the best way to clean or the best product to use. For that matter, neither does every homeowner, and that includes me!

Both sites also give tips that make cleaning easier and faster. They are USA-based sites, but bathtub rings south of the border are no different than those in Canada.

Sticky problem solving

On these sites, you can find solutions to a vast number of elusive cleaning problems such as how to remove stickers from walls and furniture, eliminate mildew from the corners of your bathtub, get gum out of fabric or erase indelible marker doodles. You will be amazed at the cleansing magic of some everyday household products not normally associated with cleaning. Before your team arrives, you can have all the necessary products to tackle those special problem areas lined up on the kitchen counter.

Creepy crawlies in your basement? Pest control is a major topic on www.allabouthome.com. If you have carpenter ants, silverfish, gypsy moths or any one of a wide selection of disturbing intruders, search here for the recommended course of action on the site.

Now that you have an action plan – a list of "must dos" for every room, you are ready for your helpers and the fun begins. From the lights on the chandelier to the floor underneath the refrigerator, you must chase down every cobweb, fingerprint and dust ball. Wipe down walls, doors – including the top edges – windowsills and frames. Every window must be polished to sparkling perfection, inside and out. Clean screens and the tracks of sliding doors.

Scrub-a-dub-dub

Take each picture from the walls; wipe down the frame and the back and polish the glass. Wipe down light-switch plates, baseboards, Venetian blinds, the heating and air intake grill plates, and every possible item that is in the room.

The kitchen and bathrooms hold high ratings for viewer appeal. In the kitchen, remove the contents of cupboards, closets and drawers and wash every square inch. Line shelves and drawers with clean liner paper that is easy to remove. Do not use wild patterns. Plain white or soft beige is always inoffensive and unobtrusive.

Clean the inside of the refrigerator, the microwave, and the oven. Put as many small appliances including coffee grinder, electric kettle and toaster, blender, and food processor inside a cupboard or drawer. Your goal is a counter with nothing on top of it.

In the bathroom, as well as all the woodwork, scrub sinks, toilets, shower stalls and bathtubs with a product designed to clear away soap scum and hard-water residue.

Polish all furniture throughout, including head and footboards on every bed. Empty the dining room buffet or hutch, clean thoroughly, polish each item and replace neatly.

Employ all those vacuum tools that seldom see the light of day so not a single corner or remote area is missed. Vacuum out the garage. And tidy up the workbench. Are the recycling blue boxes and the disposal cans squeaky clean?

Scrub the back deck and the landing outside your front door. Scrub both sides of the doors leading into the house. Wipe down outside light fixtures; polish the number sign, the door handle and the knocker. Wipe down window boxes, flowerpots and all outdoor garden decorations.

By the time they leave, your home should be sparkling enough to pass the most rigorous inspection. Don't despair; you won't have to repeat the heavy-duty cleaning every time someone phones for an appointment. Now it will be easier to maintain it on a weekly and daily basis. With everything meticulously clean and the clutter gone, it's time to repeat your survey of each room and make another list of what remains to be fixed and updated.

The finishing touches

Leaf through a design magazine and notice what is in the rooms it features. Do you see a soap dish and mangled toothpaste tube on the counter in the bathroom? Are there make-up brushes, lipstick tubes and eye shadow compacts on the vanity? What about the towels on the towel rack?

Are they faded and a little wrinkled, as yours and most average Canadians' might be?

What's on top of the bedroom dressers in the magazine photos? Probably a floral arrangement, either formal or casual, depending on the style of the room, plus a portrait in an expensive frame. Draped casually across the bed will be an expensive throw or a luxurious robe.

The rooms in magazines are a study in perfection and good taste. They don't look as though people really live in them. That is your goal. Pretend that *Canadian Homes* is planning a photo shoot of your place and you want to project a gracious milieu in every room.

Invest in a set of smashing new towels for the bathrooms and hang them just before people arrive. This is not a waste of money – they will be lovely in your new home. Once potential buyers have left, neatly roll up the towels (this eliminates crease marks) and store them in one of those drawers you emptied. The everyday towels can hide in that same drawer until the visitors leave. Your exercise in creating space pays off now, by making it easier to quickly transform a normal home into an ideal one when visitors drop by to view it.

Protect treasures

To add to the room's character, you might want to set out flowers in an antique vase or display a photograph in a handsome frame. Before doing this, consider how difficult it would be for someone to sneak those items out of the house. If there is even a remote chance theft could occur, don't do it. The rule of thumb is: Leave no valuables in your home while strangers will be walking through it. Most people are honest, and you will accompany clients through the house yourself. But it's too easy to lose track of someone for the minute it takes to sneak into a room and scoop up a curio. As well, you want to encourage prospective buyers to spend time in the house unaccompanied. They will be more comfortable without the owner. This is when the real decision-making conversation between husband and wife will unfold. You don't want to worry about checking up on them every few minutes. Or frisking them before they leave!

If you do not have a safety deposit box, rent one at your local bank or trust company and put any precious or cherished jewellery and small valuable items in it. Everything else of value should be stored in a secure haven off the premises. You think your jewellery box is safe in a bottom drawer? Don't bank on it. I would never peek into anyone's dresser drawers if I were touring a house, but there are lots of snoops who would. Don't give them the opportunity to rob you.

What's the first impression?

Now that the inside is as fresh as can be, walk outdoors, start your car and drive around the block. As you approach your house, stop at the curb and take a critical look. What does it say to you? Is it a home you would be proud to move into? Does it need paint? Is the garage door hanging straight? Are there any dangling wires, sagging eaves troughs, Christmas lights in June, empty flowerpots or neglected window boxes? Does the landscaping need sprucing up? A few well-placed pots of colourful flowers can work wonders. Fertilize the lawn, replace dead patches with sod, and trim dead branches.

Are there oil stains on the driveway? Do the interlocking bricks need resealing to restore them to pristine condition? Is your teenager's car sitting on blocks? Can you find a place for the wagon and bicycles?

Walk up to your front door and knock. Is the doorknocker solid and attached firmly? Does the doorbell work the first time it's pressed, always? Does the door glide open gracefully, or complain by squeaking? What impression flashes through your mind as you stand there waiting? What do you focus on? Is it in good repair? Is there anything shabby or dirty in front of you, around you or under your feet?

What's out back?

The backyard counts too. Are the garbage cans, recycling boxes or composter the first thing you notice? Would some strategically placed flowers give the yard a better-groomed appearance? If you have a deck or a back porch, is it solid and been either pressure blasted, freshly stained or painted? Are you storing anything on it that should be removed, other than planter boxes or large flower containers?

If this sounds like an excessive amount of work, don't let it discourage you from listing your home yourself. Any professional real estate agent will walk through your home before listing it and if she is sincerely committed to selling it, will recommend the same procedure.

In Chapter 11, you will find checklists for every room in your home plus your garage, the front of your home and the backyard. Before a potential buyer comes through your home, do a run-through with these quicklists to make sure everything is as presentable as possible. If you have done the pre-work suggested in this chapter, and can keep the housework under control on a day-to-day basis, you should be able to whisk your home into perfection on an hour's notice.

Picture perfect

Once you have the front of your home looking as impressive as possible, shoot a roll of colour pictures. Take some from the sidewalk directly in front of the house and some from across the street. Shoot some from left and right angles. Frame your shots to diminish or completely eliminate unattractive features such as telephone poles or fire hydrants. Develop the roll and select the photo that makes your home look its eye-catching best. Order 25 reprints of that photo – you'll need them for the feature sheet you will be producing to hand to prospective buyers. You'll find more about this in Chapter 10, along with a sample to guide you.

Chapter 7

Finding a buyer

The hard work is over. Now you can channel your energies into finding someone who will fall in love with your fabulous home. How can you spread the word? In all likelihood, you have already told your relatives, friends and neighbours that you are planning to sell. Contact them again with the news that you are ready to advertise. Would they like a feature sheet, in case they know anyone who might be interested? Be sure to add, “Oh, by the way, we’re selling our home without a realtor so it’s a really good deal.”

There are various ways to advertise your home. Start with the simplest and least expensive: Post a feature sheet on bulletin boards at the local grocery stores. It’s a good policy, and common courtesy, to first ask the manager for permission. Both of the above are worth doing because they cost nothing. But the odds of either method bringing in a buyer are remote.

Your strategy to reach as many potential buyers as possible will include erecting signs, advertising in newspapers and using the Internet.

Before you do any of these things, you need to decide what telephone number to use. Do you want to receive calls about the house at your current phone number? If everyone living in your house is an adult, your regular telephone line may work just fine.

For a small additional monthly fee, you can sign up for a call identification service from your telephone company. This gives you two or more numbers for the same telephone line, each identified with a different ring. Use one of those numbers on your signs, in your ads and on your brochures. Its distinctive ring will alert you that it is a call about the house giving you the opportunity to mute the TV and answer with your most polished manner.

Designate one member of the family to field the 4SBO calls – the one who is most comfortable answering questions and talking about your home's features. If anyone else answers, they should transfer the call to that person or take a message. Of course you'll have telephone profile sheets by the telephone to capture as many facts as possible about the prospect. A sample is provided at the end of this chapter.

Voice mail

If your household includes young children, consider exploring other options. To field calls about your home, you need to be able to control the background noise and handle the conversation without distractions. As any one with youngsters can attest, these are not realistic expectations when little ones run your life. You might be nursing the baby, or refereeing an argument between siblings, or bathing a toddler just before bed when someone wants details of your home.

If this describes your lifestyle, a local voice-mail service can come to the rescue. Use the number they assign you on all your signs, ads, brochures and Internet postings. Calls to that number will be answered by a message that you dictate. People who remain interested in making an appointment will leave their number. You save time and energy by not having to talk to those who realize from the recording that your home does not suit their requirements. As well, you save your sanity. Telephone calls about the house will never disrupt your family life. You will not be jarred from sleep by that thoughtless caller who happened to see your sign on his way home from the midnight shift.

On the message, describe the major features of your home (you'll find more details about how to decide what to feature later in this chapter) and politely ask the caller to leave a name and telephone number if he is interested in making an appointment to view your home and say that you will call back. Check your messages several times during the day and evening and return the call at the first lull in activity. When people leave a number, they expect a prompt reply.

Two minutes is the standard time to record a message using a private voice mail company but you can probably negotiate for more. Before you do that, write out what you plan to say and test how long it takes. You'll be amazed at how much detail you can give in two minutes without talking so fast you sound like a chipmunk

Look in your local yellow pages under *Telephone Messaging Services* or *Telephone Equipment Systems and Services* to find companies that provide this service in your area. On the Internet, search for *Voice Mail Messaging*

Systems and Services, and specify Canada only. You'll find telephone numbers for companies in most of the provinces.

Answering machines

If you aren't satisfied with either of these systems, an alternative is the answering machine hooked up to a second line installed by your telephone company. This would be a brand new number and different line. Only people calling about the house will hear the message you leave on the answering machine. This solution also frees up your original line for personal calls.

At the time of writing, the cost in Ontario for a second line from Bell would be: $75 to install a jack, $55 to activate the line and then $25 a month for service. At first glance, it seems like a lot of money for a service you will need for only a few months at most, but when you consider $155 in relation to the listing price of your home, it is insignificant.

If you use either a voice mail system or an answering machine, mention in the ad, "To hear more about this house, please dial 000-111-2222 and listen to our recording." Some people are reluctant to call a 4SBO number, preferring to be able to learn more about it from a voice message than from you directly. Using voice mail or an answering machine could increase the number of calls you receive.

Tip

If your voice does not record well, or you are nervous speaking on a recording, or your English is difficult to understand, ask a friend or relative who has none of those concerns to record the message for you.

Secrets to signs that work

Perhaps the most productive advertising tool will be the sign you post on your lawn. Ready-made signs are available from many sources, but you can make them yourself, following these guidelines:

- The important words are: 4SBO, By Appointment and a telephone number to call. A sample sign is on the next page.
- Use large letters. Most people will read it as their car goes by. They do not want to pull over to the curb and squint to see what you are trying to tell them.
- Do not handwrite the sign. People handwrite signs for garage sales. You risk conveying the message that this is a fire sale or that you are a naïve homeowner and can be talked down in price.

- Use a brightly coloured background. Neon yellow is the most visible colour in all weather conditions.
- Find a local sign maker or a print shop. If your signs are printed on paper, have them laminated to withstand Canadian weather. The print shop will be able to give you the name of a company that does this.
- Attach your signs to a sturdy post and hammer them firmly into the ground, one facing each direction. They have to be high enough to attract attention. Position one near the walkway into your home, the other near the lot line between your home and your neighbour. If either of these locations does not give the passerby an unobstructed view of the sign, find a better spot.
- You can affix a protective box for your brochures to the signpost so people wanting more information can take one. A source: www.bcislandhomes.com.

- Best idea! If you want to avoid the hassle, order signs available from 4SBO. See last page. Nothing is easier.

Price your classified ad

Before you write your ad, contact your community newspaper plus the daily from the largest nearby city and ask for advertising rates. Specify it will be a classified ad in the real estate section. If the sales representative quotes you in agate lines, tell her you need to know what an ad will cost by the column inch or centimetre.

Don't ask her to estimate how many words you'll be able to fit in a one-inch, one-column ad because that depends on the type size you choose. Here's how to figure that out for yourself. Find an ad that has the size of type you would like to use in a recent copy of each of the papers you're planning to use. Count the characters and spaces, measure the height of the each ad in inches and multiply by the per-inch rate you were quoted. You now have a rough estimate of the space charges. If the ad is two columns wide, remember to double the price because it is using twice as many column inches. There is usually an extra charge for features such as:

- Putting a box around your ad (always a good idea)
- Using darker type (called boldface) for a few words leading into your ad
- Using a headline in larger type centred above your ad
- Adding a photo to your ad. As well as paying for the extra space, there will be art department costs. Have you ever wondered why the majority of photos in the real estate sections of major daily newspapers are small and black and white? Printing

a full-colour photo adds significant costs; be sure to ask before deciding to run colour.

Feature words sell

When you are ready to advertise, it's time to figure out what to say. Gather the family around the table and talk about all the things you really love about life in your home. What will each of you miss when you leave? What made you want to move in when you first saw it? As the words and the memories start to flow, you can capture them on a list. Once that is done, list all the upgrades you have added to the home since moving in.

You could invite your closest friends in for coffee and cake and encourage them to tell you what they find most attractive about your home. Of course, you'll add all those to the list too.

When you started this process, you didn't know what to say about your home. Now, you probably have a list that is too long, so read it over and select the features that will appeal most to the next person living in your home. From this point on, the ad will be easy.

When writing an ad, don't say too little or too much and try not to reduce the words to ridiculous contractions to save space. For example here are some I found:

> Cabbagetown 2sty. TLC thruout, 3 BR. 1 ens. 2 baths + pow. rm. f/din. mn fm rm 2w/o, 2 sol. CAC, c/vac. Lge. Lot. 2pkg.

Each of these is an actual abbreviation from the classified section of The Globe And Mail – albeit, they were not all in one ad.

I think it says: A two-storey home that has had tender loving care throughout. Three bedrooms, one with an ensuite bathroom. Two full bathrooms plus a powder room. Fireplace in dining room. Main floor family room. Two walkouts and two solariums. Central air conditioning and central vacuum. Large lot. Two-car parking.

I'm not convinced I correctly cracked all the codes. F/din could mean family dining room, formal dining room or full dining room. The point is, if you want to sell your home, people should not have to guess what you're trying to tell them. In fact, if they don't understand, they won't call you – they'll move on to another ad. The features of your home are what will sell it. Spell them out. Keep it simple.

Every home is different. Every ad will be different but the basic points you should always cover include:

- Its location
- Its price
- Number of bedrooms
- Number of bathrooms (unless you have only one, then don't mention it. In most homes, you can usually find a place to install at least a powder room. You don't want to lose a sale because a potential buyer needs two.)
- Garage or parking spaces
- Your telephone number

Beyond those, you can build in your home's unique features – the ones you selected from the list developed with the input of your family and your friends. These might include the new roof, a remodelled kitchen, hardwood floors, a large fenced yard, new broadloom or a luxurious soaker tub. If it's a small starter home, its special feature may be what good value it is for the money.

Save 1,000 words!

That's what a photo is supposed to be worth. Unless your home is positioned so it is absolutely impossible to capture a flattering photograph of it, always include a photo with your ad. Colour is best, but the cost may be prohibitive. A black and white photo is better than nothing, and should fall well within your budget. The newspaper can convert a colour photo to black and white; you don't need to supply a black and white picture.

Let's look at the ad you read about in Chapter 1 that worked so well in 1982 when it ran in Toronto's Globe And Mail. Here's how it was worded:

> REGAL ESTATES. $285,000 buys you a magnificent home that reflects your unique taste and lifestyle. This 5,600 sq. ft. home is nestled midst the trees on a ravine in this most exclusive area of Unionville, Ont. Floor-to-ceiling windows in the kitchen, living room, dining room and master suite overlook three acres of mature trees, a private pond, waterfall and rustic bridge. You can relax in the bathtub and watch squirrels scampering through the branches. Five bedrooms, four bathrooms, billiards room so large the walls never interfere with a good shot, large library/den. Huge atrium with fishpond creates impressive entrance. Two fireplaces, main floor laundry room, renovated kitchen. This house, built by one of Toronto's leading architects for his family, defines its owner as a successful person who appreciates the best in life. If you are looking for an exceptional home, call and book an appointment to view this remarkable property. Private sale by owner. No agents please. 416-416-4166.

One hundred and fifty nine words. That's massive for a real estate classified ad and it was expensive. But do you know what's interesting? I remember what we sold the house for; I can't recall within a hundred dollars what the ad cost! Whatever we paid, it was worth every dollar because it sold our home when a three-month listing with an agent did not. We ran the ad over two columns and specified the same small type used by other real estate ads in that section. We assumed that people who could afford the price would be intrigued enough to read right to the bottom. We were right.

I'm not suggesting you spend 159 words to detail your home. On the contrary, size your ad so it's big enough to be noticed in the rows upon rows of tiny classifieds, but small enough to be a quick read.

How else can you spread the word?

The Internet is considered the electronic gateway to the world. You could post your home on a site and reach millions of people. But one problem stands in the way. How do they find your ad?

In the United States it's a cinch. Both AOL and Yahoo! have sites dedicated to real estate. An interested buyer can find listings specific to the area he is interested in. As well, there are literally hundreds of for-sale-by-owner sites offering similar services.

Neither of those Internet giants offers a real estate section on its Canadian networks. There are small operations posting Canadian homes on the Internet, but few have enough listings to be considered a major source for the home hunter. As 4SBO picks up steam in this country, and both sellers and buyers become more comfortable with using the Internet, the number of homes for sale on the Web should mushroom.

If you live in an area that has a 4SBO site, by all means consider listing with it. For a flat fee, you can post a photo of your home and its features on the site. Some also offer to print brochures and provide signs. I can't vouch for the effectiveness of any of them, but they are worth looking at. The following URLs are either completely dedicated to Canadian ads or have a section allocated to Canada. Some also list homes for sale by real estate agents. This list does not pretend to cover every Canadian 4SBO site. To do your own search, type in FSBO and specify Canada.

www.clickahomecanada.com	www.canada-fsbo.com
www.homeportfoliojunction.com	www.homes-canada.com
www.privatesalerealty.com	www.privatelist.com
www.canada.homesalez.com	www.topfsbo.com
www.forsalebyownercanada.com	www.cbon.com
www.actualhomes.comcanada	www.fsbosites.com
www.okhomeseller.com	www.fsbo-bc.com
www.bcislandhomes.com	www.fsbo.ca

About the Telephone Profile Form

The questions on the form that is provided for you to use when people respond to your ads, are designed to gather information about the caller so you can decide if you want to make an appointment with her. If the caller isn't interested in moving for two years, there is no sense wasting your time showing her your home.

Home ownership information helps you identify how strong a potential buyer the caller is. If the caller's home is on the market or sold, she's a better prospect than one who hasn't listed the home yet. The information about the caller's car builds in a safety feature. When the doorbell rings, you can check that it is the person you are expecting.

This form helps organize your appointments. As soon as you are finished with the call, transfer the appointment information into an agenda or onto a calendar. Then file the forms in order of appointments. The first form in the file will be your first appointment. You can read it quickly just before the caller arrives to remind yourself about the details of your conversation. By picking out something personal to say when you greet her, you make her feel welcome.

Use the area for comments and notes to jot down things you want to remember. Example: If the caller mentions how much his family would like to have a pool, dig out photos to show him your family and friends enjoying the pool.

Please make as many copies of this form as needed.

Telephone Profile

Date Called: ____________________

Name: ____

Telephone #: Day: ______________________________ Evening: ____________________

Where do you live now? ____

How did you hear about our home?

☐ Sign ☐ Ad ☐ Brochure ☐ Friend ☐ Other

How long have you been looking for a house? ______________________

When would you like to move? ______________________________________

Do you own a home? ☐ Yes ☐ No

Is it currently for sale? ☐ Yes ☐ No

Are you coming by car? ☐ Yes ☐ No

Colour and make of car? ____

Will you coming alone? ☐ Yes ☐ No

If no, who will be with you? _______________________________

Date of Appointment: ______________________________ Time: ____________________

Comments/Notes: ____

____

____

____

____

____

____

____

Chapter 8

When an agent comes to call

Just as sure as robins return in the spring, you can count on one of your first calls coming from a real estate agent. Guess what? She has the perfect client for your house. Will you co-broke? Co-what? She's asking if you will co-operate with her, in other words give her a commission if she sells the house.

What do you say? You don't want to lose a potential sale. Nor do you want to list your house with her. The agent won't be able to bring in the client until you have listed. What if she has set up this scheme to entice you to list – that "perfect client" is fictitious?

If she spills out the name of the buyer before you have entered into any kind of contract or referral arrangement with her, and you can find the telephone number, you are not breaking any law by calling. Introduce yourself and explain that you have heard he is searching for a home. Tell him yours is on the market as 4SBO. No agency commissions are involved and the price reflects that. Ask the prospect if he wants to work with you.

He may not. Many people feel more confident dealing alongside a real estate agent, primarily because agents know their way around the paperwork. Suggest he come and see the home without the agent. At that time, you will show him the material you have on hand that should build his confidence in your ability to handle the deal without an agent. If he remains reluctant to work alone, he will have lost nothing. He can still return with the agent and if you want the sale, you will have to negotiate with her.

Before you sign anything with her, read the legal advice below and remember that the six per cent commission is as flexible as a wet noodle. You have priced your home assuming there will be no commissions paid. As well, you have done most of the work a realty firm would handle if acting as the listing agent. You wrote the ad copy, paid for the advertising, supplied the signs and produced feature brochures about your home. Walk away from any agent who refuses to recognize the monetary value of your contributions and balks at cutting the commission. This is not a person you want to deal with, whether she has a genuine prospect or not.

That's my take on the subject. On the premise that sound legal advice could provide more valuable direction on how to handle the situation, I asked a colleague, who is a real estate lawyer, what he would recommend. Here's his response:

"What do you do when an agent sees your 4SBO sign or your ad in the real estate section of the newspaper and calls to say that she has a prospective buyer? Of course, before she will introduce you, she wants to discuss a commission for the referral. Here are a few things to consider if this happens.

Double dipping

"First, you should be aware that the buyer might have already signed a purchaser agency agreement with the agent. In layman's terms, this means that the agent is working for the buyer who will pay her a commission if the right house is found and the deal closes. When that happens, the agent ends up with the same commission she would have received had the house been multiple listed through another agent. If you agree to her commission demands, she will simply be double ending the deal and doubling her commission.

"Few buyers sign a buyer agency agreement. Why should they? Most realize the home seller generally pays the agent's commission. So you are reasonably safe to assume that the agent is simply house hunting for a client who has not committed to pay her commission.

"The agent needs to earn a living but she has an agreement with neither you nor the potential buyer. She faces two options:

- Persuade the buyer to sign a buyer agency agreement, or
- Convince you to sign a commission agreement.

"The simplest alternative is to arrange the commission through the buyer. You don't have to get involved at all with that agreement. However, if the buyer signs it, you will be in a stronger position to negotiate reducing or eliminating a commission on your part.

What's it worth?

"What will you do if the agent firmly says, 'No,' and insists you must cover the commission? Now you have to decide just how eager you are to connect with her client and what that meeting is worth to you. If you agree to work with her, she will suggest you sign a commission agreement. Be careful! Insist that the agreement be specific to one buyer and be limited to a very short time frame.

"Also make sure that it does not apply to a buyer you have already dealt with, or to anyone who may contact you in the future, or to anyone who may contact you without the agent's help. Most important, never sign anything until you have taken it to your lawyer for review and listened to her advice on your options.

Problems with a one-day listing

"The agent who says she has a buyer may ask you to sign a short-term (one-day) listing agreement. If possible, avoid getting involved in this complicated process. You would have to ensure that the agent removed all the clauses from the standard listing agreement that do not meet your needs or protect your interests. For example, it might state that the commission arrangement includes all buyers the agent attracts during the short-listing period. That would unfairly include those who are responding to your marketing efforts.

"Other examples of clauses you should take out of the standard listing agreement include:

- Paying a commission if your home is sold during the listing period, no matter how the buyer found out about it.
- Paying a commission if you sell your house after the listing expired, but as a result of advertising done by the agent. If an agent "splashes" an ad campaign of your property during the short-listing period, you may end up in court fighting to prove how the buyer found your home.

"These are a few of the reasons you should insist on a simple commission agreement that applies only to the one buyer the agent claims to have in the wings.

"If the agent won't accept your terms, stick to your 4SBO philosophy and let her worry about her commission with the buyer."

Chapter 9

Create Open House pizzazz

For months you have methodically prepared your home for sale. You realize that real estate agents generally introduce a new listing to the market by holding an Open House. From the Open Houses I have attended, more agents and nosy neighbours than serious buyers show up. That makes sense; the Open House provides a good opportunity for agents who do not have the listing to become familiar with the home. It might be perfect for one of their clients. And neighbours who have never been in the house get a chance to see it.

Thinking back to Open Houses that I have walked into, the house was usually cold. Why? I don't know. Perhaps the homeowners turned down the heat on the assumption a lot of people would be holding the door open and they would be wasting fuel. Or perhaps it just felt cold because of the ambiance.

The agents in those Open Houses usually sat where they could see the door and often looked as though they wished they had brought along their knitting or a good book. Those who weren't bored were working on weekly sales reports or some other business-related documents and clearly did not want to be disturbed. The atmosphere seemed tinged with solemn desperation. Instead of being excited about viewing the property, I found myself wishing I had never ventured through the door

Another idiosyncrasy I observed in many Open Houses was the agent's reluctance to move out of his chair to greet the visitor. He would toss out an obligatory hello and ask me to sign the guest book; then he would ignore me unless I was brash enough to pose a question. And to this day, I have never had a callback from one of them!

To me, Open House should translate into: "You are welcome to come in and look around and we are pleased to see you." Open House should replicate those special times when neighbours invite the whole street in. It should be friendly and warm and bustling. There should be a sense of activity, an air of excitement about the arrival of a new offering on the marketplace.

Do you need an Open House?

There is no rule that says you must hold an Open House, but if you decide you want to start your 4SBO experience with one, try to learn from the mistakes outlined above. Many of the problems I have experienced with Open Houses stem from the length of time they are open. How many people would normally visit an Open House? If we assume that 20 people show up over a three-hour period, there will probably be a group that arrives shortly after the doors are unlocked followed by the fashionably late who burst in half an hour later. Then come those long, empty lapses interrupted only by a sporadic straggler.

Let's assume you shorten the event to one hour. You will not have time to look bored. The house will be alive with people running into each other as they make their way from room to room. This is just what you want. Nothing motivates a potential buyer more than the thought he might lose the deal to one of those other couples that is taking a particularly close look at the place.

Paper trail

Shortly before you set a date for your Open House, you'll want to start preparing a number of handouts for your guests. Because you will use the same documents for all future appointments you make when people call to view your home, produce lots of copies. I suggest starting with a stack of 25 of each.

The following list covers the various materials you should supply to everyone visiting your home. Some are documents you simply need to photocopy. Others, those marked with an ✱ asterisk, are customized for your Open House. Samples are supplied at the end of the chapter for your guidance.

✱ A guest register for people to fill out when they arrive at your home

✱ A feature sheet of your home. This should cover the back and front of a standard size sheet of paper. On the front will be a colour photograph of your home. You can either scan a picture of your home into your computer and print it out, along with the information, or simply buy 25 reprints of a photo of your home. If you decide to print the photo through your computer, look for matte or glossy paper produced especially for computer-generated photos. Office supply stores or camera shops often carry this paper. It will print a more vibrant reproduction of your photo. Having said that, I must add that you can achieve acceptable results using plain bond paper. If you use photo reprints, simply glue one into position on the front of your feature sheets.

A copy of the lot plan, if available

Certificate of appraisal from a reputable appraiser (See Chapter 4)

Home inspection report plus copies of invoices showing repairs have been completed (See Chapter 4)

✱ Question and comment sheets for potential buyers to carry with them as they go through your home

A few clip boards

Business cards from a nearby mortgage broker or a mortgage specialist at a bank in your vicinity

And finally, tucked away in an accessible drawer, copies of the Agreement of Purchase and Sale. It's most unlikely someone will be eager to make an offer on the first visit, but stranger things have happened. Be prepared! Agreements of Purchase and Sale for each province are include in this book. Make a few copies to keep on hand for when you need them. It doesn't get any easier than that. As well, in Chapter 17, you'll find a completed sample of each province's Purchase Contract to guide you in how to fill it in yourself.

If you are selling a condominium, you will also want to provide:

Information about current monthly condo fees and what they cover

Tip

Photocopy the Guest Register form at the end of this chapter and cut each one in half. If you decide to produce your own, use a large, boldface font. People often forget their glasses!

The guest registers and the clipboards should be available at the front door as long as this doesn't restrict the free flow of traffic. Remember, you want to create an impression of roominess, which has to start with the entranceway.

If you have a large foyer, provide a small table or a desk and a chair so visitors can sit down to fill in the guest register. If this is impractical because of space limitations, seat them in the living room with a clipboard and the Register for the few minutes they will need to fill it out.

All of the other handouts should be neatly piled where you can access them easily when the time is right. There's a reason for this. You don't want them to be distracted trying to read about room sizes or taxes while you are walking them through the house. Their full attention should be focused on your home's features and the pleasing ambiance you have so carefully engineered.

Organize house tours

When they have filled in the guest register, the house tour will begin. Explain to them that you will walk them through first, giving them a general overview and answering questions as you go. Following that tour, you'll give each of them a clipboard, a home feature sheet with more detailed information and a Comment Form. They may spend as much time as they would like reviewing the house. Point out where they should return when they are finished. You will be waiting to answer their questions.

By working this way, you achieve two results. First, you eliminate the curious few who simply want to step in the door, scan a couple of rooms, grab all the information and depart. Second, this strategy keeps people in your home longer than if they arrived, took a feature sheet, walked through and left. Only the most ill-mannered will take the clipboard and feature sheet before they have the guided tour. Most will be courteous enough to stay for that second go-round. The longer they remain, the better the odds they will find features that attract them to your home. Your approach incubates a stronger base of prospective buyers.

Home alone

Arrange with a relative or a friend to join you at an Open House or to be on call if you have an appointment to show your home when you are alone. It's distressing that the world has deteriorated to the point that women in particular must never admit strangers if we are the only one at home. A 4SBO sign can signal a shady character that there might be easy prey to be found inside.

When a friend arrives to help with your Open House, take a few minutes to brief her on the procedure. Then, if you are walking people through when a new party arrives, she can greet and seat them and give them the guest register to fill in while waiting for you. You could also second the help of another adult family member to take visitors on the rounds. Plan a route in advance so you won't find yourselves crossing paths and arriving in the same room at the same time.

Please photocopy as many of the following forms as you need.

4SBO Guest Register

Welcome to our home. Please fill out the following information in case we need to reach you. Thank you.

Name: ______________________________

Address: ______________________________

Telephone: ______________________________

Car Make & Licence: ______________________________

How did you hear about our home? Please check all that apply:

☐ Lawn sign ☐ A friend told us

☐ Saw brochure ☐ Internet

☐ Ad in paper ☐ Other (Specify) ______________

Signature: ______________________ Date: __________

✂---

4SBO Guest Register

Welcome to our home. Please fill out the following information in case we need to reach you. Thank you.

Name: ______________________________

Address: ______________________________

Telephone: ______________________________

Car Make & Licence: ______________________________

How did you hear about our home? Please check all that apply:

☐ Lawn sign ☐ A friend told us

☐ Ad in paper ☐ Internet

☐ Saw brochure ☐ Other (Specify) ______________

Signature: ______________________ Date: __________

Stately Home facing park

Combines old-fashioned quality with contemporary comfort and conveniences

33 Whippoorwill Court $379,000

Architect has magically transformed an outdated home into a futuristic delight. This proud, three-storey house encompasses four bedrooms, four full baths and one powder room in 3,700 sq. feet.

The traditional centre-hall plan remains but small, pokey rooms have been reconstructed into vast, open concept spaces. A narrow flight of steps has been replaced with a gracious, sweeping staircase.

The first floor is designed for mingling with friends, eating and entertaining. The second floor is for escaping, rewinding and slumbering. The third floor has been converted into a soundproof, fully wired, state-of the-art office.

Even the basement has been refashioned into a bright, cheerful playroom to keep children off the street and out of your hair!

Make an appointment today to view this unique property. Partial financing available to a qualified buyer. 204-204-2044

We're relocating but our home has to stay!

This detached home has 14 rooms above ground plus a winterized sun porch facing the exclusive 20-acre Briarton Park. We lovingly restored all the original hardwood floors and installed Mexican ceramic tile in the kitchen, laundry and mudrooms. A unique wood-burning fireplace opens onto both dining and living rooms. Central vac and central air. The lot is approximately one-half acre with 80 ft. frontage. Large back deck overlooks landscaped gardens and stone barbecue. Two-car garage at back of lot is accessible by small unpaved road. This is a home you would be proud to call your own. It offers too many features to detail here – come and see for yourself before it's gone. How we'll miss it!

Rooms:	Width Feet	Length Feet
Main Floor:		
Foyer	10	14
Living room	20	28
Dining room	16	18
Kitchen	21	15
Powder room	7	6
Laundry Room	9	9
Mud room	6	8
Sunroom facing park	8	12
Second Floor:		
Master bedroom	22	22
Ensuite bathroom	16	15
Bedroom 2	10	12
Bedroom 3	12	13
Home theatre	14	16
Full bathroom	9	11
Third floor:		
Office/Library/den	30	28
Basement:		
Playroom	20	16
Gym	12	18
Three-piece bathroom	8	9
Sauna	7	9

Address:
33 Whippoorwill Court
South Platysville, Manitoba
Tel: 204.204.2042

Township: Miramar

Zoned: Residential

Construction: Brick with Board and Batten

District: South East

Schools: Earl Bronson
St. Gabriel's
Marsden High

Taxes: $2,800

Heating: Hot water/Oil. New furnace in 1999

Hydro: 200 amps

Plumbing: Copper

Water heater: Rental

Town water and sewers

Visitor Comment Form

As you look through our home, please answer a few questions and make notes about any further information you need. Thank you

Name: ______________________________

Address: ______________________________

Telephone #______________________________

What features do you particularly like about our house?

____

____

____

What could be improved?

____

____

____

Would this home suit your needs? ☐ Yes ☐ No

If no, please explain: ______________________________

Is this house good value for the price? ☐ Yes ☐ No

If no, how do you think it should be priced? $ ______________

Will you come back for a second visit? ☐ Yes ☐ No

Notes and Questions

____

____

____

____

____

____

Chapter 10

Legal support builds confidence

Selling your house through the 4SBO method can be intimidating. Here you are, playing a role that could earn a real estate agent thousands of dollars but you don't have the agent's experience to draw from. You know what you want for your house, and after reading Chapter 7 you know how to market it. But you're uncomfortable with all the details – things like drafting the Agreement or negotiating the deal.

Don't be intimidated. After you read Chapter 12, you'll be your own best negotiator, and Chapter 13 brings you up to speed on all the terminology in the Agreement. If that's your worry, you're flailing your broom at the wrong boogeyman. Your real fear, unless you are a lawyer, lies in the legal details.

To your rescue comes your trusty lawyer. Bring her in early enough to anticipate issues, to help draft the Agreement, to advise through negotiations when you need a sounding board, and finally to close your deal. Of course you'll need to pay your lawyer for the extra work, but you'll be pleasantly surprised, and probably shocked as well, to learn that your legal costs will be a pittance compared to the real estate agency's commissions. Before proceeding, I should clarify that I am using the term lawyer, but in other jurisdictions such as British Columbia and Quebec, your real estate transaction may be handled by a Notary Public or Notaire.

You are going to save a lot of money selling your house through the 4SBO method. Be smart. Spend some of that money on your lawyer.

It is important that your lawyer become involved early, starting with a review of the Agreement of Purchase and Sale. Ideally you would like to have the Agreement ready to go when you meet with the buyer for the final round of negotiations. Here's what to do: prepare your draft with all of the terms you want in it, and then run it by your lawyer in advance. You may even ask her to help you draft it, although this may add time, which translates into extra cost.

Once your Agreement has been pre-screened, as long as you and the buyer don't make too many significant changes, you should be comfortable proceeding without further review. Since you are meeting with your lawyer anyway, she could also review in advance some clauses that you think the buyer may want inserted, such as a financing condition, if it isn't already in your standard form.

Another method of protecting yourself is to sign the Agreement you have prepared, but make it conditional upon satisfactory review by a lawyer. Both you and the buyer may have such a condition. And a final option is for you and the buyer to prepare the Agreement together, but not to sign it until each of you has taken it to a lawyer. The problem with these two methods is that they break up the negotiating process and effectively allow the buyer a cooling off period, which is not traditionally a good sales tactic (see Negotiating the Deal in Chapter 12).

By bringing your lawyer in early, you will be far ahead of anyone who relies exclusively on a real estate agent. Think about it. At the end of the day the buck stops with the lawyers. They know what makes a deal succeed or fail – they see so many. They have the training and the drafting skills. Their profession is regulated by strict ethical standards; and perhaps most importantly, they are not guided by the self-serving interest of not receiving a commission until a deal is sealed.

In agent-negotiated deals it is a curious practice that the Agreement usually does not get to the lawyer until after it is signed and binding – essentially when it's too late to make any changes. A skeptic might say that this is because the agent doesn't want to bungle the deal by getting bogged down with legal issues, even at the expense of his client's best interests. In fairness, there is truth to the maxim that "people make deals, lawyers break them." Nonetheless, you will be in charge of the negotiations, you can make the deal succeed, and a good lawyer is your best defence against getting blind-sided along the way.

Agents have their place

Now might be a good time to pause and say a word in defence of real estate agents. Throughout these materials you will find references to why I think the 4SBO system is better than using a real estate agent. My references, by necessity, involve comparisons, and the comparisons, inevitably, lead to a conclusion in favour of the 4SBO method over retaining a real estate agent. However, I'm not suggesting that agents don't have their place, or that most of them are unethical or unprofessional. The greatest number of real estate agents are well-trained, knowledgeable specialists, and all-around nice people. The 4SBO method is based on a self-help philosophy for individuals who are willing to step into the shoes of the agent, take on his task, emulate his professionalism and save some significant money.

There are good real estate agents and bad ones – there are good lawyers and bad ones. With the 4SBO method, you don't have to worry about good and bad agents because you avoid them entirely, which just leaves the lawyers. How do you find a good one? First, know what you want, and second, canvass the resources to find what you want.

Defining the good lawyer

Assuming you do not already have a real estate lawyer whom you know and trust, here are a few essential qualities to look for in order of declining importance:

- Trustworthy
- Competent
- Compatible and
- Reasonably priced.

The first two, trustworthy and competent, go without saying. In the realm of competence, don't use someone who "dabbles" in real estate law. Every lawyer is licensed to practise real estate; not everyone has the experience necessary to take on your deal. Use someone seasoned in residential real estate.

What do I mean by compatible? In a 4SBO transaction you will be relying on your lawyer much more than you would in a traditional agent-driven transaction. As suggested earlier, your lawyer should be involved from the beginning, sometimes before you even have a buyer in sight. For this reason, you and your lawyer must be compatible. Put another way, there must be a good fit. Your lawyer must share your vision of how you expect the deal to proceed and be accepting of the process you are bringing to her. Your lawyer will become your confidante, your advisor and your representative - you will be a team. As a team, you must be able to communicate freely. The lawyer you are considering may be the most renowned and respected solicitor in town, but if you are not convinced that she is compatible with you, your style and your objectives, keep looking.

You will notice that I put price last. The 4SBO philosophy is obviously based on cost savings, but you can't compromise when it comes to protecting your legal interests. Legal fees may be a deciding factor, but only when all other things are equal or when there is a monstrous discrepancy in the fees being quoted. If that's the case, ask why? It may be trite to say it at this point, but with lawyers as with anything, "You get what you pay for."

So now that you know what you want, where do you find it? The single most reliable source of a good lawyer is a referral from someone you trust. Ask around. If you have no one to ask, call your local Law Society. Most of them have a lawyer referral service, but you should know that they are not screened in terms of competence. The business ad section of the phone directory works just as well. Many ads specify the areas of practice; focus on ones that stress real estate.

All other things being equal, it's a good idea to choose a lawyer in your area. A local lawyer will be more familiar with local conveyancing practices, as well as local title and regulatory issues in the event that problems come up. A local lawyer will also be more convenient for you and closer at hand for last minute closing issues and transferring trust funds between banks.

Ask the questions

Interview your lawyer. Believe it or not, real estate lawyers are hungry for business. You are the client; they are the service providers. You are paying the bill. You have a lot on the line. You are ultimately in control. Keep thinking about these things every time you feel intimidated by the prospect of interviewing a lawyer. During the interview, ask questions that will target the good lawyer criteria given above: "How much real estate do you do in a month? Are you opposed to a 4SBO transaction? Do you have any references? How much can I expect to pay?" Ask tough questions; "Are you prepared to help me through this?" The answer may be proof of your lawyer's true mettle.

What's the cost?

Establish the price. Depending on the jurisdiction you are in, a fixed price may be an option. It is becoming more and more common for lawyers to fix their price on real estate transactions. By "fixed price" I mean everything including fees and disbursements. This becomes a less reasonable expectation the more you involve your lawyer in the less predictable process of drafting and negotiating a real estate deal. Nonetheless, if you can't nail down a total fixed price, try to fix the transaction costs and pay hourly for the rest. At the very least you should fix an hourly rate, and if paying hourly you should request a reasonable estimate of what that will total in the end.

You should discuss and agree on the expectations between you in terms of the lawyer's function, time, availability and effort. Recognize that any fixed quote will be based on a "normal" transaction – one with no extra mortgages to discharge, no title problems to clean up, no writs or liens to be dealt with. Understandably, these things will involve extra costs.

Write down the anticipated fee and the retainer expectations, or have the lawyer write them down. That way, at the end of the day, she will be morally, if not professionally, bound to abide by her quote or estimate and commitment. As a general rule, always discuss cost at the outset – don't be embarrassed and don't feel you are offending the lawyer. She is providing a service and is accustomed to quoting a price to her clients. To not ask is unprofessional, and frankly, invites a big bill when your deal is through.

Chapter 11

You've found alive one – what now?

Signs are posted on your front lawn. The ads are running in the local paper, as well as in a daily newspaper in the nearest urban area - many people retire from city-based jobs and look for a more pastoral environment. Others are willing to commute to escape the traffic jams, the inflated home prices and the pollution. You've had your Open House, or not. You are ready for some response. Suddenly the phone rings and a total stranger wants to book an appointment to view your home.

This is no time to get cold feet, or work up a sweat, whichever you are prone to do in times of stress. Be confident. You have your feature sheet beside the phone so everything you want to say is at your fingertips. And you have those telephone profile forms that you photocopied from Chapter 7 to help you collect the right information.

The caller is legitimate. He has sold his home; yours is in the right neighbourhood and sounds perfect for his family. Yes indeed, your ads have hooked a live one! He and his wife are coming by immediately after work so they can see the property before dark.

Your home is in peak condition. Now is the time to consider how to set the stage so it reflects the ambiance and lifestyle you want to project. It should be cheerfully bright. Even if the sun is streaming in the windows, before anyone arrives turn on every light including the one in the garage. If your kitchen is bathed in sunlight at a specific time of the day, try to book appointments for that time. Nothing gives a warmer feeling about a home than a bright kitchen. Soft candlelight flickering in carefully selected places adds to the ambiance, as does a fire glowing in the fireplace.

Mmmm ... it smells like home

Irresistible scents should welcome your prospective buyers. You have heard about baking cookies or bread before you show your house. Don't scoff. Without doubt this adds to the overall atmosphere of contentment and pleasure. I think the aroma of a freshly baked loaf of bread is most appealing. And it's so simple to achieve! Buy a package of frozen yeast buns, ready to bake. Pop one in the oven and soon the scent will waft through the house. No one needs to know you baked only one bun!

Are you planning to have trout for dinner? Or garlic bread? I think not! Until your home is sold, your meal plans should be comprised of bland foods that you can heat up without infusing the house with unpleasant odours. Think rice pudding – it's almost perfect!

If something happens that fills your home with a bad smell when you are expecting house visitors, don't try to mask it with an aerosol room spray. Few if any of those smell natural; when your guests enter, they will sense that you are trying to cover up something. And under no circumstances grab a bottle of perfume and squirt it around. The intensity of that can be a turn-off to many people.

I use one of three solutions when faced with this situation. Either:

- Quickly light a number of small vanilla-scented candles and let them burn for at least half an hour. Keep a supply on hand for emergencies like this.
- Put a quarter teaspoon of vanilla in a small pot, add some cinnamon or nutmeg and simmer for 10 minutes, or
- Peel a thin strip of orange or lemon rind and set it either directly on the stove's element turned to its lowest setting, or if you use gas, in a fry pan over medium-low heat. The oil from the citrus will lend your room a pungent, exotic smell. A word of warning, don't leave it on the heat too long – the peel turns very acrid if scorched.

Be particularly sensitive to any unpleasant whiffs associated with pets such as dirty cat litter or bedding that has not been aired out daily. Those scents are part of your everyday life. You don't even notice them, but they will wrinkle the nose of a stranger as soon as he enters the room. Your routine until you sell should include grooming your pets, changing the litter and airing out their bedding daily.

Pet concerns

Even the friendliest pet can frighten people unaccustomed to having them around, or damage their clothes by jumping on them. Worse yet, they can do something to really humiliate you.

Many years ago when my husband and I were selling a home, a couple arrived and left their shoes on the mat inside the door. When they were preparing to leave, one of the woman's dainty slingbacks had mysteriously walked away. We found it, dripping with saliva in the jaws of our playful puppy, the back strap chewed in half. Of course we were red-faced and apologetic and offered to replace the shoes. They did not buy the house. To this day, in my mind's eye I can see her hobbling back to the car, trying to keep that soggy, maimed shoe on her foot. As humiliating as it was, the memory still brings a chuckle.

If possible, farm your pet out during appointments. Try to hire a sitter who will take him on short notice, or find a teenager from your neighbourhood to take him for a walk. Failing all else, either tether him outside or put him in a cage in the laundry room or some other warm, bright corner where he will look comfortable and well cared for. Give him a light snack, a bowl of water and a toy for company so he won't complain.

Curb the kids

Controlling the children while you hold an Open House is relatively simple because it's a one-time occurrence for an hour. Absolutely the best place for them is anyplace but home. There will be a lot going on at your place; they are safer out of the way. If they must be at home, pull out a favourite video and set them up in the family room. Explain that strangers will be walking through the house so it is important that they do not wrestle, argue or throw things about. People will be less inclined to ask them questions about the house or why you are moving if the children are attentively preoccupied with the video.

It's a stickier situation booking appointments when you have very young children. If you are a stay-at-home parent with toddlers, consider enrolling them in a day care or play centre for two or three hours every day or finding someone who will take them on a daily basis while your home is on the market. That will build in time to keep the house in shape plus it opens a window in your day for showing your home. You will know when to book appointments.

If your children are school age, call a family pow-wow to help them understand their roles in keeping the house clean. Ask for volunteers for specific chores. If no one volunteers, draw jobs out of a hat. Explain that the house must be tidy before everyone leaves every morning. Home will resemble a boot camp until it is sold. No dirty laundry on the floor of their bedrooms. Shoes are to be removed at the door and promptly put away every time they come in. Toys must be returned neatly to shelves or the toy box. No uneaten food can be left on the kitchen counter. All eating, including snacks, must be done at the table.

Review the rewards

Include the children in a discussion about what the move will mean for them. What are they most excited about in the new home? Remind them that you need a bigger house so they can all have their own bedrooms. Talk about how their friends will enjoy the new pool. Point out how much more time they will have in the new house because it's closer to the school and so they won't have to catch the bus. Add the promise of a reward once the house has been sold – perhaps a family camping expedition or a trip to Disney World. Whatever you choose, it should be something the children will consider very special. With that pot of gold at the end of the rainbow to encourage them, they will be more motivated to make the extra effort you need from them.

Plan to roll everyone out of bed half an hour earlier than normal in the morning so chores can be done. If you are working and will be booking appointments in the late afternoon or early evening, organize dinner before you leave the house so it will be quick to serve and clean up afterwards. Spend a weekend or two before advertising your home loading the freezer with casseroles and home-made TV dinners that need only to be taken out of the freezer in the morning to thaw, then heated and eaten on schedule.

From the first day you mount a sign on your lawn until the deal is closed, a meticulous home is mandatory. If you find your family is having trouble keeping up with it all, sign up for a weekly cleaning until the home is sold. You don't want cleaners there when prospects come for a viewing so book their first appointment of the day. A team of two can be in and out by 10 a.m., leaving the balance of the day free for showings.

Dealing with extra stress

When an interested person calls to set up an appointment, your preferred option is to build in a two-hour lead-time before greeting him at your door. Sometimes that won't meet his time constraints and you have to be ready within half an hour.

Or worse yet, he may have seen the sign as he drove by, ignored the by-appointment-only and is knocking on the door. Your first response is to suggest he book an appointment. If he insists, you either let him in, or risk never seeing him again. You can't afford to lose a potential sale because your home isn't ready to show.

Nightmarish situations can haunt anyone selling a home. No two are ever the same, but you can survive with your poise intact by applying this three-step strategy:

- Think with the speed of a whirling dervish
- Kick your imagination into overdrive
- Remain as cool as a Cheshire cat

If you start to panic, take a moment to focus on the reality – you are not the root of the problem. He arrived without an appointment. You are extending a courtesy by letting him in without notice. You are not the one who needs to apologize.

Here's an example. Let's pretend a couple arrives at the door and begs to see the house immediately. They are desperately looking because the husband has been transferred and they have to move to your neighbourhood within the next two months. The children are 1,500 miles away with their grandparents; the couple has flown in and has only one week to locate a new home.

What are you going to do?

Well! You certainly aren't going to say no. But your mind flashes to Jeff, your eight-month-old baby that you left sitting in the highchair in the kitchen squishing banana chunks through his fingers and flinging them to the floor.

Spiff, the dog, is under the chair licking up Jeff's spilled milk.

You calmly and quickly seat the couple in the living room, hand them the feature brochure, the assessment, the inspection report and ask them to fill out the visitor identification sheet. Brilliant! You just bought some time. Excuse yourself for a few minutes to tend to your child.

In a flash, scoop up Spiff and either put her outside or in her cage. Wash the baby and plop him in the playpen. Wipe and fold up the highchair. You cleverly keep a plastic tablecloth underneath the highchair. Roll it up, banana, milk and all and stuff it under the sink. You can retrieve it for wiping once they have left. Make a quick circuit to turn on all the lights and – presto! – in seven minutes you're back with them. No problem, they wait longer than that at the ATM machine! You casually walk over to the fireplace, switch it on, slip a CD in the player and as gentle music floats through the room, you smile and say, "Ready?" If Jeff fusses, gather him into your arms and take him along.

After your tour, invite them to go through the house alone at their own pace. You entertain the baby somewhere within sight of the front door so you can join them again before they leave.

A nightmare successfully handled by applying common sense and a little imagination. Hopefully, you will sell your home without ever being hit by a nightmare like that, but if you are, swing with it.

By keeping your home neat, clean and organized, you have the power to cope with spur-of-the-moment messes like Jeff's bananas and milk. The homeowner had the foresight to place a plastic tablecloth daily under the highchair. Without that, she could never have cleaned up so quickly.

The last pages in this chapter are checklists for the various areas of your house, designed to help you and your family maintain your home in top shape. Make copies and keep one in a drawer in each room for easy reference every morning. It's unlikely that every room will need every action every day, but the list includes them so when you do a complete check-up of your house and yard during the two hours leading up to an appointment, you won't overlook an important detail.

Quicklist

Entrance – foyer or hall

☐ Move anything that obstructs the passageway
☐ Shake mat
☐ Wipe tray for placing shoes and boots. It should be empty.
☐ Damp wipe light switches
☐ Wash both sides of door and top edge
☐ Dust woodwork
☐ Clean windows and mirror
☐ Dust hanging picture frames. Polish glass.
☐ Dust furniture
☐ Vacuum floor, mop if tile or linoleum
☐ Wipe with barely dampened cloth if hardwood
☐ Dust light fixture
☐ Organize closet
☐ Check supply of empty coat hangers

Hicks

Quicklist

and family room

- ☐ Dust all wood surfaces
- ☐ Dust all lamps including light bulbs & wall sconces
- ☐ Plump all cushions including removable seat cushions on upholstered furniture
- ☐ Vacuum fabric-covered furniture; damp-wipe leather furniture
- ☐ Damp wipe light switches/plates
- ☐ Polish brass fittings and silver picture frames
- ☐ Dust hanging picture frames
- ☐ Stash magazines and newspapers
- ☐ Tidy bookshelf
- ☐ Put away controls for entertainment equipment
- ☐ If TV can be concealed behind doors, close them
- ☐ Remove spots from hardwood flooring
- ☐ Clean windows
- ☐ Wipe top edge of door and window frames
- ☐ Clean fireplace hearth, grate and mantle
- ☐ Wipe down fireside tools and their container
- ☐ Vacuum Dining Room
- ☐ Dust all furniture
- ☐ Clean fingerprints from backs of chairs
- ☐ Polish top of table
- ☐ Clean chandelier including bulbs
- ☐ Clean windows
- ☐ Tidy up buffet
- ☐ Vacuum carpet, damp wipe hardwood floor

Quicklist

Den or office

- ☐ Dust furniture and equipment, including computer screen
- ☐ Tidy desk
- ☐ Wipe fingerprints off desk and polish
- ☐ Damp wipe keyboard and mouse
- ☐ Close laptop and wipe top and sides
- ☐ Close filing cabinet drawers
- ☐ Wipe plastic mat under office chair
- ☐ Clean wheels and base of office chair
- ☐ Dust framed pictures
- ☐ Dust all woodwork
- ☐ Clean windows
- ☐ Tidy bookshelf
- ☐ Vacuum upholstered furniture, damp wipe leather furniture
- ☐ Stash newspapers and magazines
- ☐ Wipe hardwood floor with barely damp cloth
- ☐ Vacuum broadloom

Quicklist

Kitchen

- ☐ Clear everything off countertops
- ☐ Wash counters and dry
- ☐ Wipe cupboard doors and drawers & dry with a towel
- ☐ Open drawers and wipe out any crumbs
- ☐ Wipe sticky marks from shelving inside cupboards
- ☐ Wipe out cupboard below sink
- ☐ Organize contents in pantry
- ☐ Wipe and polish all appliances
- ☐ Clean oven window, inside oven and refrigerator shelving
- ☐ Remove magnets and memos from refrigerator door
- ☐ Dust woodwork
- ☐ Clean windows
- ☐ Make sink sparkle by wiping with vinegar
- ☐ Mop floor

Quicklist

Bedrooms

- ☐ Make beds, tucking sheets under mattress all around
- ☐ Pull bedcover tightly so there are no wrinkles
- ☐ Plump pillows and shams and place neatly on bed
- ☐ Put slippers, apparel and footwear away
- ☐ Clear all personal items off dresser top
- ☐ Close drawers and doors
- ☐ Dust furniture, woodwork and picture frames
- ☐ Dust lighting fixture and bedside lamps
- ☐ Clean windows
- ☐ Vacuum if carpeted, damp wipe if hardwood floors

Children's bedrooms

- ☐ All of the above, plus
- ☐ Put toys neatly in toy box or on shelves
- ☐ Tidy up bookshelf

Quicklist

Bathrooms

- ☐ Put grooming aids and makeup in drawers or baskets under sink
- ☐ Wipe and dry countertop, doors and drawers of cabinets
- ☐ Clean mirrors and faucets
- ☐ Empty wastebasket
- ☐ Clean windows
- ☐ Shake out or vacuum mats
- ☐ Hang new towels
- ☐ Mop floor

Laundry Room

- ☐ Clean outer surface of appliances
- ☐ Put away ironing board
- ☐ Cover laundry basket
- ☐ Put away detergent and other laundry products
- ☐ Close cupboard doors
- ☐ Clean windows
- ☐ Dust all woodwork
- ☐ Mop floor

Quicklist

Basement

☐ Wipe down stairs
☐ Remove cobwebs and spiders
☐ Dust furniture and shelving units
☐ Wipe outside of freezer chest
☐ Clean windows. Make it as bright as possible.
☐ If children play in the basement, put away toys
☐ Check furnace filter and replace if necessary
☐ People will want to inspect furnace, humidifier, water heater, water softener and electrical box. Make sure nothing is blocking their way.
☐ Vacuum floor if dirty

Garage

☐ Clean doors
☐ Clean windows
☐ If there are steps leading into the house, sweep them
☐ Sweep floor
☐ Make sure garbage cans are clean and tightly closed
☐ Wipe down shelving units

Quicklist

Front Yard & Entrance

Basics like raking, trimming, weeding, and watering grass and flowers must be done on a regular basis. Here are the things you can do during a two-hour window before an appointment:

☐ Pinch off dead flowers
☐ Remove children's bikes, wagons etc.
☐ Gather up toys
☐ Remove blue boxes and garbage cans from curb
☐ Shake out doormat
☐ Sweep sidewalk, steps and landing
☐ Polish doorknob and doorknocker
☐ Wipe down door and any dirty woodwork

BackYard

☐ Clear clutter from path leading to the backyard
☐ Collect toys
☐ Sweep steps and deck or landing. Wipe down railing.
☐ Hang up barbecue tools
☐ Cover barbecue
☐ Stash away garbage cans and blue boxes

Chapter 12

Negotiating – how to play the game

Once you have taken a few prospective buyers through your home, you'll realize that most play it one of three ways. The majority will walk through quietly, nod now and then and occasionally comment on a feature or ask a simple question. A few will fall in love with your home and won't be able to hide their pleasure and excitement over it. At the other end of the scale will be those who will criticize your choice of décor or special features and exchange disparaging remarks within earshot. Don't rise to the bait - they are conspicuously laying the groundwork for a price reduction.

Don't be disappointed if no one makes an offer the first time they view your home. Even those who fall in love with it will want to revisit. When a prospect returns with a measuring tape and dimensions of certain pieces of furniture, your heart can start to beat a little faster. If the furniture fits, there is a strong possibility they will be back to negotiate.

It's time to count the beans

When you sense that someone may be on the verge of making an offer, it's time to try and determine if he can afford your home. The first thing to do is suggest he visit your mortgage broker for pre-approval. If he balks at this, suggest he drop into his own bank, explain his financial position and the fact that he wants to buy a home, and ask how much he could be pre-approved for. You don't want to have an offer come in, take your home off the market, and then find out he can't get a mortgage.

The Internet simplifies so many things in life, including calculating mortgages. Direct your potential buyers to search for "mortgage calculators Canada" and dozens of sites will pop up. At www.canadamortgage.com, they'll find a useful, easy-to-read table that charts the maximum mortgage a person should carry in relation to income. It also shows how much home a person at various income levels can afford.

Canadian banks provide a wealth of mortgage information too. At www.royalbank.com, your buyer can anonymously plug in details about his debts and assets. In a split second, it calculates the maximum price he should pay for a home. Personal identification is not required to use either of these sites.

Seldom does anyone offer the full listing price unless it is an exceptional home in an overheated market. It may be that although they love your home, they can't handle it financially. Some thrive on wrestling the price to the mat so they walk off victoriously while you limp away with nothing to show for all your work. Most will simply want to feel they won a good deal. That's basic human nature at work again – don't take it personally.

Competition helps

If you are aware that there are two or more serious contenders for your home, you are in the best possible position. You can hint there is competition and that you expect an offer in today, or tomorrow evening. Or you have set up an appointment with a party to write up an offer. Be truthful. If no such appointment exists, don't fabricate one.

Another tactic that can work in your favour when you perceive there is strong demand for your property is to set a deadline for offers. You advise prospective buyers that you will accept offers between 4:00 p.m. and 6:00 p.m. on Saturday. This notches up the pressure and pretty well guarantees a quick sale at top price. It is not unheard of in a feisty urban market such as Toronto's for homes to sell at higher-than-list price. The presentation of offers is akin to an auction with the highest bidder claiming the spoils.

This dream seldom materializes for a typical home in an average neighbourhood. Most homeowners are expected to negotiate. Before you meet your first prospect, analyze your position. On the plus side, you have given the buyer an appraisal and a home inspection. You have satisfied his need to know what your home is worth and what condition it's in. To guarantee he doesn't face expensive, unexpected repairs down the road, you are prepared to hand him a Home Warranty on closing.

Added value

Calculate the monetary value of these three items. For the purpose of this example, let's assume you paid $300 for the inspection, $400 for the appraisal and will pay $200 for the warranty, for a total of $900. Did you list your home at below or close to the appraised value? If yes, your answer when asked to shave more off the price is simple. In an unflinching voice that is neither contentious nor antagonistic, you say:

> "I spent $400 dollars on an appraisal so we both know the house is listed at fair market price. Then I saved you $300 on the home inspection. On top of that, I'm adding more value by offering to give a free home warranty worth another $200. Do you honestly believe the price is unreasonable?" You end with a friendly smile.

That couple that fell in love with your home will probably eye each other, smile back and reply, "It sounds fair. Let's get on with the paperwork!" But most buyers will squeeze a little harder.

In chapter one, I mentioned that four potential buyers came to see the house. One of them telephoned to tell me that he had driven six miles further north of my house and discovered he could buy a home comparable in size to ours for thousands of dollars less. He was fishing for a better price. As I listened, my mind raced. How should I respond?

> "You are absolutely right," I agreed "Six miles further up is not Regal Estates (fictitious name) and it's further from the city so naturally

> property values are cheaper. Only you know your financial situation and whether you can afford our home. Perhaps you should seriously consider that other house."

I spoke politely but firmly with no apologies. I was afraid I had insulted him and would ever hear from him again. Two days later, he was back with an offer – the one we accepted!

Do the math

A note pad and pencil are the tools you need to prepare for the next level of negotiations. Write down how much money you would have paid in real estate commissions if you were not listing your home as 4SBO. Now subtract how much of that commission was applied to reduce the listing price of the house. If your goal was to sell your home quickly, you may have pared the listing price by half of the commission - up to three per cent.

You need to calculate if you can reduce the price further, and if so, by how much. Analyze each of the following, making notes and recording the numbers on the note pad as you proceed:

- How quickly do you want to sell? If you can wait, you have a better chance of holding the line on the price.
- How much must you recover from the sale to pay off the mortgage and other commitments?
- If you have already bought a new home, how much do you need to meet all the closing and moving costs?

Jot down lots of numbers. In fact, fill the top page of your note pad with strings of randomly placed numbers accompanied by scribbled short notes, the way a serious number-cruncher would do. This is your worksheet – it tells the story. It's also your prop for the round of negotiations with a buyer who is tightening the screws.

Bring the notepad and its calculations to the next meeting with the buyer who is demanding a better deal. Begin by sitting very straight with your hands folded on the table in front of you. There is total silence for a minute or two while you concentrate on the worksheet in front of you. Silence is golden right now. Take time to really study the figures and notes. The buyer can see a page jammed with numbers and notations but it's positioned so he can't read anything clearly. Now you lean forward a bit, look him gently in the eye and earnestly state your case. Here's a sample of what you might say:

> "As you can see, I've spent a lot of time working and reworking the numbers. One of the reasons I chose to sell this home myself was to save the real estate fees. I have to cover some steep financial obligations. The very best I could do is give you $500 off the price (or whatever your figure is)."

Next, repeat the same logic you used in the first negotiating session we covered:

> "I invested $400 dollars on an appraisal so we both know the house is listed at fair market price. Then I spent $300 on the home inspection. On top of that, I'm offering to add more value by giving you a free home warranty worth over $200. Do you honestly believe the price is unreasonable?

> "Joe, I would like to do business with you. I think you would be a definite asset to this neighbourhood and would quickly make a lot of friends here, but I simply can't go lower." Again you end with a friendly smile.

Born to barter

It's easy if you never lose sight of the fact that this is a game society requires you to play. When our early ancestors started trading, bartering was the only way to do business. Today, many buyers will only deal if they are convinced they have reached the absolute lowest price. The driving force could be genetic, psychological or simply the challenge of the chase. Don't be nervous. Don't be afraid. Don't lose your temper or your patience. Just understand that it's a game that, with practice, you can play like a pro.

You can have fun doing the homework for your negotiating sessions. Build a few imaginary encounters between you and a buyer and practise. Sit down with a friend or relative and develop your dialogue. You want to be absolutely comfortable and in control. If you can exude a sense of confidence, the buyer will know intuitively that the best price is on the table and negotiations are over. He either agrees to your terms or leaves.

When you reach an agreement, shake hands on it and immediately turn to a fresh page in your note pad and work out the details. Emotions can run high during the negotiating process, even though both parties appear cool on the surface. The buyer may think he heard you agree to something that you didn't. Now is the time to put it all on paper and clear up any misconceptions. Make a copy and hand it to your buyer.

Once he has looked it over, you have reached the most important juncture since you made the decision months ago to sell. It's time to draw up the Agreement of Purchase and Sale. Right now, not tomorrow morning. You want that signature before he walks out the door. The next chapter tells you everything you need to know about the Agreement of Purchase and Sale. Pour a coffee and get comfortable; you are about to absorb a vast amount of very important information.

Did I just hear you say you don't care about all the small print in the agreement? Big mistake! Whether you are buying or selling a home, you must be utterly certain you know what you are signing. In all likelihood, this will be the only opportunity in your lifetime to have every clause explained to you in words that everyone, not just lawyers, can understand.

Chapter 13

Sealing the deal

The single most important document involved with selling your house is the contract between you and the buyer, the Agreement of Purchase and Sale. This Agreement sets out all of the rights and obligations between the parties. Besides simple things such as the purchase price, the property description and the closing date, it sets out important legal issues such as conditions that must be met before the Agreement is binding, or warranties about the property for which you will be held accountable.

What follows is an overview of the standard contents of an Agreement of Purchase and Sale, and some drafting tips to help you prepare your Agreement. While each province, and in some cases each municipality, may have a different form of contract, much of the required information and contract terms are substantially the same. The following discussion may not exactly follow your province's common form of agreement, but the information will likely appear in one way or another. Having said that, remember that this is a **general** overview. It is important that you always read the Agreement, consult your lawyer, and make sure you understand **everything** in it.

The Contract process

Your 4SBO kit comes complete with sample contracts for the sale of your property. The contracts have been professionally drafted and are custom tailored for each Canadian province. Pull out the contract applicable to your province and photocopy a supply for your use. If the photocopy resources are available to you, copy the form onto the size of paper that is customary in your region (standard or legal - see sample forms).

The forms have been prepared to reflect a typical Agreement of Purchase and Sale in any given province. They have not been drafted in favour of one party over another. If it appears so, it's because local laws or customs dictate it. Some of the forms will, in fact, contradict my drafting advice. For example, some forms allow for a Property Disclosure Statement, others provide for a new survey. These are both things that I recommend avoiding whenever possible; they are included in the forms because their absence will be conspicuous in certain regions. The focus is on providing accepted terms, rather than scaring away prospective buyers with a one-sided agreement. Having said this, by all means customize the forms and draft them in your favour. Consult your lawyer when doing so to make sure you don't run afoul of local customs or laws.

You'll want to prepare your Agreement in advance so it's ready to go when you have an eager buyer. Because your property is unique, and because laws change, and because every region within a province may have unique practices, you should have your agreement reviewed in advance by a lawyer before it becomes binding (see Chapter 10).

When meeting with a prospective buyer, have several copies of your Agreement on hand. You can either print multiple copies so you always have a blank copy on hand for other buyers, or you can have one master copy and make photocopies after you have completed most of the information. This will save you time when you're ready to draw up the Agreement, and will ensure that the information you filled in is accurate on every copy.

Agents traditionally prepare four identical Agreements, and have all four signed. You should have two at a minimum – one for you, one for the buyer. At every stage of the negotiation process (offer, counteroffer and acceptance), each copy must be identically worded and with original signatures and initials where applicable.

The offer

One last point before starting: You should understand the process of offer, counteroffer and acceptance. The Agreement originates, not as an agreement, but as an offer. It is usually the buyer making an offer to you, even though you may have prepared the document. The buyer offers to buy the property at the price and on the terms set out in the document. Under contract law, an offer is open for acceptance at any time until it is revoked or expires (expiry requires a time limit). In real estate transactions, offers often have irrevocable dates, which require that the offer, or counteroffer, as the case may be, stays open for a fixed period. This allows the person receiving the offer some time to think about it without worrying about it being withdrawn.

Implications of the counteroffer

Upon obtaining the offer from a buyer, you have three choices: accept it, reject it, or submit a counteroffer. A counteroffer means submitting the document back with any change on it. In this event, the parties that have made them should initial all changes. Any time a counteroffer is submitted, it has the effect of voiding the prior offer. So, you cannot change a term, find out the buyer doesn't like the change, and then hold him to his original offer. Your change clears him of any further obligation until he either accepts your new terms or presents you with a counteroffer of his own.

If your change is not accepted, and you want to go back to his last offer, you must submit a new counteroffer matching the previous terms. For these reasons, as you get closer to a deal, you may want to feel him out for terms that he will accept. And remember, it's a two-way street. The buyer will also be aware of the fact that every counteroffer that he makes provides you with an opportunity to walk away. For all he knows, you may have come up with a higher bidder just waiting for the tabled offer to be rejected.

Acceptance may be as simple as the receiving party initialling the changes made. Some agreements have specific signing sections at the end that allow for counteroffers or acceptance. Use these if they appear. Don't be intimidated by the "seal" requirement that appears on some forms. You don't need to have your own seal or even put a mark other than your signature on the document. The seal is an antiquated legal habit and the absence of your "seal" will not affect the enforceability of your contract. Once accepted, the document becomes a binding Agreement of Purchase and Sale. It may still have conditions, but depending on how the conditions are drafted, they may not allow for an escape.

So now that you understand the process, put on your 4SBO hat and let's get drafting . . .

The Agreement

Buyer/Seller

When defining the buyer and the seller, ensure that the seller is the person or persons to whom the title is registered, presumably you and anyone else you own the property with. Consult your deed if you don't know how you hold title. On many deeds, the property owners are listed as the "transferees." The "buyer," despite the use of the singular term, should be all the parties that you intend to hold accountable to the contract. In some jurisdictions the terms buyer and seller may be replaced with "purchaser" and "vendor" respectively. Avoid any buyer trying to submit an offer "in trust," or consult your lawyer about it.

Property

Describe the property as best as possible, using both the municipal address and the legal description, if available (see your deed). Be careful with dimensions (frontage, depth, etc.). Even though most agreements allow for some leeway by saying "more or less," it does happen that problems arise because it is discovered that the property does not conform to the dimensions represented in the Agreement. If you're putting it in, make sure you know.

Land is typically referred to as "Real Property," and in law – whether the contract says so or not – unless expressly excluded, it includes all buildings and structures on the land.

Price

Often the forms allow for the purchase price (and deposit) to be stated in both words and numbers, as you would do when filling out a cheque. This avoids any misunderstandings or typographical errors. Some of the common form agreements don't provide a space, but it is nonetheless prudent practice. Dollars will be deemed to be Canadian unless otherwise stated.

Deposit

The deposit should be an amount that is a reasonable estimation of your damages in the event that the buyer defaults on the deal. Such damages might include things like your carrying costs, the costs of re-selling the property, possible depreciation, etc. Having said this, deposit amounts vary dramatically from region to region and may depend on the nature of the property. Ten per cent is often an accepted standard, but that can be a lot of money for the buyer to raise immediately, and there will be other factors to consider, including how eager you are to have the buyer sign.

Most of the 4SBO forms set out what will happen to the deposit. Generally it belongs to the seller if the buyer defaults, or it is returned to the buyer if the agreement is not accepted or firmed up. There may be a single deposit or several, payable in stages. The initial deposit can be submitted with the original offer, or be produced shortly after the agreement is accepted, depending on what the agreement requires. Unlike the closing proceeds, it is not uncommon for deposits to be given by uncertified, personal cheque. You should have it cashed immediately and then confirm that it clears.

Traditionally a real estate broker would hold the deposit in trust. On a 4SBO transaction, the deposit should be made payable to you or your lawyer. The buyer will likely insist that it be held "in trust" - most common form agreements provide for this - and the buyer may also insist that it be made payable to, and be held in trust by your lawyer. If you consider the buyer's perspective, these are not unreasonable terms.

You should specify whether the deposit will include interest or not, and to whom such interest will be payable. If the deposit is being paid into a lawyer's trust account, you should be aware that some trust accounts do not bear interest, which means that if the buyer is entitled to interest under the agreement, you might find yourself paying it out of your own pocket. It is easiest to follow common practice and avoid the interest unless there is a substantial amount involved and the buyer is insisting.

Adjustments

Most agreements provide, in one way or another, that the balance due on closing will be subject to the usual adjustments. Some agreements will set out exactly what these adjustments will be. For example, property taxes will be adjusted as of the closing date. Taxes will be calculated at a daily rate, and if, on the closing date, you have overpaid your taxes you will receive a credit on closing for the overpaid amount. If, on the other hand, some of your share of the taxes have not yet come due, you will be required to compensate the buyer and your proportionate amount will be deducted from the balance due on closing.

Usually all taxes levied up to the closing date must be paid in full.

Other amounts that may be adjusted in similar fashion include water rates, local improvement charges, condominium fees, fuel oil supplied on closing and tenant rents. If you foresee issues on any of these things, consider dealing with them more expressly in advance. For example, if your property has recently been assessed for pending local improvements, discuss it with the buyer and make the agreement clear as to how these additional rates will be apportioned between you. Similarly, if there are oil or propane tanks, decide with the buyer and set out in the Agreement whether he wants the tanks filled on closing and adjusted for (which is often the standard procedure).

Closing date

The closing date should not be on a weekend or holiday, although the common form of agreement from some regions allows for the transaction to close on non-business days. Many jurisdictions cannot transact a closing unless the documents can be registered at the local Land Registry Office, which means a business day, and during regular business hours. Agents are in the habit of choosing a date at the end of the month, usually a Friday. There is no good reason for this. Unless you have a reason for doing so, a mid-month closing will avoid the month-end rush and give your lawyer more time to devote to your file. It will also make it easier to find available services such as moving companies.

The closing date is simply the subject of negotiation between you and the buyer. It can be a matter of days if your lawyers can put it together that fast. The buyer, in particular, should ask his lawyer before committing to a short closing. The buyer's lawyer will need a reasonable period of time to investigate the property, and in this regard two weeks or more is to be expected. Anything from three to 10 weeks seems to be the standard in most jurisdictions. Longer closing periods are also possible, however the buyer will need to be careful about financing commitments in this regard, as lenders will only hold a mortgage commitment for so long.

Condominiums

Selling an interest in a condominium has some unique aspects and requirements. You should always fill out the Agreement appropriately and include a special clause dealing with condominium issues.

First, a condominium is a unique form of legal interest. The deed will reflect the interest being transferred as a "condominium" and not a "freehold" or "fee simple" interest. When describing the property you must always be sure to state that it is a condominium and include (or exclude) all parking spaces, storage units or other exclusive-use parts of the condominium complex to which the unit owner is entitled.

The buyer should also be made aware that ownership of the condominium unit is subject to the Declaration, By-Laws and Rules of the Condominium Corporation. These could put limits on fundamental issues such as pets, children or the ability to make improvements. These documents also outline the geographical limits of your condominium interest (e.g., to the back side of the drywall), and any agreements that govern the daily operations of your condominium complex such as maintenance agreements and the use of common elements. The condominium documents will set out your unit's proportionate share of the regular condominium fees. For all of these reasons, all the stated condominium documents should be made readily available to the buyer for inspection before signing. Preferably these documents should be added to the Agreement, or at the very least they should be otherwise acknowledged, and confirmed as reviewed and accepted by the buyer. Among the other adjustments set out in the Agreement, the closing adjustments on a condominium transaction will typically include any condo fees or deposits, as well as any keys or garage opener deposits (assuming the latter are left behind).

A central document on a condominium purchase is the Estoppel Certificate or Certificate of Status, or whatever it might be called in your region. This is a document in which the condominium corporation certifies to the requesting party, for a fee, the economic (and other) status of the unit, the common elements and the corporation as a whole.

In some jurisdictions, it has recently become the custom for the seller to pay for and provide the certificate. This flies in the face of the traditional method of caveat emptor, in which it was the buyer's responsibility to acquire and review the certificate. The certificate may disclose a problem or deficiency, in which case it is usually left to the parties' lawyers to resolve. For the buyer's purposes, the certificate must be relatively recent, so, if you are going to acquire the certificate prior to signing, it is not recommended that you do so too far in advance of the closing date, otherwise someone will be required to suffer the cost of a new certificate at some point.

You may be requested to make a representation as to your knowledge concerning any announced or anticipated liabilities of the condominium corporation, increases in unit reserve requirements, maintenance costs, capital costs, unit fees, and the like. As always, make sure you are comfortable with the content of any such warranty, because you may be called on it.

Because of the complexity of condominium documentation and laws, it is not uncommon for the parties to make the Agreement conditional upon a satisfactory review of the Declaration, By-Laws and Rules by a lawyer, for the benefit of either party or both parties.

Lastly, you will also want to clearly set out in the Agreement the monthly condo fees, and the fact that this figure is subject to moderate change pending closing.

Conditions

Conditions are one of the types of clauses that are frequently added to and customized on pre-printed real estate forms. For this reason they can also be the most controversial. Be sure that you know what they say and have them reviewed by a lawyer.

The term "condition" in a real estate contract refers to something that must happen before the contract becomes firm. Be certain you understand the effect of the condition and how it works. Some regions tend towards the agreement being <u>firm</u>, unless the condition is communicated as being unsatisfied; other regions tend towards treating the agreement as <u>null and void</u> unless satisfaction of the condition is communicated. Also bear in mind that <u>communication</u> of the condition being satisfied or unsatisfied is usually the key.

There is a general principle – and sometimes it is stated in the common form of agreement – that the parties must use reasonable efforts to satisfy the conditions that are their responsibility, but that is a wishy-washy concept and at best difficult to prove. Practically speaking, a condition is to some degree an escape clause. So, unless they are for your benefit, you would rather not have them.

It is in everyone's interest to keep the terms of a condition clear. To this end the following are some of the details that should be included in any condition:

- What is the condition? – state clearly what is required
- Who is responsible for satisfying it?
- What constitutes satisfaction (i.e., is there discretion or is third party proof required)?
- For whose benefit is it being included?
- Can it be waived if not satisfied?
- What is the time deadline?
- What is the result if it is not met (e.g., Agreement void or firm, deposit returned, etc.)?

Representations and warranties

"Reps and Warranties" are the other types of clauses that are commonly added to and customized on pre-printed real estate forms. Again, know what they say and have them reviewed by a lawyer.

For the most part the legal doctrine of "caveat emptor" applies to real estate transactions. It means "buyer beware," or more specifically that the buyer must satisfy himself about the status of the property: title, legality, quality, etc. Reps and Warranties try to bring the seller back into the picture and for this reason they are dangerous to you. By including a warranty, in particular, you are essentially guaranteeing the buyer something about the property. Sometimes Reps and Warranties are unavoidable, and some common forms of agreement have them built in if that is the local standard. If you must give a representation or warranty, make sure you consider adding the following:

- A clear description of what is being promised
- Whether it is based on fact, or is "to the best of your knowledge"
- Will there be verification before closing – if so, how and by whom?
- What will happen if the statement turns out to be untrue?
- Is it enforceable after closing?

For example, it can become a muddy question of law and contract interpretation as to whether you are on the hook for your guarantee after the closing date. Lawyers love to argue about what is a representation and what is a warranty, and whether they have been complied with, and whether either a representation or a warranty survives closing. The best way to avoid being in the middle of such an argument, is not to make any written statements about the property unless you are 100% confident about them, and not to make any written promises that you might not be able to keep.

UFFI

It is common for the seller to provide a UFFI warranty. What is UFFI? It stands for urea formaldehyde foam insulation – a chemical foam that was once sprayed inside the exterior walls of older houses for insulation purposes. It was subsequently found to be toxic and banned.

Houses that have UFFI suffer a significantly depreciated property value and may be dangerous. Most people who have UFFI in their home know it, and have either had the insulation removed or they monitor it. You would probably know if your house had UFFI, but as with all warranties, make sure you are comfortable with a statement about whether it is in your house or not. Some of the UFFI warranties are "to the best of your knowledge," which is better than giving an absolute warranty. If you are unsure about the status of your house, and you want to know, your home inspector (see Chapter 4) should be able to tell you.

Survey

A "survey" or "surveyor's real property report" or "certificate of location" is a schematic layout of the property that accurately shows its boundaries and the locations of all dwellings, fences, structures and other relevant markings or items. In some provinces (e.g., Alberta and Quebec) it is commonplace for the seller to provide one, and in those instances it is part of the 4SBO standard forms that the seller provide a new survey. In other jurisdictions, the survey is more the subject of negotiation. Many common forms of agreement do not address the issue of a new survey, and if there is to be a new survey clause, it must be added separately. Many forms do, however, require that the seller disclose and provide any existing surveys, if any, that may be in their possession. Check the common form agreement that applies to your province.

Your preference is certainly not to pay for a survey and ideally not to have one done at all. From a seller's perspective, the only thing a survey can do is disclose problems. You may feel comfortable with a survey clause:

- If you had a survey when you bought the property, and
- If your lawyer at the time reviewed that survey and told you everything was fine, and
- If you have not made any changes since, and
- If your neighbours have not made any changes that might affect your property.

That's a lot of ifs. In the event you did not have an up-to-date survey when you bought the property, you should know that your lawyer's opinion to you was probably qualified by anything that would have been revealed by a new survey. Under these circumstances you may be sitting on a problem that you are not even aware of, and have no recourse of any kind unless you have title insurance. Worse, under the new Agreement you may be obligated to fix the problem, or the problem may ruin the deal – and all because of a survey that you paid for! So avoid a new survey unless you are confident that it won't disclose any problems.

If you agree to provide a survey, be sure you have one to give, or be prepared to pay for a new one. You may think you have a survey, but it may not meet the buyer's or the buyer's lawyer's requirements. A "sketch" of the property, or a simple boundary survey, is not the kind of survey that a buyer usually needs or expects. Technically a survey should be an original, with a surveyor's seal, showing all buildings, lot lines and fences, and noting all relevant set-back distances.

A standard survey clause will require that a survey be up-to-date in the sense that there have not been any additions or changes from the date it was prepared. Some lenders, the people your buyer is borrowing money from to purchase your property, require a survey that is not more than ten years old. How old is the one you have on hand? If you are asked to provide an existing survey, it should be attached as a schedule so the buyer knows in advance what he is getting, and the Agreement should expressly state that you make no representations or warranties regarding the suitability, accuracy or completeness of the survey.

Title insurance: a better way

A recent alternative to surveys in Canada is title insurance. A title insurance policy will insure the buyer against any deficiencies that would have been disclosed by an up-to-date survey. Title insurance can be a seller's best friend, because, not only does it save you the cost of the survey, but it avoids any problems that would have been uncovered by the survey, while still protecting the buyers interests. If you are getting hung up negotiating the cost of a new survey, present the option of title insurance and negotiate around the much lesser cost (approximately half) of a title insurance policy.

Fixtures and chattels

What is a fixture; what is a chattel; what is included? Some common forms of Agreement are clear on this, and some are not so. You should understand the distinction between fixtures and chattels, and if your agreement is not clear, simply list all the items that you expect to be included and/or excluded as part of the deal, regardless of what class they fall into.

A "fixture" generally refers to anything that is screwed, glued, nailed, bolted or otherwise attached to the property. In the same way that the law specifies that land includes all buildings and structures, so too does it include all fixtures. In other words, fixtures are deemed to be sold with the land unless expressly excluded. Ownership of the fixtures is transferred by the deed. So, for example if you want to take the chandelier with you, list it as an excluded fixture.

"Chattels" are all other items not affixed to the property, and the general rule is that they are not included in the purchase price unless the Agreement specifically provides so. Chattels include items such as refrigerators, stoves, washing machines, etc. If you are selling such chattels, ownership is transferred by a separate Bill of Sale, which is usually delivered by you on closing. Depending on the value of the chattels, provincial sales taxes may be an issue, although it is customarily ignored on incidental items. Some common forms of agreement expressly state who will pay such additional taxes. If, for example, an expensive boat is included as part of the deal, make sure your Agreement specifies that any applicable sales tax shall be "in addition to" the purchase price.

As you can imagine, relying on the distinction between chattels and fixtures leaves much room for argument. What about the basketball net, or the fountain in the backyard? Okay, so the satellite antenna is bolted to the roof, but not the converter box that runs it. What about a built-in dishwasher? Who gets the hoses and attachments for the central vacuum system, or the pool skimmer? Where window dressings are concerned, the common wisdom seems to be that drapes are not included, but all curtain rods and other mechanisms are – which may or may not make sense depending on your and your buyer's intentions. To be on the safe side, whenever there is room for doubt, be specific.

Finally, an included chattel or fixture may be a rented item. Hot water tanks or furnaces are often culprits for this oversight. Consider whether any of the items you are purporting to sell are rented and not owned. If they are rented, either exclude them from the Agreement, or better yet, obligate the buyer to assume the rental contract on its terms. Give the buyer a copy of the rental contract to review, and for greater certainty include it in the Agreement as a schedule. Of course, you will have already confirmed that the rental contract can be taken over by another person. If it is not assumable by the buyer, and you do not intend to continue the payments, you must be prepared to pay off the debt in full.

Property condition

It is a generally accepted practice that, on closing, the property should be in substantially the same condition it was when the agreement was signed (or some agreements may say when it was inspected by the buyer). Essentially this means you can't allow the property to deteriorate before closing. On the other hand, if a defect existed that the buyer could have seen by reasonable inspection, but did not (for example, a hole in the wall behind the couch), then the buyer has to accept that defect and you are not responsible for repairing it.

It is common courtesy to clean the house and tidy up the property when leaving it. It is also common practice to leave behind any extra door keys, mailbox keys, garage door openers, alarm codes and manuals and warranties for fixtures and included chattels.

Most agreements provide by default that the property will be vacant on closing. This means two things.

- First, that there are no people on the property. This includes no tenants or other ongoing occupational rights. If tenants are to continue living in the space, with or without the new owner, then this must be clearly set out elsewhere in the Agreement. Tenancy arrangements usually accompany a number of other clauses (See Chapter 19 sample clauses).
- Second, you must remove all of your chattels as well as any fixtures not included in the purchase price. In short it means you must remove all of your belongings and all of your garbage. You may not temporarily store things on the property (unless you and the buyer agreed so in writing), and you may not leave behind things you don't want, but think the buyer might like to have.

Further inspections

Some agreements provide a standard clause allowing the buyer to perform further property inspections before closing; others require that any such clauses be separately added, if desired. From a seller's perspective, further inspections are not desirable and you should try to steer away from them if possible. First, they are a nuisance, but far more importantly they may give the buyer cause for second guessing their decision. This is particularly true if the inspection is to occur after your belongings are removed, when the worn carpet becomes more apparent and only the picture hangers are left on the walls. This is not to say that an inspection clause fundamentally changes the rights or obligations of the parties, or that the inspection will entitle the buyer to an out, but simply that if there is a potential escape to be found, the buyer is apt to look for it that much harder after a disappointing inspection.

Despite the foregoing, many agreements will provide for, and many buyers will insist on, a further inspection clause. It may not be certain law, but there is case law that suggests that, in any event, a buyer may be entitled to such an inspection to ensure that there has been no substantial damage to the property prior to closing. So, if a further inspection cannot be avoided, consider addressing the following in the inspection clause:

- When can the inspection be performed (on or before a specific date)?
- How much advance notice do you require?
- How many inspections are allowed?
- What is the purpose of the inspection(s)?
- Who may be present at the inspection(s)?

Title searches

In a real estate transaction, the buyer is responsible for verifying that the title is good and that the intended use of the property as contemplated in the Agreement is legal. The buyer's lawyer will look after the necessary searches before closing, and your lawyer will answer any concerns or problems (title requisitions) that are raised. If title problems are raised, you should review your lawyer's opinion from the time you acquired the property to see if it was addressed at that time. You should also ask your lawyer to look into how a title insurance policy might be able to insure over the problem.

Reviewing the letter of opinion that you obtained from your lawyer when you purchased the property is a good idea in any event - even before you draft the new Agreement. If there were any title problems at that time, they will be set out in the opinion letter and may be dealt with proactively in your new Agreement. You should solicit your current lawyer's help in the event that custom drafting is required.

Other matters that the lawyers will look at relate to the state of the taxes and other charges, as well as the legal use of the property. By legal use I am referring to things like the existence of permits for all things that needed permits, and compliance with zoning by-laws. Some agreements deem the use contemplated in the Agreement as the current use, others require that the parties specify the legal use. If your precedent requires that you insert the legal use, more than likely it will be "single family residential." Again, to be sure, you should consult your lawyer's opinion from the time you bought the property. Certainly if you suspect any building or zoning issues, you should consult with your lawyer on those issues in advance.

Some of the Atlantic provinces will require that you insert the type of Deed you will be giving. A typical deed is a "warranty" deed, but consult with your lawyer in this regard.

Existing mortgages, encumbrances or Liens

Unless being assumed by the buyer, any existing mortgage(s) on the property will need to be paid out in full, discharged and removed from title. The logistics of this on closing are handled differently from one province to another. The 4SBO sample agreements are designed to accommodate the procedure in each province. Your lawyers will look after the details. For your part you should simply be prepared to plan your finances accordingly. Keep in mind things like prepayment penalties and discharge fees when assessing the cost of exiting your current mortgage.

You should also be aware that in most jurisdictions, outstanding judgements or court orders against you or any other co-owners may attach to your property and will likely be disclosed by the buyer's inquiries. You should be reasonably comfortable that you are clear of such judgements, or have your lawyer conduct a preliminary search before getting to the latter stages of the transaction. The preliminary search might also be prudent if you are a discharged bankrupt, or owe family support payments from the past, since old writs and judgements, although perhaps expunged, have a bad habit of hanging around.

Insurance

Most agreements obligate the seller to keep the property insured against fire and other hazards until closing. It is a good idea to do so in any event. If you fail to do so and there is a catastrophe, you might find yourself obligated to go out of pocket and rebuild the damage in order to deliver on your contract with the buyer.

GST/HST

As a general rule, residential resale transactions are not subject to Federal Goods & Services Tax [GST], or in the Atlantic provinces Harmonized Sales Tax [HST]. New home sales are subject to GST, and the sale of a substantially renovated dwelling may be subject to GST. If you are in doubt on this issue, consult your lawyer. Most agreements specifically state who shall be responsible for GST/HST if it is payable, but the accepted practice is not consistent across the country. Some standard form agreements say it shall be in addition to the purchase price, others require that it be included, which means that the seller pays it. The likelihood is that GST does not apply to the sale of your house, but you should be comfortable with this issue in advance because, as the seller, you may be required to produce a certificate to that effect on closing.

Family law issues

In most jurisdictions across Canada the rights of spouses in real estate transactions must be addressed in the Agreement. This may be in the form of an accompanying affidavit, or a spousal consent, or a simple statement by the seller as to spousal status. Consult your lawyer in this regard. Usually your spouse must sign the consent even if technically he/she is not named in the deed and is not on the title. If your spouse does hold the title with you, he/she will have to sign as a co-seller. If you have a spouse, and your spouse does not do one of these two things, you may find yourself in immediate breach of the contract.

Notice

Most agreements require that any offer, counteroffer, acceptance, or removal of a condition be in writing and communicated in order to be effective. This means that parties must know where to reach one another. One of the most reliable destinations is a lawyer's office with a fax machine, so it is recommended that you allow for such service if you and the buyer have a lawyer at the time of signing. The Agreement should specify where and by what manner such written communication, or notice, may be given. For this reason it is advisable that the Agreement provide each party's address, fax number (if any), and lawyers' information (if available at that time). Be careful, some standard forms do not necessarily allow for service of notice by fax – you must put it in if you want that option. Make sure you always know somewhere that you can reliably reach the buyer to serve them with notice.

Custom Clauses

Most standard form agreements have a blank section that allows for custom conditions or terms to be added. Your 4SBO kit comes with samples of some of the standard clauses that you may want to include, or be asked by the buyer to include. Some of the clauses may be familiar, as they appear pre-printed in some standard form documents – this is simply a matter of regional custom. Most agreements specify that any such additions take precedence over the pre-printed form, so make sure you are comfortable with them. And as always, make sure you read and understand the added clauses and have them reviewed by your lawyer before you are obligated to them under the contract.

Legal terms

There are a few legal concepts that run through virtually all of the common forms of agreement. Briefly summarized they include the following (also see the 4SBO Glossary):

"time of the essence"

This means that time limits will be strictly enforced. If you or the buyer are even one minute past a deadline, it's too bad.

"entire agreement"

This type of clause makes it clear that the entire Agreement must be in writing and within the four corners of the document. Put another way, there are no side agreements and no one is relying on things that were discussed but are not included in the document. It also follows that the Agreement should be complete. Do not leave out fundamental terms such as the parties, the price or the property description, otherwise the contract may be deemed void for being uncertain.

"tender"

This is the term used when one party presents everything it is required to produce and delivers it to the other party in an effort to show that it is (or later in court, was) ready, willing and able to close. It is also used to simply describe the act of handing over the required money, the deed, the keys, or whatever else may be critical to the closing. Tender usually is accomplished by delivery to the other lawyer.

"contra preferentem"

This is a legal principle that says if there is a discrepancy or unclear clause in the Agreement, then it should be construed against the person who drafted it. In this case that would be you - which is not something you want. Most of the 4SBO forms state that this doctrine shall not apply and the Agreement shall be interpreted equally between the parties.

The foregoing discusses most of the sections of an agreement that you may be required to complete, as well as some of the pre-printed matters that you should be aware of. There is much more. A house sale is probably one of the most complex legal transactions you will ever engage in. There is a lot there and it's all there for a reason. My advice? **Read the whole document and consult** a lawyer!

The Property Disclosure Statement

A Property Disclosure Statement is a document completed by the seller that summarizes the seller's knowledge of the property on a variety of issues. It is not mandatory in most jurisdictions.

Every region tends to have its own form of Statement. Examples of some of the more concerning questions include the following:

- Does the subject property comply with zoning?
- Are there any public projects or road widenings planned?

- Are you aware of any problems with the well or septic?
- Are you aware of any environmental problems on the property?
- Is there an existing or proposed waste site nearby?
- Are there any pending real estate developments nearby?
- Are you aware of any structural problems?
- Have all permits been obtained?
- Are there any fire code deficiencies?
- Is the fireplace/chimney in good working order?
- Is there lead in the plumbing?
- What is under the carpeting?
- Is there a home inspection report available?

I would not want to see you answer any of these questions. Since the Statement usually specifies that it is not a warranty, and allows for the questions to be answered "unknown," why put yourself in that position? The chance of the information being manipulated against the seller is great, particularly if the Statement is made part of the Agreement. Consequently, whenever possible, avoid the Property Disclosure Statement entirely.

Extended use of the Property Disclosure Statement turns the entire foundation of caveat emptor on its head. Why, and where did it come from, you ask? In most jurisdictions it arose for the benefit of real estate agents. It was originally designed as a source of information that they could rely on when listing and describing the property, and its main purpose was to fend off claims alleging that the agent knowingly misrepresented a property. Knowing that it was available, it then became commonplace for buyers to ask for the Statement. It is becoming more and more commonplace for agents to include it in the Agreements, and in some jurisdictions it has even found a place in the standard forms of agreement. Given its initial purpose, the Property Disclosure Statement has no place in a 4SBO transaction unless statutorily required.

Despite all of the foregoing, a buyer may insist on a Property Disclosure Statement and may even insist on making it part of the Agreement. It can be incorporated in the Agreement either by reference in a representation or warranty, or by attaching it as a schedule. Before doing so, consider how confident you are about the content of the Statement and make sure the Agreement specifies the manner in which it is being included (as a representation, as a warranty, to the best of your knowledge, etc.). Refer to the discussion above about Representations and Warranties regarding specific matters that should be considered in any clause. Avoid ambiguous statements like: "The Property Disclosure Statement attached hereto shall form an integral part of this Agreement."

If you are unsure about whether or not the Statement is required, or whether or not your objection to providing it is unreasonable, ask your lawyer what the common practice is in your region. Regions vary dramatically in this regard and it may be that in your region it is not uncommon for sellers to refuse to provide a Property Disclosure Statement. More importantly, ask your lawyer about the legal impact of the Statement based on your Agreement and the laws of your jurisdiction.

Chapter 14

Finding the money

To finally clutch a signed offer in your hands is to experience a surge of joy and relief. A burden slips from your shoulders like the shudder of a giant icicle collapsing from an eavestrough. Life can return to normal; no longer do you need to live in a showcase home. You can leave your slippers beside the bed, your hairbrush on the vanity and Spiff the dog sleeping on the couch. It's a gratifying sense of freedom spiked with victory. You want to shout to the world, "I sold my home!"

But have you? It's true, you have a signed Agreement of Purchase and Sale accompanied by a respectable deposit cheque made out to your lawyer, but the major chunk of the money is yet to come. Until that cheque has been delivered on closing day, you are not home free (excuse the pun).

Obtaining financing is the most critical step your buyer must take. It is not unusual for the purchase agreement to include a clause making the sale conditional on the buyer qualifying for the mortgage he needs. If you've followed the advice in the previous chapter about how to close the sale, that condition will be short-lived – for no more than one week.

The alarm bells in your head should clang frantically if the purchaser mentions that he doesn't have the funds for the down payment. This warns you that he has to borrow money for the down payment too, so will be financing more than the 75% maximum recommended by lending specialists. Consider yourself fortunate that you weren't approached to fund the deposit!

Find a broker

Three days after signing, it is not presumptuous of you to call and ask what progress he has made. If he fumbles with his answer, and you sense that he has not moved forward on this yet, suggest he contact the Canadian Institute of Mortgage Brokers and Lenders either through the Web site www.cimbl.ca or by telephone at 1-888-442-4625. They should be able to direct him to a broker in his area who can negotiate the most competitive mortgage for him. There is no cost to the buyer for this service. You have one consolation – you priced the house at market value, so the appraisal should not be a stumbling block.

Hours before the time limit on his conditional offer expires, he might turn to you for financing help. You don't want to lose the sale, but even under pressure, you must be cautious. Do not agree to anything that could end up putting you and your family at risk. Under no condition should you accept the suggestion of your continuing to hold the current mortgage on the house, and making the monthly payments while the buyer reimburses you an equal amount every month.

If you check the fine print on the agreement you signed when you took out your mortgage, you will likely find a clause that states you must pay off the mortgage when you sell the house. By accepting the new buyer's suggestion, you immediately default on your mortgage.

There's another problem with the suggestion you continue to hold that mortgage and make the payments. What happens if the new buyer stops making monthly payments to you? He now lives in your house, yet you are still responsible for the mortgage. What recourse do you have? If you go to your bank, you alert them to the fact you are in default and you will be severely penalized.

Financially, you not only have payments on your new home, you have to continue paying for the old one. My accountant describes this as the bacon and egg situation. "The chicken is involved but the pig is committed." Using his analogy, the buyer has the role of chicken while you find yourself in the same position as that pig!

How can you help?

A second mortgage held by the seller is fairly common, if you can afford to hold one. As long as the buyer has put a substantial amount down - for example $20,000 - and is not struggling under a lot of other debt, it's worth considering. Don't be shy about asking for his personal information before you commit to this. He must divulge all of his assets and liabilities to prove that he is a sound credit risk. Also ask for personal references - an employer, a clergyman, his accountant or lawyer. You'll want to ensure they have known him for a number of years and that they aren't related.

Fast credit check

If you have any doubt about analyzing the numbers, take them to your financial advisor. As well, you should insist that the buyer provide you with a credit check. This will track not only his credit history over the past few years, but his employment record too. You can see how much he owes on his credit cards, how often he has missed a payment, if he has any legal disputes or judgements against him and if he has ever been bankrupt. There are two Internet sites that will provide a speedy consumer credit report for about $15. They are www.equifax.ca and www.iquiri.com.

The instantly apparent advantage to holding a second mortgage, especially under the market conditions that exist at the time of writing, is the interest rate you can demand. Very few stock market or mutual fund portfolios today consistently return the 10% to 13% interest that a second mortgage can command, depending on the risk factor.

Watch for danger signs

The reason a second mortgage earns higher interest is because it can be a risky business no matter how thoroughly you review the buyer's financial situation. What could go wrong? The most obvious is he could default on his payments. At the first sign of difficulty, you must act quickly. At jeopardy are the interest and the remaining principal as well.

Your immediate reaction, if a cheque bounces or if he's a few days late with a payment, is to check the status of his first mortgage. If the second is shaky, it's highly probable the first is in trouble too. You want to keep that lending institution at bay for fear it will take over the house and you will lose everything. You do this by making the payments on the first mortgage yourself while you go to court to win possession of the house. That legal battle could go on for months. Once you gain possession, you can sell the house, pay off the first mortgage and if you're lucky, have enough left to cover the balance owing on the second.

Holding a second mortgage is not for the weak-hearted or for those without a solid financial base. If you are just getting by, don't consider it. The most prudent gesture you can make is to refer the buyer to a mortgage broker who will be able to suggest creative financing alternatives that will work for him.

Chapter 15

Picking the best realtor

Okay, by now, you have read enough about 4SBO homes to conclude that you simply are not cut out to sell your home by yourself. You agree it probably isn't difficult and there is not a lot of legal paperwork you couldn't figure out, but you can't see yourself walking strangers through your home and promoting all its features. No, that just isn't you.

Or maybe you read the book, listed your home yourself and it didn't sell. Now you're ready to hand it over to a professional. That would be your friendly neighbourhood real estate agent.

Before you approach a broker, you should first consider what type of listing you think you need. There are two types, exclusive listings and co-operative multi-agent listings where the home is available to a network of realtors. The concept is simple to understand: if your home is listed exclusively with a broker, agents from other brokers are not able to show it. If you agree to a multi-agent listing, you extend the reach to more potential buyers.

As discussed earlier, cracks are forming in the traditional six per cent commission structure. Internet home sales continue to inch upwards with no ceiling in sight yet, particularly in the USA. In both Canada and the USA, as more homeowners explore the 4SBO option, realtors are awakening to the realization that more of their customers fail to see a correlation between the size of the commission and the value of the services rendered. For example, home prices in Toronto have escalated to an average of $300,000. Twenty years ago, the average would have been closer to $80,000. The effort involved hasn't changed; the process remains the same to sell a $250,000 home today, as it was to sell an $80,000 one then. Twenty years ago, the commission would have been $4,500 compared to $18,000 today. That's a chunk of change to lose from the sale of a home; the Canadian consumer is digging in her heels and the real estate industry is listening.

Today, as well as the traditional agency, you have a choice of discount brokers or flat fee realtors who offer full multi-sale services for a fee much less than six per cent. You can buy a custom pack of services at various prices instead of being locked into a commission rate. You decide what services you need and then shop for an agent from a firm that can provide you with those.

Once you have decided what type of real estate firm you want to work with, you're ready to find the person who is capable of giving the best service. Where do you start? There are real estate agents in urban centres and small towns across Canada. You see their faces smiling from the pages of your community newspaper, from real estate magazines, from flyers and bus stop benches.

How do you choose? To illustrate a point, I'm going to inject another story here. My husband and I were having dinner in California. We asked for the wine list. The waiter handed us an exquisite leather-bound album of wine bottle labels. We didn't recognize any of the wines so we picked the most beautiful label. As it turned out, the label was the best thing about that bottle; its contents were dreadful! The moral of the story is: Don't pick an agent by appearance. Your decision should not revolve around studying all the photos to figure out who has the most sympathetic face, or who is the most earnest looking, or the prettiest. You need the best.

Put on your employer's hat

Talk to your friends. Can they recommend someone? I would not base a decision on another person's recommendation, but if the service was good, that agent is worth talking to. Consider yourself an employer searching for the best-qualified person to do the job. An employer first asks for resumés. Real estate agents should be able to provide you with one detailing their education, experience and achievements. Call each of the real estate firms that offers the type of service you require, explaining that you have a home for sale and are in the process of deciding which realtor to list with. Ask the realtor to have his most productive agents submit resumés to you by the end of next week. It will be interesting to see what comes in.

Pay attention to how much thought and preparation went into each resumé. Is it accompanied by a professional cover letter? Does it have spelling or grammatical errors? How creative is it? While you may not consider that spelling and grammar are critical skills for an agent, on a resumé they are clear indicators of the applicant's lack of attention to detail. If she makes basic errors on a resumé with which she is marketing herself, how can she possibly hope to get the paperwork right in selling your home? A careless resumé points to a careless individual, the kind of person who will arrive at an open house without the sign, or who advertises it for the wrong day or makes a costly error on the sales agreement.

Continue to call for resumés until you have from six to ten. Read them once, setting aside the ones that for one reason or another don't impress you. Then read the rest a second time and select your top four or five. Set up appointments for each of them and ask them to bring a portfolio of ads and marketing material they have produced. Before they come, draw up a score sheet with the names of each agent down the side. Across the top will be columns for Appearance, Personality, Education, Experience, Creativity, Integrity, and Portfolio. A sample score sheet is included at the end of this chapter for you to photocopy or reproduce.

The task is to ask

To prepare for face-to-face interviews, you need to develop questions to help you rate each applicant in those categories at the top of your score sheet. As you read each resumé, look closely at education and experience and probe into anything that strikes you as unusual or pertinent. "What were you doing for the two years between this job and that one? What was your major in University? Why did you choose that College? Why did you move to this realtor from that one? What is the major strength of the realtor you are with now?"

Ask, "How many homes did you sell in the last 12 months? And the year prior to that?" If a candidate tries to impress you with the fact she sold $1 million worth of real estate, insist on an estimate of how many properties were involved. She could be living on the laurels of one luxury home sale. Immediately dock marks for integrity – she avoided your question and tried to delude you. "How many homes did you list and not sell personally? What is the average selling time for homes you list? What do you like most about selling real estate, and least? What is your strongest point as a realtor, and your weakest? What was your best selling experience? Your worst?"

With some of these questions, you will learn more from how the candidate answers than from what she says. You gain insights into her personality and idiosyncrasies as well as experience. Body language will give you clues to subjects she is uncomfortable dealing with and areas where she is at ease.

After the questions, turn to the material in each portfolio. Don't just admire the various brochures and ads. For your purposes, you want to find out precisely what her involvement was. Ask, "Did you write that ad copy? Take the home photo? Design the feature brochure?" This will give you insights into her creativity and range of skills. Her creative thinking will come into play not only in advertising your home, but also in finding a fit between your house and a client and in putting together an offer acceptable to both parties.

Observe and record

As each candidate responds, you should listen, evaluate the nuances of the conversation and the body language and make notes. Just before the interview concludes, casually toss out: "What do you think of my home? What should I do before listing it?" This is a revealing part of the test. You want to see if the candidate is clever enough to take the initiative and ask if she can walk through prior to answering. As she prepares to leave, explain that you will call back three candidates for a second round.

Immediately after each candidate leaves, take your work sheet and rate her in each category from 1 to 10, with 10 being topnotch. For personality, factor in how you think you would get along with her, not just how she would interact with the clients. Selling a home is fraught with tension. You'll have to face some high-pressure moments together – there is no room for personality conflicts. Record the score and you're ready for the next one.

When you have seen them all, review the scores and reread your notes. You might not necessarily agree that the top three scores are your top three choices to call back. For example, one willowy young woman scored well because you gave her 10 points for her university degree in psychology – an excellent foundation for selling real estate – plus another 10 points for her fashion-forward designer suit that fitted her perfectly. But she seemed a tad arrogant; you are concerned she'll talk down to people.

You prefer the heavy-set woman who went into real estate with a Grade 12 education after raising her family. She didn't score high points for education or experience and her clean but outdated pantsuit didn't help in the appearance column either. However, she was alert, gave thoughtful answers and left no doubt about her strong work ethic and contagious sense of humour.

Follow your instincts and invite three back to evaluate your home's market price. This gives you one more opportunity to work with them, to assess how they perform this part of their job. When they return with their evaluation, ask how they arrived at the value. By now, you will know which agent will do the best job for you.

After all this effort, you might discover that the agent you want to deal with works for a traditional broker with the six per cent commission structure. Don't be afraid to negotiate. Ask for a clause to be written into the listing agreement stating the commission will be reduced to three per cent if the listing broker sells your home. You know that if an agent from a competing broker makes the sale, the listing broker will keep only three per cent at best and less if it's a multi-agency listing.

Any broker who is hungry for business will be prepared to bend a little. And if you are determined to work with the agent you selected from all the candidates, you might have to bend a little too and saw off at four per cent But that's okay; you have saved two per cent or $6,000 on a $300,000 home. That's not chickenfeed! Finally, if all attempts to negotiate a break on the commission fail, your consolation is knowing that you found the very best agent to work for you. Give her the listing and good luck!

Score Sheet For Picking The Best Realtor

Agent's Name	Education	Experience	Creativity	Personality	Appearance	Integrity	Portfolio	Total Score

Chapter 16

Checklists for separating couples

If you are a couple going through a separation, you likely feel the need to make a number of decisions. One major decision is what to do with your home. Other property, like vehicles and investments, needs to be considered. Arrangements have to be made for children. You need to plan for your future.

The following checklists will help you organize yourself and your thoughts as you begin the separation process. Some people may use them to sit down with their spouse or partner when they are ready to begin discussing these issues. Others may use them to prepare to start a court proceeding.

At the end of the chapter you will find a list of items that it will be important to talk to your lawyer about. You will want to get legal advice from a lawyer, either to help you and your partner make a separation agreement, or to help you through a court proceeding, if necessary.

Checklists for the house

Separating couples typically choose one (or a combination) of the following:

- ➢ The house is placed on the market and sold
- ➢ One person "buys out" the other person's share of the house
- ➢ One person is permitted to remain living in the house for a specified period of time

Sale of the home

- ☐ How much is the home worth? If you cannot agree on this, you will need to find a way to determine this amount. Some hire a qualified real estate appraiser together; others hire their own and take the average of the two appraisals. Some use the opinion of value from a qualified real estate agent, as opposed to an appraiser, which usually costs less. Some do their own research in newspapers and through the Internet to arrive at their best estimate as to value.
- ☐ Who will be primarily responsible for placing the home for sale on the market, or will this be a shared responsibility? If shared, how will tasks such as advertising and showing the home to potential buyers be shared?
- ☐ If a real estate agent will be used, who will that agent be and who will be responsible for all necessary arrangements with the agent?
- ☐ Do any repairs have to be made, and if so, who will be responsible for arranging for the repairs and how will the cost be shared?
- ☐ When is the most desirable time to sell, considering when the mortgage is due for

renewal, the season, school year, and various market conditions?

- ☐ Who will have the right to live in the home until it sells?
- ☐ Who will be responsible for paying the mortgage, insurance, realty taxes, utility payments and any other operating expenses before the sale?
- ☐ Which real estate lawyer will you choose to act for you on the sale?
- ☐ Will the lawyer's fees be shared by you equally and paid out of the sale proceeds?
- ☐ If there is a mortgage, will there be any prepayment penalty? Can the mortgage be transferred without penalty to a new home that one of you may purchase?
- ☐ What debts and encumbrances, such as the mortgage, will be paid out of the money that you receive for the house? For example, will debts such as credit card balances, lines of credit, and student loans be paid?
- ☐ Are there any overdue realty taxes, writs or liens that will have to be paid at the time of sale?
- ☐ Should the equity be split equally? This is a complex question requiring legal advice, and may be affected by such things as a debt registered against the property that is solely the responsibility of one spouse; a debt owed from one spouse to the other; transfer of all or a portion of one person's share of the equity to the other in exchange for settlement of other assets or debts; or child or spousal support obligations.

Buying out the other spouse's interest

- ☐ Can one person afford the costs associated with running the home?
- ☐ Does it make sense that one person, as opposed to the other, remain in the home?
- ☐ After determining the value of the home (see "sale of home" above), how much equity is left after deducting mortgages, realty tax arrears and any other debts registered against the home?
- ☐ Should the person who is buying the other person's share pay less than 50% of the equity? This is a complex question requiring legal advice, and may be affected by such things as a debt registered against the property that is solely the responsibility of one spouse; a debt owed from one spouse to the other; the settlement of other assets or debts; or child or spousal support obligations.
- ☐ When will the transfer from one person to the other occur?
- ☐ When will the spouse receive his or her money?
- ☐ Will the person who is buying out the other's share have to refinance the existing mortgage, or will the bank or lender allow the other person to be released from his or her obligations under the existing mortgage?
- ☐ Who will pay for the costs associated with the transfer of the home from one person to the other, and any costs associated with arranging a new mortgage?

Right to live in the house

- ☐ Could one person continue to live in the home for a certain period of time? For example, until children have graduated from high school, or until he or she has other housing, or has retrained to become financially independent.
- ☐ What will happen at the end of the time period? For example, will the house be sold or will one person be given the option of buying out the other's share at that time?
- ☐ Will the spouse who leaves the house be allowed to re-enter the house for any reason during that time period, and if so, for what reasons?
- ☐ Allowing one person to remain in the house is a benefit. What will the other person receive in return? Will allowing a person to remain in the house offset, for example, an obligation to provide child or spousal support?
- ☐ If any repairs have to be made, who will be responsible for arranging for the repairs and how will the cost be shared?
- ☐ Who will be responsible for paying the mortgage, insurance, realty taxes, utility payments and any other operating expenses?
- ☐ If only one person pays the mortgage payments and taxes, will this affect the sharing of the equity when the house finally sells or is purchased by the other spouse?

Checklist for other real estate

Vacant land, cottage, time-share condos

- ☐ In whose name is the property registered?
- ☐ What is the property worth?
- ☐ Are there any mortgages, liens or encumbrances registered against the property?
- ☐ Are there outstanding realty taxes or membership fees?
- ☐ If the property is owned by both of you, will it be sold or will one person transfer his or her interest in the property to the other?
- ☐ If the property is being transferred from one to the other, will any money be paid, or will there be an exchange for some other property or some other benefit?
- ☐ If it is a time-share condominium or agreement, will you sell your interest? If you are not able to sell it, how will you share it?

Checklist for property & assets

Cars/trucks/boats/personal watercraft/snowmobiles

- ☐ What is each vehicle worth?
- ☐ Who is the registered owner of each vehicle?
- ☐ Is the vehicle leased? At the end of the lease, will the vehicle have any value, or will money likely be owed to the leasing company?
- ☐ Is there a debt associated with the vehicle, such as a bank loan or loan from a family member? How much is it and when will it be paid back?

- ☐ Will a vehicle or boat be transferred from one person's name into the other's? If there is any cost associated with the transfer, who will pay it? Who will obtain the required forms for the transfer from the relevant transportation authority?
- ☐ If a boat or watercraft, whose name is on the vessel permit or license? Will it be transferred from one person's name to the other?
- ☐ Who will arrange and pay for the necessary insurance?

Household furniture and items

- ☐ Did either person own any of the items before the marriage?
- ☐ Were any items inherited?
- ☐ Were any items gifts from friends or family members?
- ☐ Are there items of sentimental value that would be important for each of you to keep?
- ☐ Will photographs and family videos be duplicated or otherwise divided?
- ☐ Are there certain items that one of you will need more than the other?
- ☐ Will you assign a value to each item, and divide the items so that each of you receives equal value?
- ☐ Alternatively, will you divide the items according to preference, practicality, or on some other basis?

Bank accounts

- ☐ How much money is in each account?
- ☐ Will joint accounts be closed or transferred into one person's name?

- ☐ Should a household account from which bills are paid remain open, and if so, for how long?
- ☐ Who should deposit money into the household account, how much, and how frequently?
- ☐ Is there an overdraft in any account, and if so, who should be responsible for paying it?

Pensions

- ☐ Will either of you apply for a division of Canada Pension Plan credits?
- ☐ Is either of you a member of a federal or provincial pension plan?
- ☐ Can the pension be divided "at source"? Who will be responsible for obtaining the necessary forms?
- ☐ Is either person a member of an employer-sponsored pension plan?
- ☐ If a person is a member of a *defined contribution* pension plan, what is the total invested value of the employer's and the person's combined contributions?
- ☐ If a person is a member of a *defined benefit* pension plan, what is the value of the pension? A professional known as an actuary may have to be hired to determine its value.

Savings Plans and Investments

- ☐ What is the value of the plan or investment according to the most recent statement?
- ☐ If it is held in both names, can and will it be divided into two separate plans? Can stocks or shares be transferred so that each person owns some in his or her own name?

- ☐ Can all or a portion of the savings or investment be transferred to the other person? Will there be any taxes to be paid if this done, or is there a way to avoid any tax? A financial planner or accountant may have to be consulted.

Business

- ☐ Do either of you have an interest in a company or partnership? If so, what is the percentage interest?
- ☐ Are there any agreements between owners that would affect the person's ownership or the value of the business?
- ☐ Do either of you operate a sole proprietorship?
- ☐ Will you need professional help to put a dollar value on your or the other's shareholder or partnership interest, or to value the sole proprietorship?
- ☐ If you both own shares in a corporation or are involved in a partnership, will one of you be transferring your shares or partnership interest to the other? What benefit will you receive for doing so? Will you also need to resign as an officer and director?

Other assets

- ☐ Do either of you own any other assets? Examples might be: Air Miles, a mortgage receivable, a debt that is owed to you by another person, or artwork or paintings.
- ☐ If so, what is the value of these assets?

Checklist for debts

- ☐ What are your debts? Which are in your joint names and which are in separate names?
- ☐ What is the amount of each debt?
- ☐ Are there assets that can be sold to pay down debts?
- ☐ Are there any loans from one of you to the other that should be paid off or forgiven?
- ☐ Which debts is each of you going to be responsible for paying?
- ☐ Can arrangements be made with the bank or lender to have one person released from the debt?
- ☐ Should the debts that each person is paying be placed solely in his or her name? For example, should a joint line of credit be closed, and the balance transferred to a new line of credit in one person's name?
- ☐ Should credit cards be destroyed?
- ☐ Consider contacting each credit card or financing company to determine what its policies are about spousal cards or to cancel authorizations.
- ☐ Should overdraft protection on any joint bank accounts be terminated?
- ☐ Should a "cap" be placed on lines of credit?
- ☐ What arrangements will be made to repay loans from family and friends, and what proof is needed when those debts are repaid?

Checklist for life insurance

- ☐ Is it a group or personal insurance policy?
- ☐ Term or whole life?
- ☐ If it is whole life, what is the cash surrender value of the policy?
- ☐ Whose life is insured under the policy?
- ☐ Who is the beneficiary? Should the beneficiary designation be changed, or is insurance needed to secure an obligation to pay child or spousal support?

Checklist for medical and dental benefits

- ☐ If either of you has a medical, extended health or dental insurance plan through your employment, will the children and the other person continue to be covered by the plan?
- ☐ For how long will the coverage continue?
- ☐ Who will submit the receipts to the insurer?
- ☐ How will the person who pays be reimbursed for dental, medical and drug expenses that he or she has paid for in advance?
- ☐ Who will pay for the cost of any items not covered under the plan?
- ☐ If there is no medical, extended health and dental insurance plan in place, how will the cost of prescription drugs, eyewear, medical services, dental and orthodontic expenses be shared?

Checklists for parenting

In addition to the following issues concerning children, consideration must be given to when and how children should be told about the separation, what specific information they should be given, how you can reduce the amount of conflict that children are exposed to, and how to ease the stress of the separation on the children.

The words "custody" and "access" are growing less popular and laws may soon be passed that end their use altogether. It may be more useful for you to specify the time-sharing arrangements and decision-making responsibilities for your children.

Parenting schedule

When will the children spend time with each of you:

I. During the week and on weekends?
II. During the Christmas school break? How will the time period between Christmas Eve and New Year's Day be divided between parents? Consider any particular family traditions or celebrations.
III. During statutory holidays, specifically Canada Day, August Civic Holiday, Labour Day weekend, Thanksgiving, Easter weekend and Victoria Day weekend?
IV. During the school March break?
V. During the summer holidays?
VI. On school professional activity days?
VII. On children's birthdays?
VIII. On Mother's Day and Father's Day?
IX. On religious holidays?

- ☐ When will the parenting arrangements be reviewed or changed? Consider what might happen as the children get older, a parent dies, a parent moves to a new location, or when a child requests a change.
- ☐ What permission needs to be granted for out-of-province travel? Consider exchanging information about destination, departure and return dates, airline flight details, and providing an emergency contact number.
- ☐ How can the children be contacted when not with you? By e-mail, an Internet "chat line" or telephone?
- ☐ Should one parent's time with the children have conditions attached to it? Examples: have one parent's time be supervised, or not permit him or her to drive a car when the children are passengers.
- ☐ Decision-making responsibility

Which parent will be responsible for making decisions about the following topics?

- ☐ Education, including tutoring and remedial programs?
- ☐ Religion?
- ☐ Health care, including elective surgery or treatments?
- ☐ Scheduling of doctor and dental appointments?
- ☐ Extracurricular activities and programs?
- ☐ Clothing purchases?
- ☐ Purchasing gifts, either for the child or from the child to others?

- ☐ Whether the child will move to a new location?
- ☐ How often the child sees extended family, like grandparents?
- ☐ Language spoken in the home?
- ☐ Whether the child's name will be changed?
- ☐ Does the other parent have to be consulted about the decision or the cost to be incurred before a decision is made about any of the topics?

Moving

- ☐ Will there be any restrictions on where either parent can live?

Information about the children

- ☐ By what method will the parents communicate about the children's needs and development, and how frequently?
- ☐ Will one or both parents have access to medical, dental, mental health and educational information about the children?
- ☐ Can both parents attend parent/teacher interviews?
- ☐ Can both parents attend school functions, extracurricular and sporting events?

Responsibility for driving

- ☐ Who will drive the children when travelling between parents' homes?
- ☐ Who will drive the children to school, to visit friends and extended family, and to extra-curricular activities and sporting events?

Resolving disagreements

- ☐ How will disagreements about the children be resolved if they arise in the future?

Checklists for financial maintenance

Child support

- ☐ Are there provincial guidelines in force that contain child support tables that can be consulted?
- ☐ Federal child support guidelines that apply across Canada to divorcing parents can be found on the Internet at www.canada.justice.gc.ca.
- ☐ What is each person's total income from all sources? Consult sections 15 to 20 of the Federal child support guidelines for the definition of "income."
- ☐ When might support terminate for a child? Consider what might happen when the child stops living with one parent, or reaches a certain age, or becomes self-supporting.
- ☐ When might the amount of support change for a child? Consider what might happen if income increases or decreases, if the health of a child or parent changes, if the child begins to earn an income, or if a parent becomes eligible for the Child Tax Credit or other supplement.
- ☐ If a child moves away from home during the year to go to college or university, should the support payments decrease during the

months that the child is living away from home?

- ☐ Will support payments be made by post-dated cheques, cash, or direct deposit?
- ☐ What day of the month is each support payment to be made?
- ☐ Which of the children's expenses should be covered by the support payments?
- ☐ Are there additional or special expenses for items such as daycare or expensive extracurricular activities? How will those costs be shared?
- ☐ Who can claim the child tax credit and equivalent-to-spouse credit for the children?
- ☐ How often should support arrangements be reviewed?
- ☐ Could the support payment be made by a one-time, lump sum payment?

Spousal support

- ☐ How much monthly support is needed?
- ☐ Spousal support payments are taxable for the person who receives the money. What will the actual monthly support payment be after the person receiving it has paid the tax?
- ☐ How much monthly support is affordable?
- ☐ Spousal support payments are tax deductible for the person who pays the money. How much will the monthly support payment actually be after the person paying it has received the tax deduction for that amount?
- ☐ For how many months or years will support be paid?
- ☐ If the time period for paying support is indefinite, under what circumstances should

it be reviewed? Consider a review after, for example, a certain time period, or after a person has gone back to school or retrained, or when his or her income reaches a certain amount.

- ☐ When can the amount of support be changed? Consider what will happen if, for example, a person retires, marries or lives with another person, has health problems or a change in employment.
- ☐ Will the amount of spousal support increase when child support ends?
- ☐ Has there been any support paid in the past, and should these payments be tax deductible for the person who made the payments?
- ☐ Instead of a spousal support payment, could arrangements be made to pay for that person's living expenses? An example would be paying a person's rent or mortgage payments. Should these payments be tax deductible?
- ☐ How often should support arrangements be reviewed?
- ☐ Could the support payment be made by a one-time, lump sum payment?

Checklist for pre-marriage assets and debts

- ☐ List all assets that you each owned before your marriage or at the start of your relationship

- ☐ List all debts that each of you owed before your marriage or at the start of your relationship

Checklists of what your lawyer needs

Even if the two of you are able to agree upon how you will settle everything, you should still take your agreement to a lawyer to have him or her review it and make it into a formally binding separation agreement. Alternatively, if you find that you are not able to settle things between you after discussion, you may decide that you want to consult with a lawyer. The lawyer will need some basic information from you. It will save you money if the lawyer does not have to spend a lot of time asking you about this basic information while you are in his or her office, so try to write out the following information before the meeting and bring it with you:

Background information

- ☐ You and your partner's full names, maiden name, and any former married names
- ☐ You and your partner's place and date of birth
- ☐ How long you and your partner have been living in the province
- ☐ You and your partner's address and phone number (home and work)
- ☐ How long each of you has been living at your current address
- ☐ An alternative address for mail if you do not want it to come to your home

- ☐ Date that you met your partner
- ☐ Date of marriage or date that you began living together
- ☐ Place of marriage
- ☐ If you have ever separated from your partner, the length and dates of those separations
- ☐ You and your partner's educational background
- ☐ The details of any significant medical problems, including psychological or emotional disorders
- ☐ The dates of any prior marriages for either of you
- ☐ Is the decision to separate final, and if so, what date was that decision made by either of you?
- ☐ The details of any marriage counselling or attempts at reconciliation
- ☐ Have you or your spouse signed a marriage contract or cohabitation agreement, or any agreements relating to your separation?
- ☐ Do you want your marriage to be permanently dissolved by a divorce, or do you want just a formal separation?

Employment

- ☐ The name and address of your present employer if you are working
- ☐ How long you have worked there
- ☐ Your salary, before and after taxes and other deductions
- ☐ The details of any benefits from your employment, including car allowances, medical/drug/dental benefits, and pension contributions by your employer

- ☐ The names of your and your partner's past employers, and the dates of each job

The children

- ☐ The names and birth dates of each child
- ☐ The name of the person your child is living with
- ☐ If you and your spouse are now in separate homes, the details of when each of you has the child in your care
- ☐ The name and address of your child's school
- ☐ Grade or level
- ☐ If your child has graduated from high school, the details of the child's employment or what they are now doing
- ☐ If your child is going to university, college, or some other educational or training program, the details of that program
- ☐ If your child is going to university, college, or some other educational or training program, the cost of the program, including tuition, living accommodation, books and supplies.
- ☐ The details of any grants, loans or bursaries received by your child
- ☐ The details of any registered educational savings plan for your child
- ☐ Daycare arrangements and cost
- ☐ The details of any significant medical problems of your children, including psychological or emotional disorders

The house

- ☐ The date you bought your present house
- ☐ Whose name is on the deed or on title?

- ☐ How much your home is worth
- ☐ Who holds your mortgage(s)?
- ☐ How much is your mortgage(s)?
- ☐ How much are the weekly or monthly payments?
- ☐ Are there any other debts (e.g., a line of credit) registered against the property?
- ☐ The details of whether either of you operates a business from the house or property
- ☐ Did either of you contribute more money than the other toward the purchase of the house?
- ☐ If you own a cottage, vacant land, or any other real estate, the same details as above
- ☐ If you have sold a house or other real estate in the past twelve months, the details of that sale (sale price, mortgages discharged or transferred, amount of sale proceeds and who received that money)
- ☐ Is there any chance that you or your spouse will buy another property that will be designated as a principal residence before the end of the current calendar year?

Other property

- ☐ Details of any life insurance policies
- ☐ Details of bank accounts of you and your partner
- ☐ Details of any investments, including RRSPs, stocks, bonds and other savings plans
- ☐ A list of any asset worth over $500, such as vehicles, boats, snowmobiles, jewellery, etc.
- ☐ Details of any money or property that you or your partner inherited

Debts

- ☐ Names of credit cards owned by you and your partner, and how much is owed on each card
- ☐ Details of any loans from banks, other financial institutions, friends or family
- ☐ Details of all other debts (e.g., dental bills, utility bills, phone bills)

Assets and debts you had before marriage

- ☐ Details of any land, houses, savings, investments, vehicles and other assets that you or your spouse owned before you were married or before you began living together
- ☐ Details of any debts that you or your spouse owed before marriage or before you began living together

Checklist of documents to take with you (not all will apply to you)

- ☐ Last three years of income tax returns and notices of assessment
- ☐ Marriage certificate
- ☐ If either of you has been divorced before, a copy of your divorce judgement
- ☐ Copies of any marriage contract, cohabitation agreement, or any agreement that you and your partner have signed relating to your separation
- ☐ Copies of your pay stubs for the past few months

- ☐ The latest mortgage statement from the bank or lender
- ☐ If you own a business or corporation, financial statements for the last three years
- ☐ Credit card and loan statements for the past twelve months
- ☐ The latest statements for your investments, RRSPs and other savings
- ☐ A copy of your latest pension statement
- ☐ Copies of your bank passbook or statements for each account for the past 12 months
- ☐ Appraisals for any property, including your house, jewellery, etc.
- ☐ The deed for your house or other real estate
- ☐ A written list of your furniture and household contents
- ☐ An organized list of all of your assets and debts, including those that you acquired before you were married or before you began living together

Glossary

Adjustments - Expenses such as property taxes and utilities that have been prepaid by the seller and need to be pro-rated and charged to the purchaser.

Agent - An individual or a company representing a buyer and/or seller.

Agreement of Purchase and Sale - a document outlining the terms and conditions under which a property is offered for purchase and sale.

Amortize - Mortgage payments that include both principal and interest, made in installments.

Amortization Period - The number of years required for reducing a mortgage debt to zero.

Amortization Schedule - A table that shows how much of each periodic mortgage payment is principal and interest.

Appraisal - Determining the market value of a property by an independent appraiser. This value is not necessarily the same as the selling price.

Appreciation - The amount by which a property has increased in value.

Approved Lender - A lending institution approved by the government to grant mortgage loans under the terms of the National Housing Act.

Asking Price - The price at which a property is listed for sale.

Assumption Agreement - A buyer assumes responsibility of an original owner's or builder's mortgage.

Balloon - The amount that is still to be paid on maturity of a mortgage.

Blanket Payment - A combined mortgage payment for more than one property.

Blended Payments - Regularly scheduled mortgage payments consisting of principal and interest.

Breaking Costs - A fee paid to the lender if a closed mortgage is paid before the maturity date.

Broker - A person licensed to operate a business providing real estate services to buyers and sellers.

Buyer's Agent (or Broker) - An individual or a firm working primarily in the interests of the buyer.

Buyer Brokerage Agreement - A contract outlining arrangements between a buyer and his agent.

Certificate of Location - A surveyor's document showing the exact size and location of a property, including a description of any buildings and their location on the property.

Chattels - Chattels in a home are items that may be connected by pipes and wires, such as refrigerators, stoves, washers and dryers. Also see "Fixtures."

Clear Title - ownership of real property that is free of any mortgages, liens or other liabilities.

Client(s) - The buyer and/or seller represented by a real estate broker or agent.

Closed Mortgage - A mortgage that cannot be renegotiated or paid off before maturity, without paying a penalty to the lender.

Closing - When the deal is finalized and the title to the property is transferred to the buyer.

Closing Date - The date when the property changes hands.

Closing Costs - All expenses related to the transfer of title to a property. These might include lawyer's fees, insurance premiums, surveys, title search or title insurance, appraisal cost, mortgage application fees, and others.

CMHC - Canada Mortgage and Housing Corporation, a government agency providing mortgage insurance and information.

Collateral - A property assigned as security for a loan.

Collateral Mortgage - A loan secured by a mortgage, but the money can be used for buying a property or for any other purpose.

Commission - The amount or percentage payable to brokers or agents upon completion of a purchase and sale.

Common Elements - Refers to all the property of a condominium development except the units owned by individual parties.

Condition - In a real estate document this term refers to something that must happen before the contract becomes firm.

Conditional Offer - An offer to purchase, but with conditions such as the selling of a present home or being able to arrange proper financing.

Condominium - A development where the land and all common elements of buildings are owned collectively by all unit owners and only a specific unit belongs to an individual owner.

Conventional Mortgage Loan - A first mortgage where the amount cannot be more than 75% of the appraised property value.

Convertible Mortgage - A short-term mortgage that can at any time be converted into a longer term closed mortgage without penalty.

Conveyance - The legal transfer of title to real estate property.

Debt-Service Ratio – The difference between gross household income and total debt payments.

Deed – A registered document that serves as evidence of ownership.

Default – Failing to make a mortgage payment when due or not fulfilling other terms and conditions of the mortgage.

Deposit – Money paid in trust, usually to a lawyer, when an offer to purchase is made.

Discharge of Mortgage – A document stating that a mortgage loan has been paid in full.

Discount Broker – A real estate firm that charges less than the normal commission rate.

Down Payment – The amount a buyer must put up himself, the difference between the full price of the property and the amount of the mortgage.

Dual Agent – A real estate broker or agent who represents both the buyer and the seller.

Easement – The right of use of another person's land for a specific purpose or reason.

Encumbrance – A legal claim against the property, a debt or a mortgage.

Equity - The value of a property less the amount of the mortgage and/or other claims against the property, if any.

Financial Institutions – Banks, Trust Companies, Credit Unions, Mortgage Lenders, Insurance Companies, etc.

Financing – Looking after monetary matters, such as deposits, down payments and mortgage arrangements.

Fire and Property Insurance - Evidence of such insurance is required by the lender and has to be arranged by the purchaser before closing.

Fixed Rate Mortgage - The interest rate remains unchanged for the term of the mortgage.

Fixtures - Fixtures are items that have been attached and have become part of the property, such as built-in closets, carpeting and light fixtures. Also see "Chattels".

Flat Fee Broker - A real estate firm charging a set amount, instead of a percentage of the purchase price.

4SBO or FSBO - For Sale By Owner. Pronounced FIZZBO. Also known as a Private Sale.

Foreclosure - A legal procedure for the lender to take possession of the property if the borrower defaults on the mortgage loan.

Gross Debt Service - The payment amount needed to cover principal, interest and taxes.

Gross Debt Service Ratio - A measurement of principal, interest and taxes as a percentage of gross household income.

High-ratio Mortgage - A mortgage loan that is in higher than the standard criteria for lending values.

Inspection - Checking the house for structural or other defects by the buyer or by an expert hired by the buyer.

Interest Rate - The percentage paid to a lender for the use of the money borrowed.

Land Survey - A certificate of location indicating boundaries of a property.

Lender - A person or a company in the business of lending money. Also known as a mortgagee.

Lending Value - The purchase price or the estimated market value of real estate.

Leverage - Monies borrowed to purchase real estate property.

Listing Agreement - A written agreement between the seller and his agent.

Maturity Date - The date on which the term of a mortgage ends.

Mechanic's Lien - A claim against a property by someone who has provided materials and/or labour and has not been paid.

Mortgage - A legal instrument assigning property as security for a loan.

Mortgage Broker - An individual or a firm bringing lender and borrower together.

Mortgage Insurance - By law, any mortgage for which the down payment is less than 25%, must be insured to protect the lender.

Mortgage Life Insurance - Insurance that guarantees the mortgage will be paid in full if the borrower dies.

Mortgage Payment - Scheduled payments that include principal and interest.

Mortgagee - An individual or a financial institution lending money secured by a mortgage.

Mortgagor - A borrower who gives title to his property as security for a mortgage loan.

Negative Amortization - When installment payment amounts are less than the interest rate on the mortgage. The principal increases and the borrower owes more than the original sum borrowed. .

Net Worth - Total assets minus total liabilities equal a person's financial net worth.

Offer of Purchase - A signed document outlining the terms under which a buyer agrees to purchase a property.

Option Agreement - A written agreement stating that for a specific deposit amount an individual has first rights to buy a property within a certain period of time.

PIT - Principal, Interest and Tax payments to be made on a regular basis, as outlined in the mortgage agreement.

Principal - The actual amount of the mortgage loan, not including interest.

Principal Balance - The remaining balance due on a mortgage loan.

Private Sale - A sale arranged directly between a vendor and a purchaser, without the involvement of any agents.

Property Disclosure Statement - This document summarizes the seller's knowledge of the property. It is not mandatory in most jurisdictions.

Realtor - A person licensed to engage in the business of buying and selling real estate.

Refinancing - Paying off an existing mortgage and arranging a new mortgage, often with a different lender.

Representations and Warranties - Legal clauses sometimes built into a buy/sell contract. Be sure to have them reviewed by your lawyer before signing the document.

Reserve Fund - Refers to that portion of condominium fees being collected and held by a condominium corporation to meet future repair and maintenance expenses.

Reverse Mortgage - Money borrowed by senior citizens using their home as collateral. This loan has to be repaid from the proceeds of the estate when the owner dies.

Second Mortgage - A loan in addition to the first mortgage, usually at a higher interest rate.

Seller's Agent - A real estate person or firm working mainly on behalf of the seller.

Term - Defines the length of time a mortgage agreement is in effect before it has to be paid off or renegotiated.

Time of the Essence - Date and time limits on a contract are strictly enforced.

Title - The proof of ownership of a property.

Title Defect - An undischarged mortgage, a lien, or a fundamental error in the legal description might constitute a title defect.

Title Insurance - A policy of insurance that protects ownership and mortgage concerns. Title insurance can also include surveys, taxes, building and zoning issues, and other local authority searches.

Title Search - An investigation of real property records at the local Land Registry Office or Land Titles Office.

Variable-Rate Mortgage - A mortgage where installment amounts remain constant, but interest rates fluctuate. If interest rates are low, more money goes towards payment of principal, or the opposite if interest rates are high.

Vendor - The seller of a property.

Vendor Take-Back - A financial arrangement between the seller and the buyer of a property. This often consists of a second mortgage the seller is willing to hold.

Zoning Bylaws - Local or regional laws governing land use for specific purposes.

Chapter 18

Sample Clauses and Conditions

The following are samples of clauses and conditions that are commonly used in residential agreements of purchase and sale. Some provinces include several of these provisions in their common form of agreement, in other provinces they must be custom added if desired. The clauses can typically be added onto the pre-printed form of Agreement if there is space, or added as a schedule. It is recommended that you read the 4SBO information on drafting your Agreement when considering the use of these clauses - and as always, consult a lawyer.

Assumption of Mortgage

The Buyer agrees to assume an existing mortgage on the property, which, on closing, shall be comprised of the following terms:

Mortgage lender	___________________________________
Priority	___________________________________
Principle amount outstanding (approx.)	___________________________________
Interest rate (calculated semi-annually, not in advance)	___________________________________
Term remaining *or* principal due date	___________________________________
Amortization	___________________________________
Regular payment amount (state if taxes included)	___________________________________
Regular payment date	___________________________________
Prepayment options	___________________________________
Other material terms	___________________________________
	___________________________________
	___________________________________
	___________________________________

This Agreement is conditional upon the Buyer being approved for assumption of the existing mortgage by the mortgage lender, on or before *[date & time]* ____.
This condition is inserted for the exclusive benefit of the Buyer and may be waived by the buyer at the Buyer's sole discretion. The Buyer shall use all reasonable efforts towards fulfillment of this condition. Any costs or fees associated with the assumption of mortgage shall be at the expense of the Buyer. The Buyer must deliver notice in writing that this condition has been satisfied or otherwise waived on or before the stated deadline, failing which this Agreement shall be null and void and the deposit shall be returned to the Buyer without interest, penalty or deduction. It is a further condition of this Agreement that any assumption of mortgage must allow for a full and final release of the Seller's obligations under the mortgage. This latter condition is inserted for the exclusive benefit of the Seller and may be waived by the Seller at the Seller's sole discretion.

Condominium

The Seller warrants that the monthly common expenses currently payable to the Condominium Corporation are approximately $ _________________, and they include the following: ____
____
The Seller further warrants that the Seller is not aware of any pending increase in the monthly common expense amount, or any supplemental levy or special assessment pending or payable to the Condominium Corporation, or any existing or pending legal actions against or initiated by the Corporation, or any pending substantial change in the assets or liabilities of the Corporation. The Seller further warrants that the Seller has not received any notice of a special or general meeting of the Condominium Corporation surrounding any of the foregoing, and if any such notice is received prior to closing, the Seller shall notify the Buyer in writing, whereupon the Buyer may, at the Buyer's sole option, upon notice in writing, terminate this Agreement, and in such event the deposit shall be returned to the Buyer without interest, penalty or deduction. The Purchase Price includes the Unit as described in the Declaration, together with a proportionate undivided tenancy-in-common interest in the common elements, and together with all parking spaces, lockers and exclusive use elements included in the Declaration, which are more specifically described as follows: Lockers:____________________________, Parking Spaces:_________________________, Exclusive Use Elements:__________________________ .
The Buyer acknowledges and accepts that the Condominium Corporation may have entered into a Management Contract for the management of the Corporation and the Property. The Seller consents to the release of an Estoppel Certificate or Certificate of Status concerning the Property, which shall be obtained at the expense of the Buyer. The Buyer agrees that, notwithstanding other title provisions of this Agreement, title shall be subject to the Declaration, By-Laws and Rules of the Condominium Corporation, which the Buyer acknowledges having reviewed, or otherwise declined to review recognizing the implications of same. In the event that consent for this transaction is required from the Condominium Corporation, then the parties shall act diligently and cooperatively in pursuing such consent as soon as reasonably possible after acceptance, and if such consent is refused, then this Agreement shall be terminated and the deposit shall be returned to the Buyer without interest, penalty or deduction.

Financing

This Agreement is conditional upon the Buyer arranging suitable financing, the suitability of which shall be at the Buyer's sole discretion, on or before *[date & time]* ____.
This condition is inserted for the exclusive benefit of the Buyer and may be waived by the buyer at the Buyer's sole discretion. The Buyer shall use all reasonable efforts towards fulfillment of this condition. The Buyer must deliver notice in writing that this condition has been satisfied or otherwise waived on or before the stated deadline, failing which this Agreement shall be null and void and the deposit shall be returned to the Buyer without interest, penalty or deduction.

Inspection

The Buyer shall be entitled to a further inspection of the Property on or before *[date]* ______________________________, provided that reasonable advance notice is given to the Seller, to satisfy him/herself that there has been no substantial damage or alteration to the Property since the Agreement was signed.

Lawyer Review

This Agreement is conditional upon the [Buyer or Seller] having the form and content of the Agreement reviewed and approved by their lawyer, on or before *[date & time]* ____.
The acceptability of the lawyer's report shall be at the [Buyer or Seller]'s sole discretion. This condition is inserted for the exclusive benefit of the [Buyer or Seller] and may be waived at their sole discretion. The [Buyer or Seller] must deliver notice in writing that this condition has been satisfied or otherwise waived on or before the stated deadline, failing which this Agreement shall be null and void and the deposit shall be returned to the Buyer without interest, penalty or deduction.

Septic

The Seller warrants that, to the best of the Seller's knowledge and belief, the septic system is in good working order and was installed in accordance with the requirements of the applicable authorities at the time. This warranty shall survive closing, however the Seller makes no warranty regarding the ongoing functionality of the septic system after closing.

Survey

The Seller is supplying the Buyer with a copy of a survey as attached hereto. The Seller warrants that he/she has not made, and is not aware of any, changes, additions or alterations to the Property other than as set out on the survey. This warranty shall survive closing. **...or...** The Seller makes no representations as to the accuracy or suitability of the survey and the Buyer shall satisfy him/herself in this regard.

Tenant(s)

On closing, possession of the Property shall be subject to the following ongoing tenancies *[set out name(s) of tenant(s), monthly rent, due date(s), deposits, portion of property, whether a tenancy agreement exists, and any other material facts surrounding the tenant(s):*

____

____

____

The Seller warrants that the tenancy agreement(s), if any, are in good standing, that there are no ongoing disputes with the tenant(s) and that all rents charged to the Closing Date will have been legal. This warranty shall survive closing. The balance due on closing shall be adjusted to the Closing Date to reflect all rents, deposits, interest and other amounts relating to the tenancies.

Vendor Take-Back Mortgage

The Seller agrees to take back a mortgage against the Property in satisfaction of that portion of the Purchase Price, on the following terms:

Priority (e.g., first, second...)	______________________
Principal amount	______________________
Interest rate (calculated semi annually, not in advance)	______________________
Term *or* principal due date	______________________
Amortization period	______________________
Regular payment amount	______________________
Regular payment date (e.g., 1st day monthly)	______________________
Prepayment options (e.g., open or closed)	______________________
Other material terms (e.g., post dated cheques)	______________________
	______________________
	______________________
	______________________

The mortgage shall be prepared at the expense of the Buyer and registered at the expense of the Seller.

Well

The Seller warrants that, to the best of the Seller's knowledge and belief, the well is in good working order and is capable of supplying a safe and sufficient supply of water to the Property for normal household use. This warranty shall survive closing, however the Seller makes no warranty regarding the ongoing functionality, supply or potability of the well after closing. The Buyer (or their representative) shall be entitled, upon reasonable advance notice to the Seller, to enter onto the Property for the purposes of viewing and taking water samples in order to satisfy him/herself as to the adequacy and potability of the water supply.

Chapter 19

Sample Purchase Contracts

Purchase agreement forms are included in this book. Samples on the following pages show you how to fill out the forms for:

British Columbia

Alberta

Saskatchewan

Manitoba

Ontario

Quebec

New Brunswick

Prince Edward Island

Nova Scotia

Newfoundland & Labrador

Yukon & Northwest Territories

The information contained in this book is not legal advice and should not be treated as a substitute for legal advice. 4SBO recommends seeking the advice of a lawyer qualified in the relevant jurisdiction in cooperation with utilizing the information contained in these materials.

British Columbia

Form of Agreement of Purchase & Sale (sample completed form)

CONTRACT

OF PURCHASE AND SALE (FOR USE IN BRITISH COLUMBIA)

SELLER: JOHN DOE
SELLER: JANE DOE
ADDRESS: 123 MAIN ST., CENTREVILLE, B.C.
PC: 1A1 B2B
PHONE: (123) 345-6789
RESIDENT OF CANADA ☒ NON-RESIDENT OF CANADA ☐
Pursuant to the Income Tax Act (Canada)

BUYER: BOB SMITH
BUYER: MARY SMITH
ADDRESS: 321 QUEEN ST. CENTREVILLE, B.C.
PC: B1B 2A2
PHONE: (123) 987-6543
OCCUPATION: SALES MANAGER

PROPERTY: Municipal Address: 123 MAIN STREET, CENTREVILLE, B.C.
Legal Description: LOT 1, PLAN 2, COUNTY OF MIDDLEFORD
(the "Property") PID No. . ....

The Buyer agrees to buy the Property from the Seller on the following terms and conditions:

1. **PURCHASE PRICE:** The purchase price shall be ONE HUNDRED & FIFTY THOUSAND ——— xx [written] Dollars CDN $ 150,000.00 [numerical] (the "Purchase Price")

2. **DEPOSIT:** A deposit of FIFTEEN THOUSAND ——— xx [written] Dollars CDN $ 15,000.00 [numerical] (the "Deposit") shall be provided by the Buyer on the following terms:

The Deposit shall be delivered and made payable " in trust" to ATTICUS LAWYER. The Deposit shall be held in trust in accordance with the *Real Estate Act* and shall be credited towards the Purchase Price on completion of this transaction. In the event that the Deposit is not received by the Seller or the Seller's authorized representative or solicitor in accordance with the terms, the Seller shall have the option of terminating this contract

3. **TERMS & CONDITIONS:** This Contract shall be subject to the following terms and conditions: CONDITIONAL UPON SUITABLE FINANCING AT BUYER'S DISCRETION. MUST BE COMMUNICATED AS SATISFIED OR WAIVED ON OR BEFORE 5:00 PM MAY 17, 2003 THIS CONDITION IS FOR BENEFIT OF BUYER WHO WILL USE REASONABLE EFFORTS TO FULFILL. COMMUNICATION MUST BE IN WRITING, AND IF NOT RECEIVED ON OR BEFORE DEADLINE THEN AGREEMENT NULL & VOID & DEPOSIT RETURNED WITHOUT INTEREST OR PENALTY
The following provisions shall be deemed to apply to each stated condition, unless otherwise indicated: 1) each condition shall be deemed to be for the sole benefit of the party indicated, if so indicated, and 2) the benefiting party shall deliver to the other party a written notice that the condition has been waived or fulfilled, as the case may be, on or before the date specified, failing which this Contract shall become null and void and the Deposit shall be returned to the Buyer in accordance with the *Real Estate Act*.

4. **CLOSING:** This Contract shall be completed on JULY 14, 2003 (the "Closing Date") at the applicable Land Title Office.

5. **POSSESSION:** The Buyer shall have vacant possession of the Property at 12:00 p.m. (noon) on the Closing Date, unless another date is set out as follows: N/A [alternate possession date, if any]; OR ALTERNATIVELY, the Buyer shall assume the existing tenancies set out as follows: (NONE) [details of tenancy or tenancies, if any].

6. **ADJUSTMENTS:** As of JULY 14, 2003 (the "Adjustment Date") the Buyer shall assume and be responsible for all taxes, rates, local improvement assessments, fuel on the Property, and other charges applicable to the Property for the period subsequent to and including the Closing Date. All closing adjustments, whether to the credit of the Buyer or Seller, shall be made as of this date unless specified otherwise herein.

7. **INCLUDED/EXCLUDED ITEMS:** All fixtures shall be included in the Purchase Price, and without limiting the generality of the foregoing, such fixtures shall include: all buildings and ancillary structures on the Property, and improvements thereto, all affixed window dressings including blinds, awnings, curtain rods, tracks and valences, all affixed storm windows, screen doors, shelves, mirrors and carpeting, and all plumbing, electric, heating, ventilating, air conditioning and alarm fixtures; BUT EXCLUDING the following fixtures: ANTIQUE LIGHT FIXTURE IN DINING ROOM.
The following items (chattels) shall also be included in the Purchase Price: WASHER & DRYER IN BASEMENT.

8. **CONDITION & RISK:** The property and all fixtures and other items included under this Contract shall on closing be in the same condition as existed when viewed by the Buyer on MAY 12, 2003, and shall remain at the risk of the Seller until closing.

9. **TITLE:** Title to the Property shall be free and clear of all liens, charges or encumbrances, save and except for: a) any conditions, restrictions or reservations, including any royalties, contained in the original grant or in any other grant or disposition from the Crown, b) any registered or pending restrictive covenants that run with the land, c) any easements or rights-of-way for utilities or public authorities, or d) any matters expressly allowed for elsewhere in this Contract.

10. **TENDER & DOCUMENTS:** Any tender of money from the Buyer to the Seller shall, unless otherwise expressly provided, be in the form of cash, Lawyer's or Notary's trust cheque, or certified cheque or bank draft drawn on a Canadian chartered bank, trust company or credit union. Any tender of documents, keys or money may be effected by personal delivery upon the Buyer or Seller, as the case may be, or their Lawyers or Notaries, if any, on or before the closing date, and any documents required to be registered shall be delivered in registrable form and shall be lodged for registration in the applicable Land Title Office on or before the Closing Date.

11. **TIME:** Time shall be of the essence throughout this Contract, including any extensions. The balance of the Purchase Price shall be paid on or before the Closing Date, and/or any formal agreement(s) regarding payment of the balance of the Purchase Price shall be entered into on or before the Closing Date, failing which the Seller may, at the Seller's option, terminate this Contract, and, without limiting any other claims or remedies available to the Seller, the Deposit shall be absolutely forfeited to the Seller in accordance with the *Real Estate Act.*

12.. **FINANCING:** If the Buyer is relying on any new mortgage financing for all or part the balance of the Purchase Price, the Buyer shall still be required to pay the Purchase Price on the Closing Date, however the Buyer may wait to pay the Purchase Price until after the transfer and new mortgage documents have been lodged for registration in the applicable Land Title Office, provided that, before such lodging, the Buyer has: a) tendered the balance of the Purchase Price not being financed by the new mortgage(s), b) satisfied all of the new mortgagee's conditions and requirements for funding except lodging the mortgage(s) for registration, and c) provided the Seller with a Lawyer's or Notary's undertaking to pay the balance of the Purchase Price upon the lodging of the transfer and new mortgage(s) and the advance by the mortgagee(s) of the mortgage proceeds.

13. **CLEARING TITLE:** If the Seller is required to clear any existing charges from title, the Seller shall still be required to clear the title, however the Seller may wait to pay and discharge such existing charges until immediately after receiving the Purchase Price, provided that the Buyer may insist that the Purchase Price be paid to a Lawyer or Notary in trust, on the Lawyer's or Notary's undertaking to pay and discharge the existing charges, and remit any balance to the Seller, the undertaking to be in the form approved by the Canadian Bar Association (BC Branch) (Real Property Section), as may be amended from time to time.

14. **COSTS:** Each party shall bear their own costs. Specifically, and without limiting the foregoing, all costs relating to the conveyance and any mortgage(s) shall be at the expense of the Buyer, and all costs related to the clearing of title shall be at the expense of the Seller.

15. **REPRESENTATIONS & WARRANTIES:** This document, together with all listed Schedules, and together with the Property Disclosure Statement if and only if included with and expressly incorporated as part of this Contract, shall constitute the entire agreement between the parties. There are no collateral agreements, representations, warranties, guarantees or promises unless expressly set out in this Contract. Any express warranties or guarantees shall survive and not merge on closing.

16. **ENFORCABILITY, ENTIRETY AND INTERPRETATION OF CONTRACT:** ***This is a legal document!*** This Contract may only be amended or extended by mutual, written agreement between the parties, or between their Lawyers or Notaries, if any. This Contract shall pass to the benefit of and be binding upon each of the parties' heirs, executors, administrators, successors and assigns. In the event of a discrepancy between the Schedules or added clauses in this Contract and the pre-formatted form of Contract, the Schedules or added clauses shall prevail to the extent of the discrepancy. Any references to gender or number of parties shall be read with the intended context applied. In the event that any specific provisions of this Contract are declared illegal, invalid or unenforceable by a court of competent jurisdiction, then the offending provision(s) may be severed and shall not impair the validity or enforceability of the balance of the Contract. This Contract shall be interpreted and enforced in accordance with the laws of the Province of British Columbia.

17. **LEGAL REPRESENTATION:** Each of the parties acknowledges: a) having read this Contract in its entirety, together with any relevant schedules, Property Disclosure Statements or information pages, b) having received a copy of this Contract, and c) having been advised to seek independent legal advice from a Lawyer or Notary prior to signing this Contract. Each of the parties further acknowledges that they have either obtained such independent advice, or have declined to seek such advice and have otherwise entered into this Contract with the knowledge that it creates firm and binding legal relations and in full comprehension of the terms and consequences set out herein. Notwithstanding the source of this document, the doctrine of "Contra Preferentem" shall not apply and the Contract shall be interpreted and construed equally among the parties.

18. **FURTHER SCHEDULES:** The following Schedules are attached to and form an integral part of this Contract: "A" (SURVEY)
[applicable Schedules, if any]

19. **OFFER:** This offer, or counter-offer, shall be open for acceptance and irrevocable until 5:00 PM [time – a.m. *or* p.m.] on MAY 13, 2003 [date].

and upon acceptance, and notification of same to the other party, there shall be a binding agreement of purchase and sale.

Dated: MAY 12, 2003.

X Witness One [Witness] X Bob Smith [Buyer] ● [Seal] BOB SMITH [Print Name]

X Witness One [Witness] X Mary Smith [Buyer] ● [Seal] MARY SMITH [Print Name]

20. **ACCEPTANCE:** The Seller accepts this offer on the terms and conditions set out herein.

Dated: MAY 13, 2003.

X Witness Two [Witness] X John Doe [Seller] ● [Seal] JOHN DOE [Print Name]

X Witness Two [Witness] X Jane Doe [Seller] ● [Seal] JANE DOE [Print Name]

Alberta

Form of Agreement of Purchase & Sale (sample completed form)

RESIDENTIAL REAL ESTATE PURCHASE CONTRACT

For use in the Province of Alberta

This Contract is hereby made between

SELLER	and	BUYER
Name JOHN DOE		Name BOB SMITH
Name JANE DOE		Name MARY SMITH

PROPERTY

1.1 The Property is comprised of the Land, Buildings, and fixtures located at the following municipal address: 123 MAIN STREET CENTREVILLE, ALBERTA

1.2 The legal description of the Property is as follows:
a) If freehold:
Plan 2 Block 3 Lot 1
or
b) If Condominium:
Condominium Plan ______ Unit ______ Parking Unit ______

Jurisdiction MIDDLEFORD COUNTY

Other ______

1.3 All fixtures attached to the Property shall be included, save and except the following: ANTIQUE LIGHT FIXTURE IN DINING RM.

1.4 The Following chattels shall be included and remain on the Property: WASHER & DRYER IN BASEMENT

PURCHASE PRICE

2.1 The Purchase Price shall be paid in full on the Closing Date.

2.2 The balance due on closing set out below shall be paid by Lawyer's trust cheque, certified cheque or bank draft drawn on a Canadian chartered bank, trust company or credit union, or through such consideration as may be otherwise agreed upon herein.

2.3 **The Purchase Price includes any applicable Goods and Services Tax (GST)**, unless otherwise agreed upon herein.

2.4 The Purchase Price shall be paid as follows:

$ 15,000.00	Deposit # 1
$ /	Deposit # 2
$ 112,000.00	New Mortgage
$ / (approx. principal on closing)	Mortgage to be assumed
$ /	Mortgage back to Seller
$ /	Other
$ 23,000.00	Balance Due on Closing
$ 150,000.00	**Purchase Price**

DEPOSIT(S)

3.1 The Deposit(s) shall be made by cash or personal cheque payable to ATTICUS LAWYER, IN TRUST.

3.2 Deposit # 1 shall be delivered to the Seller within 2 days of acceptance and formation of this Contract.

3.3 Deposit # 2, if any, shall be delivered within 2 days of N/A

3.4 The Deposit(s) shall be held in trust for the benefit of the Seller and the Buyer as their respective interests appear herein. No interest shall be payable on the deposit(s), unless otherwise agreed upon herein.

3.5 The Deposit(s) shall be subsequently:

a) applied towards the Purchase Price as set out in section 2,

b) returned to the Buyer in the event that this document in the form of an offer or counter offer is not accepted, or the transaction does not close due to any conditions not being satisfied or default on the part of the Seller, or

c) forfeited to the Seller in the event that the transaction does not close due to default on the part of the Buyer.

INITIALS BS MS JD

CLOSING DATE

4.1 This Contract shall be completed on

JULY 14, 2003.
[Closing Date]

4.2 Possession of the Property shall be delivered by the Seller on or before 12:00 p.m. (noon) on the Closing Date, and such possession shall be vacant unless otherwise provided for herein.

4.3 If the Parties elect that the Closing Date shall occur on a day other than a day on which the Land Titles Office is open, then payment of the Purchase Price and all conveyancing matters shall occur on or before 12:00 p.m. (noon) on the last day on which the Land Titles Office is open immediately prior to the Closing Date, notwithstanding that possession shall be delivered on the Closing Date agreed upon above.

CONDITIONS

5.1 This Contract is conditional upon the Buyer...
(choose if applicable, stroke out if inapplicable)

☑ a) Financing:
obtaining written approval of mortgage financing
☑ (i) on terms acceptable to the Buyer at the Buyer's sole discretion

or

☐ (ii) on the following terms:
Principle amount $ ____________
(plus high ratio mortgage insurance premiums, if applicable)
Interest Rate not greater than ________ %
Term not shorter than ____________
Amortization not shorter than ____________
☐ Open ☐ Closed ☐ Limited Prepayment Options
Other material terms required by Buyer
____

This condition shall be satisfied on or before
5:00 PM on MAY 17, 2003,
[time – a.m. or p.m.] [date]

☐ b) Property Inspection Report:
obtaining an acceptable property inspection report prepared by a qualified home inspector,
☐ (i) the acceptability of which shall be at the sole discretion of the Buyer

or

☐ (ii) which shall not disclose any material deficiency that the Seller is unable or unwilling to remedy, at the Seller's option
This condition shall be satisfied on or before
________ on ________,
[time – a.m. or p.m.] [date]

☐ c) Sale of Buyer's property:
entering into an unconditional and binding agreement of purchase and sale of the Buyer's property located at
____
This condition shall be satisfied on or before
________ on ________,
[time – a.m. or p.m.] [date]

☑ d) Lawyer approval:
obtaining an acceptable lawyer's review and opinion on the form and content of this Contract, the acceptability of which shall be at the sole discretion of the Buyer.
This condition shall be satisfied on or before
5:00 PM on MAY 15, 2003,
[time – a.m. or p.m.] [date]

☐ e) Condominium Documents:
satisfying the Buyer's Condition re Condominium Documents as set out in the schedule attached.
This condition shall be satisfied on or before
________ on ________,
[time – a.m. or p.m.] [date]

☐ f) Other Buyer conditions:
____
____
This condition shall be satisfied on or before
________ on ________,
[time – a.m. or p.m.] [date]

____
____
This condition shall be satisfied on or before
________ on ________,
[time – a.m. or p.m.] [date]

5.2 This Contract is conditional upon the Seller...
(choose if applicable, stroke out if inapplicable)

☐ a) Lawyer approval:
obtaining an acceptable lawyer's review and opinion on the form and content of this Contract, the acceptability of which shall be at the sole discretion of the Seller.
This condition shall be satisfied on or before
________ on ________,
[time – a.m. or p.m.] [date]

☐ b) Other Seller conditions:
____
____
This condition shall be satisfied on or before
________ on ________,
[time – a.m. or p.m.] [date]

____
____
This condition shall be satisfied on or before
________ on ________,
[time – a.m. or p.m.] [date]

5.3 Purchaser's conditions shall be for the benefit of the Purchaser and Seller's conditions shall be for the benefit of the seller, and all conditions shall be deemed to be for the sole and exclusive benefit of the parties so stated, unless provided for otherwise.

5.4 Any Conditions may be waived at the sole option of the beneficial party, unless provided for otherwise.

5.5 Conditions shall be considered satisfied if, and only if, the beneficial party delivers written notice to the other party that the condition has been satisfied or otherwise waived.

5.6 If any condition is not satisfied within the required time limit, then this Contract shall be immediately terminated and the Deposit(s) returned in accordance with section 3.

TITLE

Title to the Property shall be free and clear of any liens, encumbrances, registrations or obligations, save and except any of the following:

a) registered or pending restrictive covenants that run with the land that do not materially affect the marketability of the Property,

b) encumbrances or obligations imposed by law,
c) easements or rights-of-way for utilities or public authorities that do not materially affect the marketability of the Property,
d) homeowner association agreements, restrictions, encumbrances or similar registrations that do not materially affect the marketability of the Property, or
e) matters expressly allowed for elsewhere in this Contract.

SURVEYOR'S REAL PROPERTY REPORT / TITLE INSURANCE

Seller shall furnish the Buyer with an up-to-date Surveyor's Real Property Report (RPR) at least 10 business days prior to the Closing Date. The RPR shall certify as to the current state of the property and shall be accompanied by written evidence regarding the status of municipal compliance. Alternatively, by acknowledging hereunder, the parties agree to obtain a title insurance policy in lieu of an RPR, provided that the policy shall be unqualified with respect to any losses that would have been addressed by obtaining the RPR and compliance report.

Buyer shall accept title insurance: ☑

CLOSING ARRANGEMENTS

8.1 The Buyer shall be provided with documents and shall have a reasonable period of time before the Closing Date to confirm registration of documents at the Land Titles Office and to obtain advances under any new mortgage(s).

8.2 If the Seller fails to deliver the required closing documents, then payment of the Purchase Price shall be delayed until the Buyer has received the documents and has had a reasonable period of time to register them and confirm registration in accordance with the above. In such event, any interest payable on the balance of the Purchase Price shall be waived pending the expiry of such reasonable time.

8.3 In the event that the Seller agrees to accept late payment of the whole or any part of the balance of Purchase Price, then interest shall be payable to the Seller on the amount so outstanding at 3% above the rate of the Province of Alberta Treasury Branches as published on the Closing Date, or alternatively the last business day prior to the Closing Date. Interest shall be calculated on a daily basis from and including the Closing Date, but excluding the date of subsequent payment. Payment tendered on any day after 12:00 p.m. (noon) shall be deemed paid on the following business day.

8.4 The Purchase Price may be used by the **Seller's** Lawyer to pay out any liens, charges or other obligations that affect title and that are the responsibility of the Seller to discharge and vacate. The Seller shall ensure that his/her lawyer provides the Buyer or the Buyer's lawyer with evidence of all discharges, including, where necessary, a certified copy of the certificate of title, within a reasonable time after the Closing Date.

COSTS

Each party shall bear their own costs. Specifically, and without limiting the foregoing, the costs shall be allocated as follows:

The Seller shall be responsible for: (i) the preparation of closing documents, (ii) the preparation, registration and discharge of any Seller's caveat(s) under this Contract, and(iii) the RPR and evidence of municipal status, or title insurance premium(s), pursuant to section 7.

The Buyer shall be responsible for: (i) the registration of the transfer, and (ii) the preparation, registration and discharge of any Buyer's caveat(s) under this Contract.

). ADJUSTMENTS

10.1 The balance due on closing shall be subject to the usua adjustments, which shall include, without limitation and among other things expressly agreed upon: property taxes, amortizec local improvement charges, utilities and any homeowner association fees.

10.2 In the case of condominiums such adjustments shall further include, without limitation, condominium fees and other amounts payable in the ordinary course of condominium ownership.

10.3 The Closing Date itself shall be apportioned to the Seller.

I. RISK & INSURANCE

11.1 On closing, the Property and all chattels included herein shall be in substantially the same condition they were in upon acceptance of this Contract.

11.2 The Property and all fixtures and chattels contemplated under this Contract shall remain at the risk of the Seller until closing.

11.3 All related insurance policies held by the Seller, if any, as well as any proceeds paid under such policies, shall be held in trust for the benefit of the parties in relation to their respective interests under this Contract. In the event of damage and subsequent payment under such policies the Buyer shall have the option of terminating this Contract or receiving the said payment and closing the transaction as scheduled with all other terms and conditions remaining the same. In the event that the Contract is terminated pursuant to this section, the deposit shall be returned to the Buyer in the same manner as if a condition had been unsatisfied under this Contract.

2. REPRESENTATIONS & WARRANTIES

12.1 The Seller represents and warrants that the following are, and as of the Closing Date shall be, true:

a) The Seller has the legal right to sell the Property,
b) The fixtures and chattels contemplated herein are in good working order,
c) The Seller is not a "non-resident" within the meaning of the *Income Tax Act (Canada)*,
d) The current use of the Land is in compliance with applicable zoning and land use by-laws,
e) The buildings, fences or other structures are located wholly within the lot lines of the Property, except where a continuing encroachment agreement exists with the adjoining property,
f) No buildings, fences or other structures are improperly located on any easements or utility Rights-of way, except where a continuing encroachment agreement.
g) The location of all buildings, fences and other structures on the Property does not violate any municipal regulations or by-laws, or alternatively that the locations of all buildings or other structures on the Property is legal non-conforming as that term is defined under the *Municipal Government Act (Alberta)*.

12.2 Any action or remedy in connection with any representation or warranty contained in this Contract, must be brought within 1 year of the Closing Date

12.3 This document, together with all listed Schedules, constitutes the entire Contract between the parties and there shall be no collateral agreements, representations or warranties.

12.4 All warranties contained herein shall survive and not merge on closing.

3. ADDITIONAL TERMS

3.1 Time shall be of the essence throughout this Contract, including any extensions, and all deadlines and date requirements shall be strictly construed and enforced. Stated times shall be interpreted as Alberta standard time.

3.2 This Contract shall enure to the benefit of and be binding upon each of the **parties'** heirs, executors, administrators, successors and assigns.

3.3 Any references to gender or number of parties shall be read with the intended context applied.

3.4 In the event that the contract is terminated, such portions shall remain enforceable as to give effect to the intent of the Contract and the reasonable equities between the parties.

3.5 In the event of a discrepancy between the Schedules or added clauses in this Contract and the pre-formatted form of Contract, the Schedules or added clauses shall prevail to the extent of the discrepancy.

3.6 In the event that any specific provisions of this Contract are declared illegal, invalid or unenforceable by a court of competent jurisdiction, then the offending provision(s) may be severed and shall not impair the validity or enforceability of the balance of the Contract.

3.7 The following Schedules are attached to and form an integral part of this Contract

3.8 This Contract shall be subject to the following additional terms and conditions:

N/A

4 ENFORCABILITY, ENTIRETY AND INTERPRETATION

14.1 Upon acceptance, this Contract shall constitute a binding agreement of purchase and sale.

14.2 The parties agree to act in good faith and to use reasonable effort and diligence in pursuing the satisfaction of conditions and carrying out the terms and intent of this Contract, and to instruct their Lawyers to act reasonably and in accordance with accepted practice in carrying out the terms and intent of this Contract.

14.3 This Contract may only be amended or collaterally agreed to by mutual, written agreement between the parties, or between their lawyers, if any, as such lawyers may be noted herein or as otherwise reasonably established during the course of this transaction.

14.4 This Contract shall be interpreted and enforced in accordance with the laws of the Province of Alberta.

5. LEGAL REPRESENTATION

15.1 Each of the parties acknowledges having received a copy of this Contract and having been advised to seek independent legal advice prior to signing. Each of the parties further acknowledges that they have either obtained such independent legal advice, or have declined to seek such advice and have otherwise entered into this Contract with the knowledge that it creates firm and binding legal relations and in full comprehension of the terms and consequences set out herein.

15.2 Notwithstanding the source of this document, the doctrine of "Contra Preferentem" shall not apply and the Contract shall be interpreted and construed equally among the parties.

5. NOTICE

16.1 Any notice given between the parties shall be deemed effected upon delivery and receipt through one of the following methods:

1) personal delivery to the addresses of the parties noted herein,

2) registered mail to the addresses of the parties noted herein (in which case receipt shall be deemed to be three days after mailing),

3) fax to the fax numbers noted by the parties herein, if any, or

4) delivery or fax to either party's lawyer, if any, as noted herein or as otherwise reasonably established during the course of the transaction.

16.2 Contacting the Buyer:

Address 321 QUEEN ST., CENTREVILLE, B1B 2A2

Phone (day) (123) 987-6543 (night) (SAME)
Fax (NONE)

16.3 Contacting the Seller:

Address 123 MAIN ST., CENTREVILLE, 1A1 B2B

Phone (day) (123) 345-6789 (night) (SAME)
Fax (NONE)

16.4 Buyer's lawyer, if any:

Name PENELOPE SOLICITOR
Firm
Address 345 BARRISTERS ROW
CENTREVILLE, C2C 3D3
Phone (123) 246-1357
Fax (123) 246-1375

16.5 Seller's lawyer, if any:

Name ATTICUS LAWYER
Firm
Address 234 CHANCERY LANE
CENTREVILLE, C2C 3D4
Phone (123) 246-3579
Fax (123) 246-3597

17. OFFER

This offer or counter offer shall be open for acceptance and irrevocable by the Buyer until

5:00 PM on MAY 13, 2003,
[time – a.m. *or* p.m.] [date]

Signed, sealed and delivered at the time of

4:45 PM on MAY 12, 2003
[time – a.m. *or* p.m.] [date]

in CENTREVILLE, Alberta
[jurisdiction]]

Bob Smith [Buyer] Witness One [Witness]

Mary Smith [Buyer] Witness One [Witness]

18. COUNTER OFFER(S)

18.1 The preceding offer or counter offer is hereby rejected and this counter offer shall now be open for acceptance and irrevocable by the

______ until
[Buyer *or* Seller]

______ on ______,
[time – a.m. *or* p.m.] [date]

Signed, sealed and delivered at the time of

______ on ______
[time – a.m. *or* p.m.] [date]

in ______, Alberta
[jurisdiction]]

name: ______ [Witness] ______

name: ______ [Witness] ______

18.2 The preceding counter offer is hereby rejected and this counter offer shall now be open for acceptance and irrevocable by the

______ until
[Buyer *or* Seller]

______ on ______,
[time – a.m. *or* p.m.] [date]

Signed, sealed and delivered at the time of

______ on ______
[time – a.m. *or* p.m.] [date]

in ______, Alberta
[jurisdiction]]

name: ______ [Witness] ______

name: ______ [Witness] ______

18.3 The preceding counter offer is hereby rejected and this counter offer shall now be open for acceptance and irrevocable by the

______ until
[Buyer *or* Seller]

______ on ______,
[time – a.m. *or* p.m.] [date]

Signed, sealed and delivered at the time of

______ on ______
[time – a.m. *or* p.m.] [date]

in ______, Alberta
[jurisdiction]]

name: ______ [Witness] ______

name: ______ [Witness] ______

18.4 The preceding counter offer is hereby rejected and this counter offer shall now be open for acceptance and irrevocable by the

______ until
[Buyer *or* Seller]

______ on ______,
[time – a.m. *or* p.m.] [date]

Signed, sealed and delivered at the time of

______ on ______
[time – a.m. *or* p.m.] [date]

in ______, Alberta
[jurisdiction]]

name: ______ [Witness] ______

name: ______ [Witness] ______

19. ACCEPTANCE

The preceding offer or counter offer is hereby accepted by the

SELLER on the terms and conditions set out herein.
[Buyer *or* Seller]

Signed, sealed and delivered at the time of

9:00 AM on MAY 13, 2003
[time – a.m. *or* p.m.] [date]

in CENTREVILLE, Alberta
[jurisdiction]]

name: John Doe [Witness] Witness Two

name: Jane Doe [Witness] Witness Two

BS MS JD
INITIALS

Saskatchewan

Form of Agreement of Purchase & Sale (sample completed form)

RESIDENTIAL CONTRACT OF PURCHASE AND SALE

For use in the Province of Saskatchewan

I / We BOB SMITH & MARY SMITH OF 321 QUEEN ST., CENTREVILLE
the "Buyer" [address]
HEREBY OFFERS TO BUY

Business Phone: N/A
Residence Phone: 987-6543
Fax: NONE

From JOHN DOE & JANE DOE OF 123 MAIN ST., CENTREVILLE
the "Seller" [address]

Business Phone: N/A
Residence Phone: 245-6789
Fax: NONE

The property legally described as LOT 2, PLAN 2, COUNTY OF MIDDLEFORD

And municipally described as 123 MAIN STREET, CENTREVILLE, SASK., 1A1 B2B (the "Property")

For the purchase price of ONE HUNDRED & FIFTY THOUSAND —— xx dollars (CDN); $ 150,000 –

To be paid in the following manner:

a) $ 15,000.– Deposit by cash or cheque, payable to ATTICUS LAWYER, IN TRUST, within 2 days after acceptance, to be held in trust pending completion or other termination of this Agreement, and to be credited towards the purchase price on closing.

b) $ 112,000.– New mortgage(s) on terms set out below and/or as may be set out in attached schedule

c) $ — Assumed mortgage(s) on terms set out in attached schedule

d) $ — Other

e) $ 23,000.– Balance due on closing, subject to adjustments as provided for herein, by cash, lawyer's trust cheque or certified cheque drawn on a Canadian chartered bank, trust company or credit union, payable to the Seller or Seller's lawyer, in trust, or as may be redirected by them.

1. This offer is conditional upon the following *[complete as applicable or stroke out]*:
   a) The buyer shall, at the buyer's sole expense, use every reasonable effort to obtain approval of new mortgage financing on or before ______ at the rate and on the terms as follows: INTEREST RATE NOT GREATER THAN 7%, CLOSED, 5 YEAR TERM 25 YEAR AMORTIZATION
   b) NIL
2. The following schedules are attached hereto and shall form an integral part of this Agreement: "A" (SURVEY)
3. If any portion of the purchase price is not paid on the Closing Date (not including any assumed mortgage(s)) pursuant to usual conveyancing practices, the Buyer shall pay the Seller interest at a rate of 7.0 % per annum on the amount so outstanding from the possession date up to and including the date of subsequent payment.
4. This transaction shall be completed on JULY 14, 2003 (the "Closing Date"), at or before 12:00 p.m. (noon), at which time the Seller shall deliver vacant possession of the Property unless otherwise provided for herein
5. Except as otherwise provided for herein, title to the Property shall be conveyed free and clear of any mortgages, liens or encumbrances, save and except the reservations and exceptions appearing in the existing Certificate of Title.
6. The balance due on closing shall be subject to the usual adjustments as of the Closing Date for taxes and other incoming and outgoing amounts relating to the property.
7. a. The following items (chattels) are included: WASHER & DRYER IN BASEMENT. These chattels shall remain with the property on closing, and the Seller warrants that they shall be free of any encumbrances or liens, and shall be in the same good working order and condition as they were at the time this Agreement was signed.
   b. All items attached to the property (fixtures) are included in the purchase price and shall remain with the property on closing, save and except the following fixtures which are not included: ANTIQUE LIGHT FIXTURE IN DINING ROOM
   c. The following items are rented or leased, and the Buyer agrees to assume the rental contracts or leases in connection with same: HOT WATER TANK
8. The parties agree to execute all usual and reasonable documents required to complete this transaction. The Seller shall be responsible for the preparation of the Transfer of Title, and the Seller shall discharge all existing mortgages or encumbrances at the Seller's expense. The Buyer shall be responsible for the cost of registering the Transfer of Title under the *Land Titles Act*, and the Buyer shall be responsible for all costs associated with arranging and registering financing. Otherwise, each party shall bear their own costs, and the cost of any Agreement for Sale shall be borne equally by the Parties.
9. In the event that this offer or any counter-offer is not accepted, or in the event that any condition is not fulfilled or performed after the responsible party has made every reasonable effort to fulfil or perform same, then this Agreement shall be null and void and the deposit shall be returned to the Buyer without interest penalty or deduction. In the event that the Buyer defaults on the completion of this Agreement pursuant to its terms, the Buyer will forfeit the above deposit in addition to any other claims the Seller may have against the Buyer.
10. The Property and all fixtures and chattels contemplated under this Agreement shall remain at the risk of and insured by the Seller until closing. No insurance policies shall be transferred on closing unless otherwise provided herein.
11. The Seller warrants that the Seller is a resident of Canada as defined under the *Income Tax Act*, and the Seller shall furnish satisfactory evidence of same on closing.
12. Upon acceptance this Agreement shall constitute a binding agreement of purchase and sale. This document, together with all listed Schedules, constitutes the entire Agreement between the parties and there shall be no collateral agreements, representations or warranties. This Agreement may only be amended or extended by mutual, written agreement between the parties, or between their lawyers, if any. Time shall be of the essence throughout this offer and Agreement, including any extensions. This Agreement shall pass to the benefit of and be binding upon each of the parties' heirs, executors, administrators, successors and assigns. In the event of a discrepancy between the Schedules or added clauses in this Agreement and the pre-formatted form of Agreement, the Schedules or added clauses shall prevail to the extent of the discrepancy. Any references to gender or number of parties shall be read with the intended context applied. In the event that any specific provisions of this Agreement are declared illegal, invalid or unenforceable by a court of competent jurisdiction, then the offending provision(s) may be severed and shall not impair the validity or enforceability of the balance of the Agreement. This Agreement shall be interpreted and enforced in accordance with the laws of the Province of Saskatchewan.
13. Each of the parties acknowledges having received a copy of this Agreement and having been advised to seek independent legal advice prior to signing. Each of the parties further acknowledges that they have either obtained such independent legal advice, or have declined to seek such advice and have otherwise entered into this Agreement with the knowledge that it creates firm and binding legal relations and in full comprehension of the terms and consequences set out herein. Notwithstanding the source of this document, the doctrine of "Contra Preferentem" shall not apply and the Agreement shall be interpreted and construed equally among the parties.
14. Unless revoked sooner, this offer shall be open for acceptance by the seller until 5:00 PM *[a.m. or p.m.]* on MAY 13, 2003

OFFER:
SIGNED, SEALED AND DELIVERED at CENTREVILLE *[place]* on MAY 12, 2003 *[date]*, and in the presence of:

Witness One *[Witness]* — Bob Smith *[Buyer]*
Witness One *[Witness]* — Mary Smith *[Buyer]*

ACCEPTANCE: This offer is hereby accepted on the terms and conditions set out herein.

SIGNED, SEALED AND DELIVERED at CENTREVILLE *[place]* on MAY 13, 2003 *[date]*, and in the presence of:

Witness Two *[Witness]* — John Doe *[Seller]*
Witness Two *[Witness]* — Jane Doe *[Seller]*

Buyer's Lawyer: PENELOPE SOLICITOR
FAX: (123) 246-1375
PHONE: (123) 246-1357

Seller's Lawyer: ATTICUS LAWYER
FAX: (123) 246-3597
PHONE: (123) 246-3579

Manitoba

Form of Agreement of Purchase & Sale (sample completed form)

CONTRACT

OF PURCHASE AND SALE (FOR USE IN MANITOBA)

To JOHN DOE & JANE DOE (herein the "Vendor")

Vendor's Address for service 121 MAIN ST., CENTREVILLE, MANITOBA, 1A1B2C

Phone (123) 345-6789 Fax (NONE)

I / We BOB SMITH & MARY SMITH (herein the "Purchaser")

Purchaser's address for service 321 QUEEN ST., CENTREVILLE, MANITOBA, B1B2A2

Phone (123) 987-6543 Fax (NONE)

Hereby offers to purchase the Property set out below on the terms and conditions set out below:

SUBJECT PROPERTY

1. (a) The Property that is the subject matter of this Agreement is the land described as follows together with all structures and improvements thereon:

123 MAIN STREET, CENTREVILLE, BEING LOT 1,
[civic address or legal description]

PLAN 2, COUNTY OF MIDDLEFORD (herein the "Property")
[... continued]

(b) The Property shall include all items affixed to the Property (fixtures), including without limitation all of the following: light fixtures, HVAC and plumbing fixtures, built-in vacuum, fitted carpets, fixed shelves and mirrors, window dressing hardware such as curtain rods and drapery tracks, screens and storm windows and doors, imbedded plants and shrubs, fountains, T.V antennae or dishes, fixed basketball nets, and the like as are now on the Property; however the following fixtures are expressly excluded:

ANTIQUE LIGHT FIXTURE IN DINING ROOM

(c) All items not affixed to the Property (chattels) which are not fixtures shall be excluded; however the following chattels are expressly included:

WASHER & DRYER IN BASEMENT.

(d) The following items are rented and are not included, and if assumable the Purchaser agrees to assume the rental contracts as of the Possession Date:

HOT WATER HEATER

PURCHASE PRICE AND PAYMENT TERMS

2. (a) The Purchase Price to be paid on the Possession Date is $ 150,000.00 (herein the "Purchase Price")

(b) The Purchase Price shall be arranged and paid on the following terms:

(i) Initial deposit
~~☐ presented with this offer~~
☑ to be provided within 48 hours after acceptance $ 15,000.00

(ii) Additional deposit to be provided on or upon

______ $ /

[date or satisfaction of condition]

(iii) Proceeds of new mortgage(s)
~~☐ for which Purchaser has prior approval~~
☑ to be arranged pursuant to financing condition herein $ 112,000.00

(iv) Assumption of existing mortgage(s) having a total balance outstanding on the Possession Date of not more than approximately $ ______ $ /
(Mortgage Assumption Schedule attached hereto)

(v) Mortgage back to Vendor in ______ priority $ /
(Vendor Take-Back Mortgage Schedule attached hereto)

(vi) Other: ______ $ /

(vii) Balance Due on Possession Date $ 23,000.00

TOTAL PURCHASE PRICE: $ 150,000.00

(c) If the Purchaser will be relying on the proceeds of a new mortgage to satisfy part of the Purchase Price, payment of that amount may be postponed for such time as the Purchaser reasonably requires to register the mortgage at the Land Titles Office and to report same and obtain the proceeds from the mortgage lender. In such event the amount so outstanding shall bear interest at the same rate set out in the proposed new mortgage payable to the Vendor immediately upon and until the date of subsequent payment. Payment tendered on any day after 12:00 p.m. (noon) shall be deemed paid on the following business day. The Vendor shall have a lien on the Property for the unpaid portion of the Purchase Price as contemplated in this section, and the lien shall also have the benefit of interest as set out in this section.

(d) The Deposit(s) shall be made by cash or personal cheque payable to ATTICUS LAWYER, IN TRUST The Deposit(s) shall be held in trust for the benefit of the Vendor and the Purchaser as their respective interests appear herein. The Deposit(s) shall be subsequently:

i. applied towards the Purchaser Price as set out in this section,

ii. returned to the Purchaser in the event that this offer or any counter offer is not accepted, or the transaction does not close due to any conditions not being satisfied or default on the part of the Vendor, or,

iii. forfeited to the Vendor in the event that the transaction does not close due to default on the part of the Purchaser.

(e) The Balance Due on the Possession Date shall be payable only by Lawyer's trust cheque, certified cheque or bank draft drawn on a Canadian chartered bank, trust company or credit union, or through such consideration as may be otherwise agreed upon in writing.

POSSESSION

3. (a) The Vendor shall provide possession of the Property at or before 12:00 PM [time – a.m. or p.m.] on JULY 14, 2003 [date] (the "Possession Date")

(b) On the Possession Date the property shall be vacant, unless otherwise provided for herein. Any chattels expressly included in this Agreement shall be left on the Property, and all other items, including those fixtures expressly excluded, shall be removed from the Property.

(c) Notwithstanding the foregoing, by acknowledging below, the Purchaser agrees to assume the existing tenancy(s) in connection with the Property (Tenancy Schedule attached hereto)

☐ Tenancy: N/L

TITLE

4. (a) Title to the Property, including all fixtures and chattels contemplated in this Agreement, shall be free and clear of all liens, mortgages, encumbrances or claims, whether registered or valid though unregistered, save and except any of the following:

i. Private or public restrictions, agreements or caveats relating to the buildings, structures or use of the Property, provided they have been complied with,

ii. Public utility easements or rights-of-way for services that supply the Property (and perhaps other properties),

iii. Easements, provided they were readily apparent at the time this initial offer was made,

iv. Existing mortgage(s) that is/are the responsibility of the Vendor to vacate and discharge, provided the requirements of section 2 have been met,

v. Matters which have been caused by, or are the responsibility of, the Purchaser, or

vi. Other liens, mortgages, encumbrances, claims or registrations listed as follows, or otherwise expressly agreed to herein:

N/L

(b) The Vendor shall, or shall have the right to, be in and convey personal and peaceable possession and occupation of the Property on the Possession Date, unless otherwise agreed to herein.

PROPERTY CONDITION

5. (a) On the Possession Date, the Property and all fixtures and included chattels shall be in substantially the same condition as they were in at the time this initial offer was made.

(b) The building(s), structures or improvements on the Property are located wholly within the lot lines of the Property.

(c) The building(s), structures or improvements on the Property do not illegally or without permission encroach onto any easements or rights-of-way located on the Property.

(d) The building(s), structures or improvements on any adjoining properties do not encroach onto the subject Property.

(e) Notwithstanding the foregoing, the Purchaser acknowledges and accepts the following encroachments and/or building or zoning non-compliance matters:

NIL

CONDITIONS

6. (a) This Agreement shall be conditional upon the following:

(i) Conditions for the benefit of the Purchaser *[check if applicable – stroke out provision entirely if not applicable]*

☐ 1. Financing

The Purchaser obtaining written approval of mortgage financing as set out in section 2.

This condition must be satisfied on or before 5:00 PM *[time – a.m. or p.m.]* on MAY 17, 2003 *[date]*,

☐ 2. Lawyer Approval

Review and approval of the terms and content of this Agreement by the Purchaser's lawyer.

This condition must be satisfied on or before 5:00 PM *[time – a.m. or p.m.]* on MAY 13, 2003 *[date]*,

☐ 3. Other

NIL

This condition must be satisfied on or before ______ *[time – a.m. or p.m.]* on ______ *[date]*,

(ii) Conditions for the benefit of the Vendor *[check if applicable – stroke out provision entirely if not applicable]*

☐ 1. Lawyer Approval

Review and approval of the terms and content of this Agreement by the Purchaser's lawyer.

This condition must be satisfied on or before ______ *[time – a.m. or p.m.]* on ______ *[date]*,

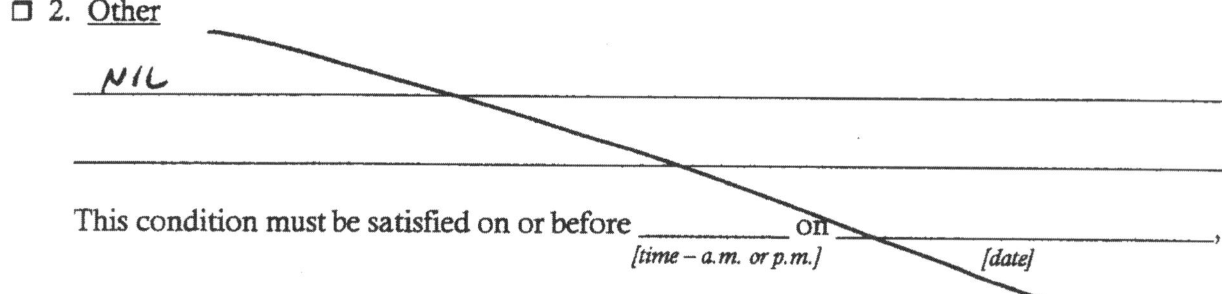

(b) Unless all of the foregoing conditions are satisfied, this agreement shall be null and void. A condition shall be deemed satisfied if, and only if, on or before the time specified, the party for whose benefit the condition exists delivers notice in writing to the other party that the condition has been satisfied or otherwise waived.

(c) The parties shall act in good faith and use reasonable efforts in fulfilling their conditions.

(d) Unless stated otherwise, each condition shall be for the sole and exclusive benefit of the party so stated, and may be waived by that party at their sole option.

GENERAL TERMS

7. (a) GST

The Vendor warrants that this transaction is not subject to Federal Goods and Services Tax [GST], and the Vendor shall furnish a certificate confirming same on closing.

(b) Closing Adjustments

The Balance Due on the Possession Date shall be subject to the usual adjustments, including, without limitation, taxes and any improvement levies for the current year. The Possession Date itself shall be the responsibility of the Purchaser.

(c) Risk & Insurance

The Property and all fixtures and chattels contemplated under this Agreement shall remain at the risk of the Vendor until closing. In the event of substantial damage to the Property, which the Vendor, acting in good faith, is unable or unwilling to put back into the same condition it was in prior to the damage, then this Agreement shall be null and void in the same manner as if a condition had been established as unsatisfied. No insurance policies shall be transferred on closing.

(d) Remedies

In addition to the agreed upon terms surrounding the deposit(s) set out in section 2, in the event of default by either party (herein the "Aggrieved Party) against the other party (herein the "Defaulting Party"), the Aggrieved Party shall have the benefit of any additional remedies available in law, and retainer or return of the deposit alone shall not constitute termination of this Agreement.

(e) Lawyers' Trust Conditions

The Vendor and Purchaser hereby agree and authorize their respective lawyers to enter into agreements whereby they impose and undertake certain trust conditions to fulfill the letter and intent of this Agreement, provided that the contractual obligations of the parties otherwise remain intact.

(f) Time

Time shall be of the essence throughout this Agreement. All times stated shall be deemed to be Manitoba time zone.

(g) Succession

This Agreement shall pass to the benefit of and be binding upon each of the party's successors, assigns and personal representatives. ,

(h) Enforceability, Entirety and Interpretation

Upon acceptance, **THIS AGREEMENT SHALL CONSTITUTE A BINDING AGREEMENT OF PURCHASE AND SALE. IT SHOULD BE READ IN ITS ENTIRETY!** This document, together with all listed Schedules, constitutes the entire Agreement between the parties and there shall be no collateral agreements, representations or warranties. This Agreement may only be amended by mutual, written agreement between the parties, or between their lawyers, if any, as set out herein or as may be have been reasonably established through the course of this transaction. Any references to gender or number of parties shall be read with the intended context applied. In the event that any specific provisions of this Agreement are declared illegal, invalid or unenforceable by a court of competent jurisdiction, then the offending provision(s) may be severed and shall not impair the validity or enforceability of the balance of the Agreement. Any representations or promises made by the Vendor shall survive closing only if expressly provided herein or if required by law. This Agreement shall be interpreted and enforced in accordance with the laws of the Province of Manitoba.

(i) Legal Representation

Each of the parties acknowledges having received a copy of this Agreement and having been advised to seek independent legal advice prior to signing. Each of the parties further acknowledges that they have either obtained such independent legal advice, or have declined to seek such advice and have otherwise entered into this Agreement with the knowledge that it creates firm and binding legal relations and in full comprehension of the terms and consequences set out herein. Notwithstanding the source of this document, the doctrine of "Contra Preferentem" shall not apply and the Agreement shall be interpreted and construed equally among the parties.

The Purchaser's lawyer, if any, is:

PENELOPE SOLICITOR, 345 BARRISTER'S ROW, CENTREVILLE, M.B., C2C 3D3
[name & address of lawyer]

Phone (123) 246-1357 Fax (123) 246-1375

The Vendor's lawyer, if any, is:

ATTICUS LAWYER, 234 CHANCERY LANE, CENTREVILLE, C2C 3D4
[name & address of lawyer]

Phone (123) 246-3579 Fax (123) 246-3597

(j) Notice

Any notice required under this Agreement shall be deemed effective if delivered to the receiving party or their respective lawyers, if any, as set out herein or as may be or have been reasonably established through the course of this transaction, by one of the following methods:

i. by personal delivery to the addresses of the parties noted herein,

ii. by registered mail to the addresses of the parties noted herein
(in which case receipt shall be deemed to be three days after mailing),

iii. by fax to the fax numbers noted by the parties herein, if any.

(k) Tender

Any monies, keys, documents or other items required to be delivered pursuant to this Agreement may be tendered by delivery of same to the respective lawyers, if any, as set out herein or as may be or have been reasonably established through the course of this transaction, or failing which upon the parties themselves.

(l) Schedules

The following Schedules are attached hereto and shall form an integral part of this Agreement

A. ***Homesteads Act Declaration*** C. ______

B. SURVEY ______ D. ______

In the event of a discrepancy between the Schedules or added clauses in this Agreement and the pre-formatted form of Agreement, the Schedules or added clauses shall prevail to the extent of the discrepancy.

ADDITIONAL TERMS

8. NIL ______

______

______

______

OFFER

9. This offer from the Purchaser shall be open for acceptance and irrevocable, but shall expire completely at the following time and date:

5:00 P.M. on MAY 13, 2003.
[time – a.m. or p.m.] *[date]*

Signed at 4:45 P.M. on MAY 12, 2003.
[time – a.m. or p.m.] *[date]*

Witness One ______ Bob Smith ______
[Witness] *[Purchaser]*

Witness One ______ Mary Smith ______
[Witness] *[Purchaser]*

ACCEPTANCE of OFFER - or COUNTER-OFFER

10. This offer is hereby *[check if applicable – stroke out alternate provision entirely]*:

☑ accepted by the Vendor on the terms set out herein

or

☐ The Vendor submits a counteroffer on the terms set out herein as amended and initialed and/or as follows:

____

____

____

____

This counteroffer from the Vendor shall be open for acceptance and irrevocable, but shall expire completely at the following time and date:

______________ on ______________________________.
[time – a.m. or p.m.] *[date]*

Signed at 9:00 A.M. on MAY 13, 2003 _____.
[time – a.m. or p.m.] *[date]*

Witness Two *[Witness]* John Doe *[Vendor]*

Witness Two *[Witness]* Jane Doe *[Vendor]*

ACCEPTANCE of COUNTEROFFER

11. This counteroffer is hereby accepted by the Purchaser on the terms set out herein.

Signed at ______________ on ______________________________.
[time – a.m. or p.m.] *[date]*

__________________ *[Witness]* __________________ *[Purchaser]*

__________________ *[Witness]* __________________ *[Purchaser]*

Schedule A

HOMESTEADS ACT DECLARATION

I / We, the Vendor(s) in the attached offer and final Agreement of Purchase and Sale (the "Agreement") do solemnly, and severally, if applicable, declare *[delete and initial all inapplicable statements]*:

1. The person who has signed the acceptance to the offer from the Purchaser is my spouse.
2. The person who has consented to the disposition of the homestead provided for by this Agreement is my spouse.
3. I am not a married person.
4. The land being bought and sold under this Agreement is not my homestead within the meaning of *The Homesteads Act*.

(SEVERALLY) DECLARED before me at)
CENTREVILLE, MANITOBA)
)
)
)
this 12th day of MAY, 2003)

John Doe
Jane Doe

Another Lawyer (OR)
Commissioner for Oaths, A Notary Public, etc.

Ontario

Form of Agreement of Purchase & Sale (sample completed form)

AGREEMENT OF PURCHASE AND SALE
(FOR USE IN ONTARIO)

BUYER: BOB SMITH & MARY SMITH (the "Buyer") hereby agrees to buy from
[legal name of Buyer]

SELLER: JOHN DOE & JANE DOE (the "Seller") the real property
[legal name of Seller]

PROPERTY: municipally described as: 123 MAIN ST., CENTREVILLE, ONT., 1A1 B2B
[full street address]

fronting on the NORTH side of MAIN STREET
[east, west, north, south] [street name]

with a total frontage of 80 FEET more or less, by a depth of 200 FEET more or less
[feet or metres] [feet or metres]

and legally described as LOT 1, PLAN 2, COUNTY OF MIDDLEFORD (PIN#...) (the "Property").
[legal description]

PRICE: The agreed upon price is ONE HUNDRED & FIFTY THOUSAND ——— xx Dollars (Canadian); $150,000.00
[written] [numerical]

payable as follows:

DEPOSIT: a Deposit of FIFTEEN THOUSAND ——— xx Dollars (Canadian); $15,000.00
[written] [numerical]

payable UPON ACCEPTANCE to ATTICUS LAWYER, IN TRUST,
[upon acceptance or herewith] [person to whom deposit is payable]

and, unless otherwise provided herein, the Balance payable on closing by cash or certified cheque, payable to the Seller or Seller's lawyer, or as they may redirect, and subject to the usual adjustments.

THIS AGREEMENT SHALL BE CONDITIONAL UPON FINANCING, THE SUITABILITY OF WHICH SHALL BE AT THE BUYER'S SOLE DISCRETION, ON OR BEFORE 5:00 PM ON MAY 17, 2003. THIS CONDITION IS FOR THE BENEFIT OF THE BUYER AND MAY BE WAIVED BY THE BUYER AT THE BUYER'S SOLE DISCRETION. THE BUYER SHALL USE ALL REASONABLE EFFORTS TOWARDS FULFILLMENT OF THIS CONDITION. THE BUYER MUST DELIVER NOTICE IN WRITING THAT THIS CONDITION HAS BEEN SATISFIED OR OTHERWISE WAIVED ON OR BEFORE THE STATED DEADLINE, FAILING WHICH THIS AGREEMENT SHALL BE NULL AND VOID AND THE DEPOSIT SHALL BE RETURNED TO THE BUYER WITHOUT INTEREST, PENALTY OR DEDUCTION.

SCHEDULES: The following Schedules are attached to and form an integral part of this Agreement: "A" (SURVEY)
[applicable Schedules, if any]

1. ITEMS INCLUDED / EXCLUDED
The following items (chattels) are included: WASHER & DRYER IN BASEMENT

The following items (fixtures) are excluded: ANTIQUE LIGHT FIXTURE IN DINING ROOM

The following items are rented and are not included, and if assumable the Purchaser agrees to assume the rental contracts: HOT WATER TANK

2. IRREVOCABILITY
This offer to reach Agreement shall be open for acceptance and irrevocable by the BUYER until 5:00 PM on MAY 13, 2003
[Buyer or Seller] [time – a.m. or p.m.] [date]
failing which this offer shall become null and void and the deposit shall be returned to the Buyer without interest, bonus or deduction.

3. CLOSING/POSSESSION DATE: This Agreement shall be completed on JULY 14, 2003 between 9:00 am and 6:00 pm (the "Closing Date")
[closing date]
On the Closing Date the Seller shall provide the Buyer with vacant possession of the Property, unless otherwise provided herein.

4. GST: The Buyer and Seller agree that this transaction is not subject to Federal Goods and Services Tax [GST], and the Seller shall furnish a certificate confirming same on closing.

5. DUE DILIGENCE: The Buyer shall have until 5:00 PM on JUNE 13, 2003 (Requisition Date)
[time – a.m. or p.m.] [date]
to investigate title to the Property, and until the earlier of:

A) 30 days from the later of
(i) the Requisition Date, or (ii) the date on which any conditions of this Agreement are communicated as fulfilled or otherwise waived, or
B) 5 days before the Closing Date,

to satisfy him/herself(s) that the Property can be lawfully used for the purposes of SINGLE FAMILY RESIDENTIAL USE,
[legally authorized use]
that there are no outstanding work orders, on-record violations or deficiency notices affecting the Property, and that the principle building(s) may be insured against risk of fire and other usual property casualties. Title to the Property shall be clear of any defects, liens, charges, registered restrictions or encumbrances, provided that title matters expressly allowed for and contemplated as acceptable shall include: A) registered restrictions or covenants that run with the land provided they are complied with, B) registered agreements with municipal authorities or public utilities, provided they are complied with or funds have been posted to secure compliance and the completion of same, C) minor easements for the supply of domestic utility, telephone or cable service to the Property or adjoining properties, D) easements for utility, telephone or cable lines, drainage, storm or sanitary sewers, or other services which do not have any material adverse affect on the use of the Property as contemplated herein, and E) any matters expressly allowed for elsewhere in this Agreement. If the Buyer makes a valid objection in writing to the matters contemplated in this section within the specified time periods, and if the Seller is unable or unwilling to remedy or satisfy the objection, and if the Buyer is then unwilling to waive the objection, then this Agreement shall be at an end and the deposit shall be returned to the Buyer without interest, bonus or deduction and without any further obligation for costs or damages between the parties. If the Buyer does not make a valid objection in writing within the specified time periods, or within any overriding limitation periods that may be otherwise prescribed by law, then the Buyer shall be deemed to have conclusively accepted the status of the Seller's title to the Property. All investigations shall be at the Buyer's own expense. Acceptance of this offer shall constitute the Seller's consent to the release of information by municipal, governmental or quasi governmental authorities concerning the legal status of the Property, and Seller agrees to provide such further written authorizations as may be reasonably required to give effect to the intent of this provision.

6. CLOSING DETAILS: If this transaction is to be completed by electronic registration, it is agreed that the exchange of closing funds, keys and ancillary documents or items shall be subject to the following: A) the exchange will not occur simultaneously with the registration of Deeds, Mortgages or other contemplated registered documentation, and B) the exchange will be governed by the terms of a Document Registration Agreement (DRA) between the lawyers retained by the parties, and the DRA shall provide that all deliveries shall be held in trust by the receiving lawyer and not released until all other terms of the DRA have been met. The exchange will occur at the applicable Land Registry Office, unless otherwise agreed.

7. DISCLOSURE AND PRODUCTION OF DOCUMENTS: In the event that the Seller is in possession or control of any deed, survey or other evidence of title, then, upon request, the Seller shall deliver such documentation to the Buyer as soon as possible and in any event prior to the Requisition Date.

8. PREPARATION OF DOCUMENTS: The Transfer/Deed shall be prepared in registrable form at the expense of the Seller. The Buyer shall be responsible for the Land Transfer Tax Affidavit and any ancillary documents that may be required pursuant to this Agreement, unless the Seller is expressly required to provide otherwise. If requested, the Seller agrees to execute statements on the Transfer/Deed relating to subdivision compliance pursuant to Section 50(22) of *The Planning Act, R.S.O. 1990*, and the Seller agrees to instruct his/her solicitor to execute such statements.

9. **DISCHARGE OF MORTGAGES:** In the event that the Seller will be discharging a mortgage or mortgages in favour of a Chartered Bank, Trust Company, Credit Union, Caisse Populaire, Insurance Company or a corporation under *The Trust And Loan Companies Act (Canada)*, then the Buyer shall be obligated to accept the Seller's lawyer's Undertaking, in a form acceptable to the Buyer's lawyer, to obtain and register a discharge within a reasonable period of time following the Closing Date, provided that the Seller shall also furnish the Buyer's lawyer with a copy of a Mortgage Discharge Statement from the mortgagee which sets out the balance required to discharge the mortgage as of the Closing Date, and the Seller shall execute a Direction instructing his/her lawyer to pay the closing proceeds in the required manner.

10. **INSPECTION:** The Buyer acknowledges having inspected the Property and the parties agree that the Property shall be delivered in the same condition as existed at the time of inspection.

11. **INSURANCE:** The Property and all fixtures and chattels contemplated under this Agreement shall remain at the risk of the Seller until the Closing Date. All related insurance policies held by the Seller, if any, as well as any proceeds paid under such policies, shall be held in trust for the benefit of the parties in relation to their respective interests under this Agreement. In the event of damage and subsequent payment under such policies the Buyer shall have the option of terminating this Agreement or receiving the said payment and closing the transaction as scheduled with all other terms and conditions remaining the same. In the event that the Agreement is terminated pursuant to this section the deposit shall be returned to the Buyer without interest, bonus or deduction. No insurance policies shall be transferred on closing.

12. **PLANNING ACT COMPLIANCE:** The Seller shall be obligated to obtain all consents and take all steps necessary to complete this transaction in compliance with *The Planning Act, R.S.O. 1990*. Such efforts, if necessary, shall be at the sole expense of the Vendor. In the event that such efforts are unsuccessful, this Agreement shall be at an end and the deposit shall be returned to the Buyer without interest, bonus or deduction.

13. **RESIDENCY STATUS:** On closing the Seller shall furnish a certificate confirming that the Seller is not a "non-resident" within the meaning of the *Income Tax Act*, failing which the Buyer shall be entitled to hold back funds in accordance with prudent legal practice sufficient to satisfy the Buyer's obligations under the Act.

14. **FAMILY LAW STATUS:** The Seller warrants that he/she is not a spouse and that no spousal consent is necessary to give full effect to this Agreement, or alternatively that the person executing the necessary consent below is the Seller's spouse.

15. **CLOSING ADJUSTMENTS:** The amount due on closing shall be adjusted and apportioned between the parties to reflect their obligations as of the Closing Date for the following items, as may be applicable: realty taxes, local improvement rates, unmetered utility charges and unmetered fuel costs. These amounts as they relate to the Closing Date itself shall be the responsibility of the Buyer.

16. **TIME CONSTRAINTS:** Time shall be of the essence throughout this Agreement. The Closing Date and any other deadlines may only be extended or amended by agreement in writing.

17. **TENDER:** Any tender of documents, keys or money may be made upon the Buyer or Seller, as the case may be, or their lawyers, if any, on or before the time specified on the Closing Date. Tender shall be validly effected if delivered personally upon the Buyer or Seller, as the case may be, or upon their respective lawyers, if any. Money tendered must be in the form of bank draft or certified cheque issued by a Chartered Bank, Trust Company, Credit Union, Caisse Populaire or Province of Ontario Savings Office.

18. **UFFI:** The Seller warrants that he/she has not caused or allowed any buildings on the Property to be insulated with ureaformaldehyde, and further that, to the best of the Seller's knowledge, none of the buildings on the Property have been insulated with ureaformaldehyde. This warranty shall survive and not merge on closing.

19. **NOTICE:** Offer, acceptance or any notice or communication required under this Agreement shall be deemed delivered and received if given in writing by any of the following methods: 1) by personal delivery to the addresses of the parties noted herein, 2) by registered mail to the addresses of the parties noted herein (in which case receipt shall be deemed to be three days after mailing), 3) by fax to the fax numbers noted by the parties herein, if any, or 4) by delivery or fax to either party's lawyer, if any, as noted herein or as otherwise reasonably established.

20. **SUCCESSORS AND ASSIGNS:** This Agreement shall pass to the benefit of and be binding upon each of the parties' successors and assigns.

21. **ENFORCABILITY, ENTIRETY AND INTERPRETATION OF AGREEMENT:** Upon acceptance this Agreement shall constitute a binding agreement of purchase and sale. This document, together with all listed Schedules, constitutes the entire Agreement between the parties and there shall be no collateral agreements, representations or warranties. This Agreement may only be amended by mutual, written agreement between the parties, or between their lawyers, if any, as such lawyers may be noted herein or as otherwise reasonably established. In the event of a discrepancy between the Schedules or added clauses in this Agreement and the pre-formatted form of Agreement, the Schedules or added clauses shall prevail to the extent of the discrepancy. Any references to gender or number of parties shall be read with the intended context applied. In the event that any specific provisions of this Agreement are declared illegal, invalid or unenforceable by a court of competent jurisdiction, then the offending provision(s) may be severed and shall not impair the validity or enforceability of the balance of the Agreement. This Agreement shall be interpreted and enforced in accordance with the laws of the Province of Ontario.

22. **LEGAL REPRESENTATION:** Each of the parties acknowledges having received a copy of this Agreement and having been advised to seek independent legal advice prior to signing. Each of the parties further acknowledges that they have either obtained such independent legal advice, or have declined to seek such advice and have otherwise entered into this Agreement with the knowledge that it creates firm and binding legal relations and in full comprehension of the terms and consequences set out herein. Notwithstanding the source of this document, the doctrine of "Contra Preferentem" shall not apply and the Agreement shall be interpreted and construed equally among the parties.

Dated: MAY 12, 2003

Signed sealed and delivered in the presence of:	Signed sealed and delivered by:		
Witness One (Witness)	Bob Smith (Buyer)	● (Seal)	Date: May 12/03
Witness One (Witness)	Mary Smith (Buyer)	● (Seal)	Date: May 12, 2003

Dated: MAY 13, 2003

Signed sealed and delivered in the presence of:	Signed sealed and delivered by:		
Witness Two (Witness)	John Doe (Seller)	● (Seal)	Date: May 13, 2003
Witness Two (Witness)	Jane Doe (Seller)	● (Seal)	Date: May 13, 2003

SPOUSAL CONSENT: The person signing below is the spouse of the Seller and hereby consents to this transaction pursuant to *The Family Law Act, R.S.O. 1990*, and further agrees with the Buyer to execute any further assurances necessary to complete this transaction.

N/A

(Witness)	(Consenting Spouse)	● (Seal)	Date:

NOTICE

The Buyer's address for service is:	The Seller's address for service is:
Address: 321 QUEEN ST., CENTREVILLE, D1B 2A2	Address: 123 MAIN ST., CENTREVILLE, ONT., 1A1 B2B
Phone: (123) 987-6543	Phone: (123) 345-6789
Fax: NONE	Fax: NONE

LEGAL REPRESENTATION

The Buyer's solicitor, if any, until further notification, is:	The Seller's solicitor, if any, until further notification, is:
Name: PENELOPE SOLICITOR	Name: ATTICUS LAWYER
Address: 345, BARRISTERS ROW, CENTREVILLE, C2C 3D3	Address: 234 CHANCERY LANE, CENTREVILLE, C3C 3D4
Phone: (123) 246-1357	Phone: (123) 246-3579
Fax: (123) 246-1375	Fax: (123) 246-3597

Quebec

Form of Agreement of Purchase & Sale (sample completed form)

OFFER TO PURCHASE

IMMOVABLE PROPERTY

For use in the Province of QUEBEC

I have requested that this contract be drafted in English. J'ai demandé que ce contrat soit rédigée en anglais

I/We, BOB SMITH & MARY SMITH (the Buyer), residing at the following address: 321 QUEEN STREET, CENTREVILLE, QUEBEC, B1B 2A2, hereby **offer to purchase** from JOHN DOE & JANE DOE (the Seller), at the price and on the terms set out herein, the immovable land and buildings, which have been inspected and found to be satisfactory, located at the following address: 123 MAIN STREET, CENTREVILLE, QUEBEC (the Property). The Property is designated in the Cadastre of MIDDLEFORD (1 01234' A12) as Lot(s) Number(s) 1, PLAN 2, and having dimensions of 80 FEET FRONTAGE, 200 FEET DEEP, more or less. In the case of a co-ownership, the Property is further described as set out in section 5.4

1. PURCHASE PRICE AND PAYMENT TERMS

The Price is ONE HUNDRED & FIFTY THOUSAND ——— xx dollars (the Purchase Price), and shall be paid on the following terms:

1.1 DEPOSIT. The Buyer submits with this offer a deposit in the amount of: $ 15,000.00
The deposit shall be by cash or personal cheque payable to ATTICUS NOTARY "in trust" and shall be held in trust, without interest unless otherwise provided for herein, by the trustee in accordance with the terms of this Agreement. The deposit shall be applied towards the purchase price at the signing of the Deed of Sale.

1.2 MORTGAGE ASSUMPTION. The Buyer shall assume an existing mortgage which, on the date of signing of the Deed of Sale, will have an approximate principle amount outstanding of: $ NIL
The assumed mortgage shall be on the terms further set out in the attached schedule. This Agreement is conditional upon the mortgage being transferable to the Buyer, failing which this Agreement shall be at an end and the deposit shall be returned to the buyer without interest penalty or deduction

1.3 SELLER'S HYPOTHEC. The Buyer shall pay to the Seller the amount of: $ NIL
which shall be secured by a vendor's privilege and a hypothec ranking in .... priority, and if there shall be any prior security it, shall not, in the aggregate, exceed $ ....
The Vendor's privilege and hypothec shall be on the terms further set out in the attached schedule.

1.4 BALANCE DUE. The Buyer shall, upon the signing of the Deed of Sale, and subject to the foregoing, remit the balance of the Purchase Price in the amount of: $ 135,000.00
This balance due shall be tendered by certified cheque(s) drawn to the order of the acting Notary "in trust". The Notary may hold back the sums owed to the Seller until the Deed of Sale has been registered and recorded in the Index of Immovables free and clear of any lien or encumbrance detrimental to the holder of the registered right and not otherwise contemplated herein. The balance due shall include any sums that must be obtained and secured through any new mortgage financing as contemplated in section 2.1 below.

1.5 OTHER. .... $ NIL

TOTAL: $ 150,000.00

2. BUYER'S OBLIGATIONS

2.1 FINANCING. The Buyer shall, at the Buyer's sole expense, apply for new mortgage financing as soon as reasonably possible following acceptance of this offer to purchase. The financing shall be on the following terms: principle amount $ 112,000.00 *(including any high ratio mortgage insurance premiums, if applicable)*, interest rate not greater than 7.00 % *(calculated semi-annually, not in advance)*, term not shorter than 5 YEARS, amortization not shorter than 25 YEARS, ☐ Open or ☑ Closed or ☐ Limited Prepayment Options, priority FIRST, other material terms required by Buyer NIL
The Buyer shall provide the Seller with a copy of a written approval of the foregoing, or otherwise waive the financing requirement, on or before MAY 17, 2003, in which event this agreement shall be firm and binding. If such notice of approval or waiver is not received by the stated date, then the Seller shall have the option, upon written notice to the Buyer delivered within three days of the aforementioned date, of requiring the Buyer to resubmit the application on the same terms to a financing source of the Seller's choice. If all of the foregoing attempts to secure financing are unsuccessful and the financing requirement is not otherwise waived by the Buyer, then this offer to purchase shall be at an end and the deposit shall be returned to the Buyer without interest, penalty or deduction.

2.2 DEED OF SALE. The Buyer shall sign the Deed of Sale on or before JULY 14, 2003, in the presence of the BUYER's Notary.

2.3 CERTIFICATE OF LOCATION. The Buyer shall, if required or desired, bear the expense of a new Certificate of Location, unless it discloses additions or changes that have taken place subsequent to the date of the Certificate of Location being supplied by the Seller.

3. SELLER'S OBLIGATIONS

3.1 PROPERTY CONDITION. The Property and all included items shall be delivered in substantially the same condition they were in when inspected by the Buyer at the time this offer was presented.

3.2 TITLE. The Seller shall provide the Buyer with: (i) good and marketable title, free and clear of all liens, encumbrances and other real estate rights, save and except those expressly allowed for herein, (ii) any Title Deed that may be in the possession or control of the Seller, as soon as possible after acceptance of this offer, and (iii) an up-to-date Certificate of Location (unless the Property is a divided co-ownership) as soon as possible after acceptance of this offer.

3.3 DEED OF SALE. The Seller shall sign the notarized Deed of Sale within the time required herein, and shall be responsible for the full payment and discharge of any existing mortgage loans and the cancellation of any existing hypothecs.

4. SELLER'S DECLARATIONS

4.1 REAL RIGHTS AND ILLEGALITIES. The Property is not subject to any right, servitude or illegality, save and except any servitudes granted for public utilities, any liens, mortgages or encumbrances expressly contemplated elsewhere in this Agreement, or any of the following: TO BE DECLARED

4.2 RESIDENCY STATUS. The Seller certifies that he/she is not a "non-resident" within the meaning of the *Income Tax Act (Canada)*, and the Seller agrees to provide an affidavit confirming same or include a statement to that effect in the notarized Deed of Sale, failing which the Buyer shall be entitled to hold back funds in accordance with prudent legal practice sufficient to satisfy the Buyer's obligations under the Act.

4.3 SPOUSAL STATUS. The Seller certifies that he/she is not a spouse; or alternatively that anyone with a spousal interest in the Property is named as a co-Seller in this Agreement; or alternatively that their spouse has consented below concurrent with acceptance of this offer; or alternatively that, as soon as reasonably possible after acceptance of this offer, the Seller shall deliver to the Buyer the required consent from the Seller's spouse together with their agreement to cooperate towards and to execute the notarized Deed of Sale, or a copy of a judgment authorizing the Seller to sell the Property without spousal consent. In the absence of any of the foregoing, the Buyer may, upon written notice, terminate this agreement in which event the deposit shall be returned to the Buyer without interest, penalty or deduction.

4.4 PROPERTY COMPLIANCE. The Seller certifies that, to the best of the Seller's knowledge, there are no existing or outstanding notices of non-compliance issued by any municipal or provincial government or other local authority, save and except as may be contemplated elsewhere in this Agreement or as follows: TO BE DECLARED

4.5 UFFI. The Seller certifies that, to the best of the Seller's knowledge, the Property has not been insulated with urea-formaldehyde foam insulation.

5. OTHER TERMS AND CONDITIONS

5.1 CLOSING DATE. The Buyer shall become the owner of the Property upon the signing of the Deed of Sale and, subject to any tenancies expressly allowed for herein, the Buyer shall be entitled to occupancy of the Property on JULY 14, 2003

5.2 ITEMS INCLUDED / EXCLUDED.

The following items are included: permanent electrical fixtures and heating, ventilating and air conditioning equipment, as well as WASHER & DRYER IN BASEMENT

The following items are excluded: window dressings, curtain rods and blinds, as well as ANTIQUE LIGHT FIXTURE IN DINING ROOM

The following items are rented and are not included, and if assumable the Buyer agrees to assume the rental contracts: HOT WATER TANK

5.3 ADJUSTMENTS. Upon the signing of the Deed of Sale, adjustments shall be made as of .... between the Buyer and the Seller for their proportionate share of all general and special taxes, as well as, without limitation, any of the following as may be applicable to this transaction: fuel, co-ownership expenses, mortgage interest, rents and equipment leases.

5.4 CO-OWNERSHIPS. If the Property involves a co-ownership, the following shall apply: (i) type of ownership: ☐ divided, or ☐ undivided
(ii) parking space (if any) number(s) ....
(iii) storage space (if any) number(s) ....
(iv) other inclusions (if any) ....

N/A

The Buyer agrees to pay the Buyer's proportionate share of the ongoing co-ownership expenses, accept the reserve fund as of the date on which the Deed of Sale is signed, and respect the Declaration of Co-Ownership. The Seller certifies that the Seller is not aware of any pending increase in the co-ownership expenses, or any supplemental levy or special assessment pending or payable to the co-ownership, or any existing or pending legal actions against or initiated by the co-ownership, or any pending substantial change in the assets or liabilities of the co-ownership, or any upcoming special or general meetings of the co-ownership at which any of the foregoing will be addressed.

5.5 VACANT POSSESSION / TENANCIES. On the date of occupancy (above), the Buyer shall acquire vacant possession of the property unless tenancies are expressly agreed to as follows: NIL

The details of the tenancy arrangement(s) are set out in the attached schedule. The Buyer agrees to respect any tenancy obligations assumed in connection with the foregoing.

5.6 COSTS. Each party shall bear their own costs in connection with this transaction. Specifically and without limitation, the Buyer shall bear the expense of the Deed of Sale, its registration and the production of any copies of same, as well as any applicable property transfer taxes, special taxes or church tax assessments that are the responsibility of the Buyer.

5.7 LANGUAGE. The Deed of Sale shall be drafted in French, or alternatively in English if expressly consented to as follows:

Initial if English desired ... BS MS (Buyer's Initials) [initials] JD (Seller's Initials)

5.8 ENFORCABILITY, ENTIRETY AND INTERPRETATION OF AGREEMENT. Upon acceptance, this Agreement shall constitute a binding agreement of purchase and sale. This document, together with all listed Schedules, constitutes the entire Agreement between the parties and there shall be no collateral agreements, representations or warranties. This Agreement may only be amended by mutual, written agreement between the parties, or between their Notaries, if any, as such Notaries may be set out herein or as otherwise reasonably established during the course of this transaction. In the event of a discrepancy between the Schedules or added clauses in this Agreement and the pre-formatted form of Agreement, the Schedules or added clauses shall prevail to the extent of the discrepancy. Time shall be of the essence throughout this Agreement and any deadlines or time limitations may only be extended or amended by agreement in writing. Any references to gender or number of parties shall be read with the intended context applied. In the event that any specific provisions of this Agreement are declared illegal, invalid or unenforceable by a court of competent jurisdiction, then the offending provision(s) may be severed and shall not impair the validity or enforceability of the balance of the Agreement. This Agreement shall be interpreted and enforced in accordance with the laws of the Province of Quebec.

5.9 LEGAL REPRESENTATION. Each of the parties acknowledges having read and understood this offer to purchase, and having received a copy of the Agreement, and having been advised to seek independent legal advice prior to signing. Each of the parties further acknowledges that they have either obtained such independent legal advice, or have declined to seek such advice and have otherwise entered into this Agreement with the knowledge that it creates firm and binding legal relations and in full comprehension of the terms and consequences set out herein. Notwithstanding which party drafted this Agreement, it shall be interpreted and construed equally among the parties.

5.10 ADDITIONAL TERMS OR CONDITIONS. NIL

5.11 SCHEDULES. The following Schedules are attached to and form an integral part of this Agreement: "A" (CERTIFICATE OF LOCATION)

5.12 IRREVOCABILITY. This offer to purchase is open for acceptance and irrevocable by the Buyer until 5:00 PM [a.m. or p.m.] on MAY 13, 2003, after which time, if not accepted, this offer shall become null and void and the deposit shall be returned to the Buyer without interest, penalty or deduction. Any counteroffer shall also render the initial offer null and void to the same effect. Signed at *[location]* CENTREVILLE on *[date]* MAY 12, 2003, at *[time]* 4:45 PM *[a.m. or p.m.]*

Bob Smith *[Signature of Buyer]* — Mary Smith *[Signature of Buyer]* — Witness One *[Signature of Witness]*

SELLER'S RESPONSE

I/We, JOHN DOE & JANE DOE (the Seller), residing at the following address: 123 MAIN STREET, CENTREVILLE, QUEBEC, 1A1 B2B,

[choose one – delete other]

☑ hereby **accept** this offer to purchase from the Buyer

~~☐ hereby **reject** this offer to purchase from the Buyer~~

~~☐ make the attached **counteroffer** to the Buyer~~

Signed at *[location]* CENTREVILLE on *[date]* MAY 13, 2003, at *[time]* 9:00 AM *[a.m. or p.m.]*

John Doe *[Signature of Seller]* — Jane Doe *[Signature of Seller]* — Witness Two *[Signature of Witness]*

~~**SPOUSAL CONSENT** *[delete if not applicable]*~~

I, ...

residing at the following address: ....,

declare that I am the spouse of the aforementioned Seller. I hereby consent to the acceptance of this offer on its terms and I agree to cooperate towards and to execute the notarized Deed of Sale.

Signed at *[location]* .... on *[date]* ...., at *[time]* .... *[a.m. or p.m.]*

[Signature of Seller one's spouse] — *[Signature of Seller two's spouse]* — *[Signature of Witness]*

ACKNOWLEDGEMENT OF RECEIPT BY BUYER

I hereby acknowledge having received a copy of this executed response from the Seller.

Signed at *[location]* CENTREVILLE on *[date]* MAY 13, 2003, at *[time]* 10:00 AM *[a.m. or p.m.]*

Bob Smith *[Signature of Buyer]* — Mary Smith *[Signature of Buyer]* — Witness One *[Signature of Witness]*

New Brunswick

Form of Agreement of Purchase & Sale (sample completed form)

AGREEMENT OF PURCHASE AND SALE
(FOR USE IN NEW BRUNSWICK)

The BUYER, BOB SMITH & MARY SMITH,
[legal name of Buyer(s)]

hereby offers to buy from the SELLER, JOHN DOE & JANE DOE,
[legal name of Seller(s)]

the real property located at 123 MAIN ST., CENTREVILLE, BEING LOT 1, PLAN 2, COUNTY OF MIDDLEFORD (P.I.D. #.....)
[street address and legal description]

which comprises land the size of 80' FRONTAGE BY 200' DEPTH, more or less,
[feet *or* metres]

at a purchase price of ONE HUNDRED & FIFTY THOUSAND ——— xx Dollars CDN ($ 150,000.00)
[written] [numerical]

on the following terms and conditions.

1. FINANCING & PROCEEDS

(a) The Buyer submits with this offer an initial deposit of FIFTEEN THOUSAND ——— xx Dollars CDN ($ 15,000.00)
[written] [numerical]

by cash or cheque payable to ATTICUS LAWYER, IN TRUST
[person to whom deposit is payable]

to be held in trust pending completion or other termination of this Agreement. On closing the deposit shall be credited towards the purchase price.

(b) This Agreement is conditional upon the Buyer obtaining written approval of financing, mortgage or otherwise, for the approximate amount of $ 112,000.00, representing 75 % of the purchase price, at current interest rates. The Buyer shall provide the Seller with a written waiver of this financing condition on or before 5:00 PM on MAY 17, 2003,
[time – a.m. *or* p.m.] [date]

failing which this offer shall become null and void and the deposit shall be returned to the Buyer without interest, penalty or deduction.

(c) The Buyer agrees to increase the deposit to a total amount of N/A Dollars CDN ($______),
[written] [numerical]

representing ______ % of the purchase price, within 24 hours of financing approval, to be held in trust and payable in the manner set out above.

(d) Unless otherwise provided herein, the balance of the purchase price shall be due on completion by cash, lawyer's trust cheque, or certified cheque drawn on a Chartered Canadian Bank, Trust Company or Credit Union, payable to the Seller or Seller's lawyer, or as they may redirect.

2. CLOSING & POSSESSION DATE This Agreement shall be completed on JULY 14, 2003 (Closing Date),
[date]

on which date the Seller shall provide the Buyer with vacant possession of the Property, unless otherwise provided herein.

3. PRE-CLOSING INSPECTION The Buyer shall have the right to conduct a pre-closing inspection of the property to ensure that the property is in the same condition as it was in at the time this Agreement was signed. Such inspection shall be performed on or before JULY 7, 2003, and at such time the property SHALL NOT be vacant.
[date] [shall *or* shall not]

4. ITEMS INCLUDED / EXCLUDED

(i) The following items (chattels) are included in the purchase price: WASHER & DRYER IN BASEMENT. Such chattels shall remain with the property on closing, free of any encumbrances or liens, and shall be in the same good working order and condition as they were at the time this Agreement was signed.

(i) All items attached to the property (fixtures) are included in the purchase price and shall remain with the property on closing, save and except the following fixtures which are not included: ANTIQUE LIGHT FIXTURE IN DINING ROOM.

(i) The following items are leased, and the Buyer agrees to assume the leases in connection with same:

Buyer(s) BS MS Seller(s) [signature] JD
[acknowledging initials required]

Hot Water Tank ✓ Furnace/Heating System _____ Propane Tank _____

Other: __________

5. TITLE SEARCH & STATUS The seller shall provide the Buyer with the legal description of the subject property. The property is to be conveyed free and clear of any liens or encumbrances, unless otherwise specified herein. The Buyer shall have until JUNE 13, 2003
[date]

to investigate title to the Property. If the Buyer makes a valid objection to the title in writing, and if the Seller is unable or unwilling to remedy or satisfy the objection, and if the Buyer is then unwilling to waive the objection, then this Agreement shall be null and void and the deposit shall be returned to the Buyer without interest, penalty or deduction and without any further obligation for costs or damages between the parties. If the Buyer does not make a valid objection in writing within the specified time periods, then the Buyer shall be deemed to have conclusively accepted the status of the Seller's title to the Property. All investigations shall be at the Buyer's own expense.

6. PREPARATION OF DOCUMENTS The Deed shall be prepared in registrable form at the expense of the Seller, and shall be tendered on closing in exchange for the purchase price. The Buyer shall be responsible for any ancillary documents that may be required pursuant to this Agreement, unless the Seller is expressly required to provide otherwise. If any survey work, permits or applications are required to put the conveyance in registrable form, such measures shall be taken at the Seller's expense.

7. INSURANCE The property and all fixtures and chattels contemplated under this Agreement shall remain at the risk of the Seller until closing. All related insurance policies held by the Seller, if any, as well as any proceeds paid under such policies, shall be held in trust for the benefit of the parties in relation to their respective interests under this Agreement. In the event of damage and subsequent payment under such policies the Buyer shall have the option of terminating this Agreement or receiving the said payment and closing the transaction as scheduled with all other terms and conditions remaining the same. In the event that the Agreement is terminated pursuant to this section, the deposit shall be returned to the Buyer without interest, penalty or deduction. No insurance policies shall be transferred on closing.

Acknowledgement of completion: *Buyer's initials* BS MS *Seller's initials* [signature] JD

. ADJUSTMENTS & TAXES
(i) The amount due on closing shall be adjusted and apportioned between the parties to reflect their obligations as of the closing date for the following items, as may be applicable: taxes, rates, assessments and fuel remaining on the property. These amounts as they relate to the closing date itself shall be the responsibility of the Buyer. Any charges for municipal improvements that have been completed as of the day this Agreement is signed – including, but without limitation, capital charges for municipal utilities or services, or betterment charges – unless otherwise provided in this Agreement shall be the responsibility of the Seller and shall be paid in full on or before closing. The Seller shall confirm that he/she is not a "non-resident" within the meaning of the Income Tax Act, failing which the Buyer shall be entitled to hold back funds in accordance with prudent legal practice sufficient to satisfy the Buyer's obligations under the Act.
(ii) If this transaction is subject to any applicable government taxes, then, unless otherwise provided in this Agreement, such taxes shall be in addition to and not included in the purchase price.

. TENDER Any tender of documents, keys or money may be effected by personal delivery upon the Buyer or Seller, as the case may be, or their awyers, if any, on or before the closing date.

0. UFFI The Seller warrants that he/she has not caused or allowed any buildings on the Property to be insulated with urea formaldehyde insulation, and urther that, to the best of the Seller's knowledge, none of the buildings on the Property have been insulated with urea formaldehyde insulation. This varranty shall survive and not merge on closing.

1. SURVEYOR'S REAL PROPERTY REPORT The Seller shall deliver to the Buyer any Surveyor's Real Property Report(s) concerning the property that s/are in the Seller's possession or control; however, subject to any survey work required for a registrable conveyance, any new Surveyor's Real Property Report shall be the responsibility of the Buyers, unless otherwise agreed upon herein.

2. HOME INSPECTION The Buyer DOES NOT [does *or* does not] require an inspection of the property on or before ______ [date – must complete if inspection required] by a qualified home inspector at the Buyer's expense. In the event that the report is not satisfactory to the Buyer, the Buyer shall have the option of terminating this Agreement upon written notice delivered to the Seller within _____ days following the date stated above, failing which this condition shall be deemed waived. In the event of such termination, the deposit shall be returned to the Buyer without interest, penalty or deduction. The Seller agrees to allow the inspector reasonable access to the property prior to the date stated above for the purpose of conducting the inspection.

3. ENVIRONMENTAL INSPECTION The Buyer DOES NOT [does *or* does not] require an inspection of the property on or before ______ [date – must complete if inspection required] by a qualified environmental inspector at the Buyer's expense. In the event that the report is not satisfactory to the Buyer, the Buyer shall have the option of terminating this Agreement upon written notice delivered to the Seller within _____ days following the date stated above, failing which this condition shall be deemed waived. In the event of such termination, the deposit shall be returned to the Buyer without interest, penalty or deduction. The Seller agrees to allow the inspector reasonable access to the property prior to the date stated above for the purpose of conducting the inspection.

4. WATER TEST The Buyer DOES NOT [does *or* does not] require a water potability test regarding the water supply on or before ______ [date – must complete if test required]. The test shall be conducted at the expense of the Buyer. In the event that the test discloses that the water supply of the property does not meet the requirements of the New Brunswick Department of Health, the Buyer shall have the option of terminating this Agreement upon written notice delivered to the Seller within _____ days following the date stated above, failing which this condition shall be deemed waived. In the event of such termination, the deposit shall be returned to the Buyer without interest, penalty or deduction. The Seller agrees to allow the buyer or their representative reasonable access to the property prior to the date stated above for the purpose of taking water samples.

15. PROPERTY DISCLOSURE STATEMENT The Seller SHALL NOT [shall *or* shall not] provide a Property Condition Disclosure Statement to the Buyer within 36 hours of acceptance of this offer, and the Statement shall be acknowledged and signed by the Buyer on or before ______ [date - must complete if statement provided].

16. FURTHER TERMS & CONDITIONS This Agreement is subject to the following further terms and conditions: NIL

17. FURTHER SCHEDULES: The following Schedules are attached to and form an integral part of this Agreement: "A" (SURVEY) [applicable Schedules, if any]

18. ENFORCABILITY, ENTIRETY AND INTERPRETATION OF AGREEMENT: Upon acceptance this Agreement shall constitute a binding agreement of purchase and sale. In the event that the Buyer defaults in the completion of this Agreement, the Buyer will forfeit the above deposit in addition to any other claims the Seller may have against the Buyer. This document, together with all listed Schedules, constitutes the entire Agreement between the parties and there shall be no collateral agreements, representations or warranties. This Agreement may only be amended or extended by mutual, written agreement between the parties, or between their lawyers, if any. Time shall be of the essence throughout this Agreement, including any extensions. This Agreement shall pass to the benefit of and be binding upon each of the parties' heirs, executors, administrators, successors and assigns. In the event of a discrepancy between the Schedules or added clauses in this Agreement and the pre-formatted form of Agreement, the Schedules or added clauses shall prevail to the extent of the discrepancy. Any references to gender or number of parties shall be read with the intended context applied. In the event that any specific provisions of this Agreement are declared illegal, invalid or unenforceable by a court of competent jurisdiction, then the offending provision(s) may be severed and shall not impair the validity or enforceability of the balance of the Agreement. This Agreement shall be interpreted and enforced in accordance with the laws of the Province of New Brunswick.

19. LEGAL REPRESENTATION: Each of the parties acknowledges having received a copy of this Agreement and having been advised to seek independent legal advice prior to signing. Each of the parties further acknowledges that they have either obtained such independent legal advice, or have declined to seek such advice and have otherwise entered into this Agreement with the knowledge that it creates firm and binding legal relations and in full comprehension of the terms and consequences set out herein. Notwithstanding the source of this document, the doctrine of "Contra Preferentem" shall not apply and the Agreement shall be interpreted and construed equally among the parties.

Acknowledgement of completion: *Buyer's initials* BS MS *Seller's initials* JD JD

20. OFFER This offer to purchase shall be open for acceptance and irrevocable by the Buyer until 5:00 PM [time – a.m. or p.m.] on MAY 13, 2003 [date].

Signed at CENTREVILLE in the Province of New Brunswick, at 4:45 PM [time – a.m. or p.m.] on MAY 12, 2003 [date].

Signed sealed and delivered in the presence of: Witness One [Witness] Witness One [Witness]

Signed sealed and delivered by: Bob Smith [Buyer] [Seal] Mary Smith [Buyer] [Seal]

21. ACCEPTANCE

(i) The Seller accepts this offer on the terms and conditions set out herein.

Signed at CENTREVILLE in the Province of New Brunswick, at 9:00 AM [time – a.m. or p.m.] on MAY 13, 2003 [date].

Signed sealed and delivered in the presence of: Witness Two [Witness] Witness Two [Witness]

Signed sealed and delivered by: John Doe [Seller] [Seal] Jane Doe [Seller] [Seal]

(ii) The Seller confirms that this offer was presented and not accepted, and returns herewith the deposit.

Signed at ______ in the Province of New Brunswick, at ______ [time – a.m. or p.m.] on ______ [date].

Signed sealed and delivered in the presence of: ______ [Witness] ______ [Witness]

Signed sealed and delivered by: ______ [Seller] [Seal] ______ [Seller] [Seal]

22. COUNTEROFFER

(i) The undersigned confirms that they have read and understood this Agreement and have modified the offer as initialed herein and/or as follows:

______

(ii) This counteroffer shall be open for acceptance and irrevocable by the Seller until ______ [time – a.m. or p.m.] on ______ [date].

after which time, if not accepted by the Buyer, this counteroffer shall be null and void and the deposit shall be returned to the Buyer without interest, penalty or deduction.

Signed at ______ in the Province of New Brunswick, at ______ [time – a.m. or p.m.] on ______ [date].

Signed sealed and delivered in the presence of: ______ [Witness] ______ [Witness]

Signed sealed and delivered by: ______ [Seller] [Seal] ______ [Seller] [Seal]

(iii) The Buyer accepts the modifications contained in this counteroffer, having initialed same, together with the remaining terms and conditions set out in this Agreement.

Signed at ______ in the Province of New Brunswick, at ______ [time – a.m. or p.m.] on ______ [date].

Signed sealed and delivered in the presence of: ______ [Witness] ______ [Witness]

Signed sealed and delivered by: ______ [Buyer] [Seal] ______ [Buyer] [Seal]

Acknowledgement of completion: *Buyer's initials* BS MS *Seller's initials* JD JD.

Prince Edward Island

Form of Agreement of Purchase & Sale (sample completed form)

AGREEMENT OF PURCHASE AND SALE
(FOR USE IN PRINCE EDWARD ISLAND)

The BUYER, BOB SMITH & MARY SMITH [legal name(s) of Buyer(s)], hereby offers to buy from

the SELLER, JOHN DOE & JANE DOE [legal name(s) of Seller(s)], the real property described as

the PROPERTY: 123 MAIN STREET, CENTREVILLE, P.E.I. BEING LOT 2, PLAN 2, COUNTY OF MIDDLEFORD [street address and legal description], at a purchase price of

the PRICE: ONE HUNDRED & FIFTY THOUSAND ——xx [written] Dollars CDN ($ 150,000.00 [numerical])

on the following terms and conditions.

1. a) The Buyer submits with this signed offer an initial deposit by cash or cheque payable to ATTICUS LAWYER, IN TRUST [person to whom deposit is payable] in the amount of FIFTEEN THOUSAND ——xx [written] Dollars CDN ($ 15,000.00 [numerical]) to be held in trust pending closing or other termination of this Agreement.

   b) On closing the deposit shall be credited towards the purchase price. In the event that this transaction does not close, or the Agreement is otherwise terminated, other than due to default on the part of the Buyer, the deposit shall be returned to the Buyer without interest, penalty or deduction. In the event that the Buyer defaults in the completion of this Agreement, the Buyer will forfeit the above deposit in addition to any other claims the Seller may have against the Buyer.

   c) Unless otherwise provided herein, the balance of the purchase price shall be due on completion by cash, lawyer's trust cheque, or certified cheque drawn on a Chartered Canadian Bank, Trust Company or Credit Union, payable to the Seller or Seller's lawyer, or as they may redirect.

2. This Agreement shall be completed on JULY 14, 2003 [date] (the "Closing Date"), on which date the Seller shall provide the Buyer with vacant possession of the Property, unless otherwise provided herein.

3. (i) The following items (chattels) are included in the purchase price: WASHER & DRYER IN BASEMENT

   Such chattels shall remain with the property on closing, free of any encumbrances or liens, and shall be in the same condition and working order as they were at the time this Agreement was signed.
   (i) All items attached to the property (fixtures) are included in the purchase price and shall remain with the property on closing, save and except the following fixtures which are not included: ANTIQUE LIGHT FIXTURE IN DINING ROOM

   (i) The following items are leased, and the Buyer agrees to assume the leases in connection with same: HOT WATER TANK

4. The seller shall provide the Buyer, as soon as reasonably possible after acceptance, with a legal description of the subject property together with copies of any surveys or boundary plans of the Property that may be in the Seller's possession or control. After receipt of this information, the Buyer shall be allowed 14 days to investigate title to the Property. If the Buyer makes a valid objection to the title in writing within such time, and if the Seller is unable or unwilling to remedy or satisfy the objection, and if the Buyer is then unwilling to waive the objection, then this Agreement shall be null and void and the deposit shall be returned to the Buyer without interest, penalty or deduction and without any further obligation for costs or damages between the parties. If the Buyer does not make a valid objection in writing within the specified time period, then the Buyer shall be deemed to have conclusively accepted the status of the Seller's title to the Property. All investigations shall be at the Buyer's expense.

5. The conveyance of the subject property shall be by WARRANTY Deed prepared in registrable form at the expense of the Seller, and shall be tendered on closing in exchange for the purchase price. The Buyer shall be responsible for any ancillary documents that may be required pursuant to this Agreement, unless the Seller is expressly required to provide otherwise. The Seller shall obtain and register a discharge of all existing mortgages, and the property shall be conveyed free and clear of any mortgages, liens or encumbrances, save and except any easements, registered restrictions or covenants that affect the property but do not materially affect the enjoyment or marketability of the property, and except as specifically allowed for elsewhere in this Agreement. The conveyance shall be in compliance with any provincial family law legislation.

6. The property and all fixtures and chattels contemplated under this Agreement shall remain at the risk of the Seller until closing. All related insurance policies held by the Seller, if any, as well as any proceeds paid under such policies, shall be held in trust for the benefit of the parties in relation to their respective interests under this Agreement. In the event of damage and subsequent payment under such policies, the Buyer shall have the option of terminating this Agreement or receiving the said payment and closing the transaction as scheduled with all other terms and conditions remaining the same. In the event that the Agreement is terminated pursuant to this section, the deposit shall be returned to the Buyer without interest, penalty or deduction. No insurance policies shall be transferred on closing unless otherwise provided herein.

7. The balance due on closing shall be subject to the usual adjustments for property related expenses and receipts, including, without limitation, all property taxes, rates and assessments. The closing date itself shall be the responsibility of the Buyer. Any charges for municipal improvements that have been completed as of the day this Agreement is signed – including, but without limitation, capital charges for municipal utilities or services, or betterment charges – whether billed or not, unless otherwise provided in this Agreement, shall be the responsibility of the Seller and shall be paid in full on or before closing.

8. Any Harmonized Sales Tax (HST) payable pursuant to the *Excise Tax Act* shall be [choose one and initial]

   Seller(s): JD JD Buyer(s): BS MS [initials required]

   ☐ included in the purchase price

   OR

   ☑ in addition to the purchase price

   If there is no HST payable, the Seller agrees to provide a Certificate in a form satisfactory to the buyer's lawyer certifying that there is no HST payable.

Date of Offer: MAY 12, 2003

All parties acknowledge having read and understood this Agreement as evidenced by their initials on this page 1 of 3

Initials of Buyer: BS MS   Witness: W1

Initials of Seller: JD JD   Witness: W2

9. On closing the Seller shall furnish a certificate confirming that the Seller is not a "non-resident" within the meaning of the Income Tax Act, failing which the Buyer shall be entitled to hold-back funds in accordance with prudent legal practice sufficient to satisfy the Buyer's obligations under the Act.

10. Any tender of documents, keys or money may be effected by personal delivery upon the Buyer or Seller, as the case may be, or their lawyers, if any, on or before the closing date.

11. All representations and warranties contained in this Agreement shall survive closing unless otherwise stated herein. The Seller represents and warrants as follows *[attach additional schedules if necessary]*:

a) The Seller has not caused or allowed any buildings on the Property to be insulated with urea formaldehyde insulation, and further, to the best of the Seller's knowledge, none of the buildings on the Property have been insulated with urea formaldehyde insulation.

b) NIL

c)

d)

12. This Agreement is further conditional upon the following *[attach additional schedules if necessary]*:

(a) This Agreement is conditional upon the Buyer obtaining written approval of financing on terms satisfactory to the Buyer or as otherwise specified in this Agreement. The Buyer must notify the Seller in writing on or before 5:00 PM [time – a.m. or p.m.] on MAY 17, 2003 [date] that the financing is unavailable and that the condition cannot be satisfied. In the event that such notice is not given on or before the specified date, the condition shall be deemed fulfilled or waived and this Agreement shall, subject to any further outstanding conditions, be deemed to be firm and binding. In the event that such notice is given on or before the specified date, the this Agreement shall be null and void and the deposit shall be returned to the Buyer without interest, penalty or deduction. This condition is for the sole benefit of the Buyer and may be waived by the Buyer on or before the specified time.

(b) NIL

(c)

13. The following Schedules are attached to and form an integral part of this Agreement: "A" (SURVEY) [applicable Schedules, if any].

14. Upon acceptance, this Agreement shall constitute a binding agreement of purchase and sale. This document, together with all listed Schedules, constitutes the entire Agreement between the parties and there shall be no collateral agreements, representations or warranties. This Agreement may only be amended or extended by mutual, written agreement between the parties, or between their lawyers, if any. Time shall be of the essence throughout this Agreement, including any extensions. This Agreement shall pass to the benefit of and be binding upon each of the parties' heirs, executors, administrators, successors and assigns. In the event of a discrepancy between the Schedules or added clauses in this Agreement and the pre-formatted form of Agreement, the Schedules or added clauses shall prevail to the extent of the discrepancy. Any references to gender or number of parties shall be read with the intended context applied. In the event that any specific provisions of this Agreement are declared illegal, invalid or unenforceable by a court of competent jurisdiction, then the offending provision(s) may be severed and shall not impair the validity or enforceability of the balance of the Agreement. This Agreement shall be interpreted and enforced in accordance with the laws of the Province of Prince Edward Island.

15. Each of the parties acknowledges having received a copy of this Agreement and having been advised to seek independent legal advice prior to signing. Each of the parties further acknowledges that they have either obtained such independent legal advice, or have declined to seek such advice and have otherwise entered into this Agreement with the knowledge that it creates firm and binding legal relations and in full comprehension of the terms and consequences set out herein. Notwithstanding the source of this document, the doctrine of "Contra Preferentem" shall not apply and the Agreement shall be interpreted and construed equally among the parties.

16. Offer, acceptance or any notice or communication required under this Agreement shall be deemed delivered and received if given in writing by any of the following methods: 1) by personal delivery to the addresses of the parties noted herein, 2) by registered mail to the addresses of the parties noted herein (in which case receipt shall be deemed to be three days after mailing), 3) by fax to the fax numbers noted by the parties herein, if any, or 4) by delivery or fax to either party's lawyer, if any, as noted herein or as otherwise reasonably established during the course of this transaction.

Buyer's address: 321 QUEEN ST. CENTREVILLE, B1B 2A2
Phone: (123) 987-6543 Fax: (NONE)
Lawyer name: PENELOPE SOLICITOR
address: 345 BARRISTERS ROW CENTREVILLE, C2C 3D3
Phone: (123) 246-1357 Fax: (123) 246-1375

Seller's address: 123 MAIN ST, CENTREVILLE, 1A1 B2B
Phone: (123) 345-6789 Fax: (NONE)
Lawyer name: ATTICUS LAWYER
address: 234 CHANCERY LANE CENTREVILLE C2C 3D4
Phone: (123) 246-3579 Fax: (123) 246-3599

Date of Offer: MAY 12, 2003
Initials of Buyer: BS MS Witness: W1
Initials of Seller: JD JD Witness: W2

17. This offer to purchase shall be open for acceptance and irrevocable by the Buyer until 5:00 PM [time — a.m. or p.m.] on MAY 13, 2003 [date].

Signed at CENTREVILLE in the Province of Prince Edward Island, at 4:45 PM [time — a.m. or p.m.] on MAY 12, 2003 [date].

Signed sealed and delivered in the presence of:	Signed sealed and delivered by:	
Witness One [Witness]	Bob Smith [Buyer]	[Seal]
Witness One [Witness]	Mary Smith [Buyer]	[Seal]

18. *[choose one – delete others]*

(i) The Seller hereby accepts this offer on the terms and conditions set out herein.

Signed at CENTREVILLE in the Province of Prince Edward Island, at 9:00 A.M. [time — a.m. or p.m.] on MAY 13, 2003 [date].

Signed sealed and delivered in the presence of:	Signed sealed and delivered by:	
Witness Two [Witness]	John Doe [Seller]	[Seal]
Witness Two [Witness]	Jane Doe [Seller]	[Seal]

(ii) The Seller confirms that this offer was presented and not accepted, and returns herewith the deposit.

Signed at ______ in the Province of Prince Edward Island, at ______ [time — a.m. or p.m.] on ______ [date].

Signed sealed and delivered in the presence of:	Signed sealed and delivered by:	
[Witness]	[Seller]	[Seal]
[Witness]	[Seller]	[Seal]

(iii) The Seller hereby modifies this offer in the manner set out herein, which amendments are initialed, including any further amendments as follows (counteroffer):

This counteroffer shall be open for acceptance and irrevocable by the Seller until ______ [time — a.m. or p.m.] on ______ [date] after which time, if not accepted by the Buyer, this counter offer shall be null and void and the deposit shall be returned to the Buyer without interest, penalty or deduction.

Signed at ______ in the Province of Prince Edward Island, at ______ [time — a.m. or p.m.] on ______ [date].

Signed sealed and delivered in the presence of:	Signed sealed and delivered by:	
[Witness]	[Seller]	[Seal]
[Witness]	[Seller]	[Seal]

19. The Buyer accepts the modifications contained in this counteroffer together with the remaining terms and conditions set out in this Agreement.

Signed at ______ in the Province of Prince Edward Island, at ______ [time — a.m. or p.m.] on ______ [date].

Signed sealed and delivered in the presence of:	Signed sealed and delivered by:	
[Witness]	[Buyer]	[Seal]
[Witness]	[Buyer]	[Seal]

All parties acknowledge having read and understood this Agreement as evidenced by their initials on this page 3 of 3

Date of Offer: MAY 12, 2003

Initials of Buyer: BS MS Witness: W1

Initials of Seller: JD JD Witness: W2

Nova Scotia

Form of Agreement of Purchase & Sale (sample completed form)

AGREEMENT OF PURCHASE AND SALE
(FOR USE IN NOVA SCOTIA)

The BUYER, BOB SMITH & MARY SMITH [legal name of Buyer(s)],

of 321 QUEEN ST., CENTREVILLE, N.S. [address of Buyer(s)], has inspected and hereby offers to buy from

the SELLER, JOHN DOE & JANE DOE [legal name of Seller(s)],

of 123 MAIN ST., CENTREVILLE, N.S. [address of Seller(s)], the real property described as

123 MAIN STREET, CENTREVILLE, NOVA SCOTIA
BEING LOT 2, PLAN 2, COUNTY OF MIDDLEFORD (P.I.D. #....). [street address and legal description]

at a purchase price of ONE HUNDRED & FIFTY THOUSAND —— xx [written] Dollars CDN ($ 150,000.00 [numerical])

on the following terms and conditions.

1. a) The Buyer submits, on execution of this offer, an initial deposit by cash or cheque payable to ATTICUS LAWYER, IN TRUST [person to whom deposit is payable] in the amount of FIFTEEN THOUSAND —— xx [written] Dollars CDN ($ 15,000.00 [numerical]) to be held in trust pending closing or other termination of this Agreement. On closing the deposit shall be credited towards the purchase price.

   (b) This Agreement is conditional upon the Buyer obtaining written approval of financing for the approximate amount of $ 112,000.00 representing 75 % of the purchase price, at an interest rate of not more than 7.00 %. The Buyer must notify the Seller in writing on or before 5:00 PM [time – a.m. or p.m.] on MAY 17, 2003 [date] that the financing is unavailable and that the condition cannot be satisfied. In the event that such notice is not given on or before the specified date, the condition shall be deemed fulfilled or waived and this Agreement shall, subject to any further outstanding conditions, be deemed to be firm and binding. In the event that such notice is given on or before the specified date, then either party may declare the Agreement null and void and in such event the deposit shall be returned to the Buyer without interest, penalty or deduction.

   (c) Unless otherwise provided herein, the balance of the purchase price shall be due on completion by cash, lawyer's trust cheque, or certified cheque drawn on a Chartered Canadian Bank, Trust Company or Credit Union, payable to the Seller or Seller's lawyer, or as they may redirect.

2. This Agreement shall be completed on JULY 14, 2003 [date] (the "Closing Date"), on which date the Seller shall provide the Buyer with vacant possession of the Property, unless otherwise provided herein.

3. (i) The following items (chattels) are included in the purchase price: WASHER & DRYER IN BASEMENT

   Such chattels shall remain with the property on closing, free of any encumbrances or liens, and shall be in the same good working order and condition as they were at the time this Agreement was signed.
   (i) All items attached to the property (fixtures) are included in the purchase price and shall remain with the property on closing, save and except the following fixtures which are not included: ANTIQUE LIGHT FIXTURE IN DINING ROOM

   (i) The following items are leased, and the Buyer agrees to assume the leases in connection with same:
   Seller(s) JD JD Buyer(s) BS MS [initials required] HOT WATER TANK

4. The seller shall provide the Buyer with a metes & bounds description of the subject property. After receipt of the description the Buyer shall be allowed 14 days to investigate title to the Property. If the Buyer makes a valid objection to the title in writing within such time, and if the Seller is unable or unwilling to remedy or satisfy the objection, and if the Buyer is then unwilling to waive the objection, then this Agreement shall be null and void and the deposit shall be returned to the Buyer without interest, penalty or deduction and without any further obligation for costs or damages between the parties. If the Buyer does not make a valid objection in writing within the specified time periods, then the Buyer shall be deemed to have conclusively accepted the status of the Seller's title to the Property. All investigations shall be at the Buyer's own expense.

5. The conveyance of the subject property shall be by WARRANTY Deed prepared in registrable form at the expense of the Seller, and shall be tendered on closing in exchange for the purchase price. The Buyer shall be responsible for any ancillary documents that may be required pursuant to this Agreement, unless the Seller is expressly required to provide otherwise. The Seller shall obtain and register a discharge of all existing mortgages, and the property shall be conveyed free and clear of any mortgages, liens or encumbrances, save and except any easements, registered restrictions or covenants that affect the property but do not materially affect the enjoyment of the property, and except as specifically allowed for elsewhere in this Agreement. The conveyance shall be in compliance with the provisions of the *Matrimonial Property Act*.

6. The property and all fixtures and chattels contemplated under this Agreement shall remain at the risk of the Seller until closing. All related insurance policies held by the Seller, if any, as well as any proceeds paid under such policies, shall be held in trust for the benefit of the parties in relation to their respective interests under this Agreement. In the event of damage and subsequent payment under such policies, the Buyer shall have the option of terminating this Agreement or receiving the said payment and closing the transaction as scheduled with all other terms and conditions remaining the same. In the event that the Agreement is terminated pursuant to this section, the deposit shall be returned to the Buyer without interest, penalty or deduction. No insurance policies shall be transferred on closing unless otherwise provided herein.

Date of Offer: MAY 12, 2003

Initials of Buyer: BS MS Witness: [signature]

Initials of Seller: JD JD Witness: [signature]

7. a) All taxes, rates and Assessments shall be adjusted to the Closing Date, as well as any of the usual adjustments, including the following as may be applicable: interest, rents, security deposits and insurance premiums. The closing date itself shall be the responsibility of the Buyer. Any charges for municipal improvements that have been completed as of the day this Agreement is signed – including, but without limitation, capital charges for municipal utilities or services, or betterment charges – whether billed or not, unless otherwise provided in this Agreement, shall be the responsibility of the Seller and shall be paid in full on or before closing.

b) Any Harmonized Sales Tax (HST) payable pursuant to the *Excise Tax Act* shall be [choose one and initial]

Seller(s)	Buyer(s)	
JD	BS MS	☐ included in the purchase price
		OR
[initials required]		☑ in addition to the purchase price

c) If there is no HST payable, the Seller agrees to provide a Certificate in a form satisfactory to the buyer's lawyer certifying that there is no HST payable.

8. Any tender of documents, keys or money may be effected by personal delivery upon the Buyer or Seller, as the case may be, or their lawyers, if any, on or before the closing date.

9. The Buyer shall have the right to conduct a pre-closing inspection of the property to ensure that the property is in the same condition as it was in at the time this Agreement was signed. Such inspection shall be performed on or before JULY 7, 2003 [date], and only upon reasonable advance notice to the Seller.

10. All representations and warranties contained in this Agreement shall survive closing unless otherwise stated herein. The Seller represents and warrants as follows:

a) The Seller has not caused or allowed any buildings on the Property to be insulated with urea formaldehyde insulation, and further, to the best of the Seller's knowledge, none of the buildings on the Property have been insulated with urea formaldehyde insulation.

b) NIL

c)

d)

11. This Agreement is further conditional upon the following [initial clauses that apply, or stroke them out]:

BS MS JD a) The Buyer shall obtain a satisfactory report from a qualified home inspector of the Buyer's choice, at the Buyer's expense. This condition is for the benefit of the Buyer and in the event that the report is not satisfactory to the Buyer, the Buyer shall have the option of terminating this Agreement upon written notice delivered to the Seller on or before [date] MAY 17, 2003, failing which this condition shall be deemed waived. In the event of such termination, the deposit shall be returned to the Buyer without interest, penalty or deduction. The Seller agrees to allow the inspector reasonable access to the property, upon giving the Seller reasonable advanced notice for the purpose of conducting the inspection.

~~b) The Seller shall provide the Buyer with a Property Condition Disclosure Statement within ______ hours of acceptance of this Agreement. In the event that the information disclosed by the Statement is not satisfactory to the Buyer, the Buyer shall have the option of terminating this Agreement upon written notice delivered to the Seller on or before [date] ______, failing which this condition shall be deemed waived. In the event of such termination, the deposit shall be returned to the Buyer without interest, penalty or deduction. This condition is for the benefit of the Buyer. If a Statement is provided pursuant to this section, the Seller warrants that the Statement shall be current and accurate to the best of the Seller's knowledge, and the Seller agrees to advise the buyer of any change pending closing.~~

BS MS JD c) The Buyer shall have this Agreement reviewed by a lawyer of the Buyer's choice, at the Buyer's expense. This condition is for the benefit of the Buyer and in the event that the lawyer is not satisfied with the form or content of this Agreement, the Buyer shall have the option of terminating this Agreement upon written notice delivered to the Seller on or before [date] MAY 13, 2003, failing which this condition shall be deemed waived. In the event of such termination, the deposit shall be returned to the Buyer without interest, penalty or deduction.

~~d) The Seller shall have this Agreement reviewed by a lawyer of the Seller's choice, at the Seller's expense. This condition is for the benefit of the Seller and in the event that the lawyer is not satisfied with the form or content of this Agreement, the Seller shall have the option of terminating this Agreement upon written notice delivered to the Buyer on or before [date] ______, failing which this condition shall be deemed waived. In the event of such termination, the deposit shall be returned to the Buyer without interest, penalty or deduction.~~

e) NIL

f)

12. The Seller shall deliver to the Buyer any Surveyor's Real Property Report(s) or plot plan(s) concerning the property that are in the Seller's possession; however, any new Surveys or plans shall be the responsibility of the Buyers, unless otherwise required or agreed upon herein.

13. The following Schedules are attached to and form an integral part of this Agreement: "A" (SURVEY) [applicable Schedules, if any].

All parties acknowledge having read and understood this Agreement as evidenced by their initials on this page 2 of 3

Date of Offer: MAY 12, 2003

Initials of Buyer: BS MS. Witness: [initials]

Initials of Seller: JD Witness: [initials]

14. Upon acceptance this Agreement shall constitute a binding agreement of purchase and sale. In the event that the Buyer defaults in the completion of this Agreement, the Buyer will forfeit the above deposit in addition to any other claims the Seller may have against the Buyer. This document, together with all listed Schedules, constitutes the entire Agreement between the parties and there shall be no collateral agreements, representations or warranties. This Agreement may only be amended or extended by mutual, written agreement between the parties, or between their lawyers, if any. Time shall be of the essence throughout this Agreement, including any extensions. This Agreement shall pass to the benefit of and be binding upon each of the parties' heirs, executors, administrators, successors and assigns. In the event of a discrepancy between the Schedules or added clauses in this Agreement and the pre-formatted form of Agreement, the Schedules or added clauses shall prevail to the extent of the discrepancy. Any references to gender or number of parties shall be read with the intended context applied. In the event that any specific provisions of this Agreement are declared illegal, invalid or unenforceable by a court of competent jurisdiction, then the offending provision(s) may be severed and shall not impair the validity or enforceability of the balance of the Agreement. This Agreement shall be interpreted and enforced in accordance with the laws of the Province of Nova Scotia.

15. Each of the parties acknowledges having received a copy of this Agreement and having been advised to seek independent legal advice prior to signing. Each of the parties further acknowledges that they have either obtained such independent legal advice, or have declined to seek such advice and have otherwise entered into this Agreement with the knowledge that it creates firm and binding legal relations and in full comprehension of the terms and consequences set out herein. Notwithstanding the source of this document, the doctrine of "Contra Preferentem" shall not apply and the Agreement shall be interpreted and construed equally among the parties.

16. This offer to purchase shall be open for acceptance and irrevocable by the Buyer until 5:00 PM [time – a.m. or p.m.] on MAY 13, 2003 [date].

Signed at CENTREVILLE in the Province of Nova Scotia, at 4:45 PM [time – a.m. or p.m.] on MAY 12, 2003 [date].

Signed sealed and delivered in the presence of: Signed sealed and delivered by:

Witness One [Witness] — Bob Smith [Buyer] [Seal]

Witness One [Witness] — Mary Smith [Buyer] [Seal]

17. *[choose one – delete others]*

(i) The Seller hereby accepts this offer on the terms and conditions set out herein.

Signed at CENTREVILLE in the Province of Nova Scotia, at 9:00 A.M. [time – a.m. or p.m.] on MAY 13, 2003 [date].

Signed sealed and delivered in the presence of: Signed sealed and delivered by:

Witness Two [Witness] — John Doe [Seller] [Seal]

Witness Two [Witness] — Jane Doe [Seller] [Seal]

(ii) The Seller confirms that this offer was presented and not accepted, and returns herewith the deposit.

Signed at ______ in the Province of Nova Scotia, at ______ [time – a.m. or p.m.] on ______ [date].

Signed sealed and delivered in the presence of: Signed sealed and delivered by:

______ [Witness] ______ [Seller] [Seal]

______ [Witness] ______ [Seller] [Seal]

(iii) The Seller hereby modifies this offer in the manner set out herein, which amendments are initialed, including any further amendments as follows (counteroffer): ______

This counteroffer shall be open for acceptance and irrevocable by the Seller until ______ [time – a.m. or p.m.] on ______ [date]

after which time, if not accepted by the Buyer, this counteroffer shall be null and void and the deposit shall be returned to the Buyer without interest, penalty or deduction.

Signed at ______ in the Province of Nova Scotia, at ______ [time – a.m. or p.m.] on ______ [date].

Signed sealed and delivered in the presence of: Signed sealed and delivered by:

______ [Witness] ______ [Seller] [Seal]

______ [Witness] ______ [Seller] [Seal]

18. The Buyer accepts the modifications contained in this counteroffer together with the remaining terms and conditions set out in this Agreement.

Signed at ______ in the Province of Nova Scotia, at ______ [time – a.m. or p.m.] on ______ [date].

Signed sealed and delivered in the presence of: Signed sealed and delivered by:

______ [Witness] ______ [Buyer] [Seal]

______ [Witness] ______ [Buyer] [Seal]

All parties acknowledge having read and understood this Agreement as evidenced by their initials on this page 3 of 3

Date of Offer: MAY 12, 2003

Initials of Buyer: BS MS Witness: W1

Initials of Seller: JD JD Witness: W2

Newfoundland & Labrador

Form of Agreement of Purchase & Sale (sample completed form)

AGREEMENT OF PURCHASE AND SALE

(FOR USE IN NEWFOUNDLAND & LABRADOR)

The BUYER, BOB SMITH & MARY SMITH [legal name(s) of Buyer(s)], hereby offers to buy from

the SELLER, JOHN DOE & JANE DOE [legal name(s) of Seller(s)], the real property described as

the PROPERTY: 123 MAIN STREET, CENTREVILLE, NEWFOUNDLAND BEING LOT 2, PLAN 2, COUNTY OF MIDDLEFORD [street address and legal description], at a purchase price of

the PRICE: ONE HUNDRED & FIFTY THOUSAND ——— xx [written] Dollars CDN ($ 150,000.00 [numerical])

on the following terms and conditions.

1. a) The Buyer submits with this signed offer an initial deposit by cash or cheque payable to ATTICUS LAWYER, IN TRUST [person to whom deposit is payable] in the amount of FIFTEEN THOUSAND ——— xx [written] Dollars CDN ($ 15,000.00 [numerical]) to be held in trust pending closing or other termination of this Agreement.

   b) On closing the deposit shall be credited towards the purchase price. In the event that this transaction does not close, or the Agreement is otherwise terminated, other than due to default on the part of the Buyer, the deposit shall be returned to the Buyer without interest, penalty or deduction. In the event that the Buyer defaults in the completion of this Agreement, the Buyer will forfeit the above deposit in addition to any other claims the Seller may have against the Buyer.

   c) Unless otherwise provided herein, the balance of the purchase price shall be due on completion by cash, lawyer's trust cheque, or certified cheque drawn on a Chartered Canadian Bank, Trust Company or Credit Union, payable to the Seller or Seller's lawyer, or as they may redirect.

2. This Agreement shall be completed on JULY 14, 2003 [date] (the "Closing Date"), on which date the Seller shall provide the Buyer with vacant possession of the Property, unless otherwise provided herein.

3. (i) The following items (chattels) are included in the purchase price: WASHER & DRYER IN BASEMENT

   Such chattels shall remain with the property on closing, free of any encumbrances or liens, and shall be in the same condition and working order as they were at the time this Agreement was signed.

   (i) All items attached to the property (fixtures) are included in the purchase price and shall remain with the property on closing, save and except the following fixtures which are not included: ANTIQUE LIGHT FIXTURE IN DINING ROOM

   (i) The following items are leased, and the Buyer agrees to assume the leases in connection with same: HOT WATER TANK

4. The seller shall provide the Buyer, as soon as reasonably possible after acceptance, with a legal description of the subject property together with copies of any surveys or boundary plans of the Property that may be in the Seller's possession or control. After receipt of this information, the Buyer shall be allowed 14 days to investigate title to the Property. If the Buyer makes a valid objection to the title in writing within such time, and if the Seller is unable or unwilling to remedy or satisfy the objection, and if the Buyer is then unwilling to waive the objection, then this Agreement shall be null and void and the deposit shall be returned to the Buyer without interest, penalty or deduction and without any further obligation for costs or damages between the parties. If the Buyer does not make a valid objection in writing within the specified time period, then the Buyer shall be deemed to have conclusively accepted the status of the Seller's title to the Property. All investigations shall be at the Buyer's expense.

5. The conveyance of the subject property shall be by WARRANTY Deed prepared in registrable form at the expense of the Seller, and shall be tendered on closing in exchange for the purchase price. The Buyer shall be responsible for any ancillary documents that may be required pursuant to this Agreement, unless the Seller is expressly required to provide otherwise. The Seller shall obtain and register a discharge of all existing mortgages, and the property shall be conveyed free and clear of any mortgages, liens or encumbrances, save and except any easements, registered restrictions or covenants that affect the property but do not materially affect the enjoyment or marketability of the property, and except as specifically allowed for elsewhere in this Agreement. The conveyance shall be in compliance with any provincial family law legislation.

6. The property and all fixtures and chattels contemplated under this Agreement shall remain at the risk of the Seller until closing. All related insurance policies held by the Seller, if any, as well as any proceeds paid under such policies, shall be held in trust for the benefit of the parties in relation to their respective interests under this Agreement. In the event of damage and subsequent payment under such policies, the Buyer shall have the option of terminating this Agreement or receiving the said payment and closing the transaction as scheduled with all other terms and conditions remaining the same. In the event that the Agreement is terminated pursuant to this section, the deposit shall be returned to the Buyer without interest, penalty or deduction. No insurance policies shall be transferred on closing unless otherwise provided herein.

7. The balance due on closing shall be subject to the usual adjustments for property related expenses and receipts, including, without limitation, all property taxes, rates and assessments. The closing date itself shall be the responsibility of the Buyer. Any charges for municipal improvements that have been completed as of the day this Agreement is signed – including, but without limitation, capital charges for municipal utilities or services, or betterment charges – whether billed or not, unless otherwise provided in this Agreement, shall be the responsibility of the Seller and shall be paid in full on or before closing.

8. Any Harmonized Sales Tax (HST) payable pursuant to the *Excise Tax Act* shall be [choose one and initial]

Seller(s)	Buyer(s)	
JD JD	BS MS	☐ included in the purchase price
[initials required]		OR
		✓ in addition to the purchase price

   If there is no HST payable, the Seller agrees to provide a Certificate in a form satisfactory to the buyer's lawyer certifying that there is no HST payable.

All parties acknowledge having read and understood this Agreement as evidenced by their initials on this page 1 of 3

Date of Offer: MAY 12, 2003

Initials of Buyer: BS MS **Witness:** W1

Initials of Seller: JD JD **Witness:** W2

9. On closing the Seller shall furnish a certificate confirming that the Seller is not a "non-resident" within the meaning of the Income Tax Act, failing which the Buyer shall be entitled to hold-back funds in accordance with prudent legal practice sufficient to satisfy the Buyer's obligations under the Act.

10. Any tender of documents, keys or money may be effected by personal delivery upon the Buyer or Seller, as the case may be, or their lawyers, if any, on or before the closing date.

11. All representations and warranties contained in this Agreement shall survive closing unless otherwise stated herein. The Seller represents and warrants as follows *[attach additional schedules if necessary]*:

a) The Seller has not caused or allowed any buildings on the Property to be insulated with urea formaldehyde insulation, and further, to the best of the Seller's knowledge, none of the buildings on the Property have been insulated with urea formaldehyde insulation.

b) NIL

c) ______

d) ______

12. This Agreement is further conditional upon the following *[attach additional schedules if necessary]*:

(a) This Agreement is conditional upon the Buyer obtaining written approval of financing on terms satisfactory to the Buyer or as otherwise specified in this Agreement. The Buyer must notify the Seller in writing on or before 5:00 PM *[time – a.m. or p.m.]* on MAY 17, 2003 *[date]* that the financing is unavailable and that the condition cannot be satisfied. In the event that such notice is not given on or before the specified date, the condition shall be deemed fulfilled or waived and this Agreement shall, subject to any further outstanding conditions, be deemed to be firm and binding. In the event that such notice is given on or before the specified date, the this Agreement shall be null and void and the deposit shall be returned to the Buyer without interest, penalty or deduction. This condition is for the sole benefit of the Buyer and may be waived by the Buyer on or before the specified time.

(b) NIL

(c) ______

13. The following Schedules are attached to and form an integral part of this Agreement: "A" (SURVEY) *[applicable Schedules, if any]*.

14. Upon acceptance, this Agreement shall constitute a binding agreement of purchase and sale. This document, together with all listed Schedules, constitutes the entire Agreement between the parties and there shall be no collateral agreements, representations or warranties. This Agreement may only be amended or extended by mutual, written agreement between the parties, or between their lawyers, if any. Time shall be of the essence throughout this Agreement, including any extensions. This Agreement shall pass to the benefit of and be binding upon each of the parties' heirs, executors, administrators, successors and assigns. In the event of a discrepancy between the Schedules or added clauses in this Agreement and the pre-formatted form of Agreement, the Schedules or added clauses shall prevail to the extent of the discrepancy. Any references to gender or number of parties shall be read with the intended context applied. In the event that any specific provisions of this Agreement are declared illegal, invalid or unenforceable by a court of competent jurisdiction, then the offending provision(s) may be severed and shall not impair the validity or enforceability of the balance of the Agreement. This Agreement shall be interpreted and enforced in accordance with the laws of the Province of Newfoundland & Labrador.

15. Each of the parties acknowledges having received a copy of this Agreement and having been advised to seek independent legal advice prior to signing. Each of the parties further acknowledges that they have either obtained such independent legal advice, or have declined to seek such advice and have otherwise entered into this Agreement with the knowledge that it creates firm and binding legal relations and in full comprehension of the terms and consequences set out herein. Notwithstanding the source of this document, the doctrine of "Contra Preferentem" shall not apply and the Agreement shall be interpreted and construed equally among the parties.

16. Offer, acceptance or any notice or communication required under this Agreement shall be deemed delivered and received if given in writing by any of the following methods: 1) by personal delivery to the addresses of the parties noted herein, 2) by registered mail to the addresses of the parties noted herein (in which case receipt shall be deemed to be three days after mailing), 3) by fax to the fax numbers noted by the parties herein, if any, or 4) by delivery or fax to either party's lawyer, if any, as noted herein or as otherwise reasonably established during the course of this transaction.

Buyer's address: 321 QUEEN ST. CENTREVILLE, B1B 2A2	Seller's address: 123 MAIN ST, CENTREVILLE, 1A1B2B
Phone: (123) 987-6543 Fax: (NONE)	Phone: (123) 345-6789 Fax: (NONE)
Lawyer name: PENELOPE SOLICITOR	Lawyer name: ATTICUS LAWYER
address: 345 BARRISTERS ROW CENTREVILLE C2C3D3	address: 234 CHANCERY LANE CENTREVILLE, C3C 3D4
Phone: (123) 246-1357 Fax: (123) 246-1375	Phone: (123) 246-3579 Fax: (123) 246-3597

All parties acknowledge having read and understood this Agreement as evidenced by their initials on this page 2 of 3

Date of Offer: MAY 12, 2003

Initials of Buyer: BS MRS Witness: W1

Initials of Seller: JD JD Witness: W2

17. This offer to purchase shall be open for acceptance and irrevocable by the Buyer until 5:00 PM [time — a.m. or p.m.] on MAY 13, 2003 [date].

Signed at CENTREVILLE in the Province of Newfoundland & Labrador, at 4:45 PM [time — a.m. or p.m.] on MAY 12, 2003 [date].

Signed sealed and delivered in the presence of:	Signed sealed and delivered by:	
Witness One [Witness]	Bob Smith [Buyer]	[Seal]
Witness One [Witness]	Mary Smith [Buyer]	[Seal]

18. *[choose one – delete others]*

(i) The Seller hereby accepts this offer on the terms and conditions set out herein.

Signed at CENTREVILLE in the Province of Newfoundland & Labrador, at 9:00 AM [time — a.m. or p.m.] on MAY 13, 2003 [date].

Signed sealed and delivered in the presence of:	Signed sealed and delivered by:	
Witness Two [Witness]	John Doe [Seller]	[Seal]
Witness Two [Witness]	Jane Doe [Seller]	[Seal]

(ii) The Seller confirms that this offer was presented and not accepted, and returns herewith the deposit.

Signed at ______________ in the Province of Newfoundland & Labrador, at ________ [time — a.m. or p.m.] on ______________ [date].

Signed sealed and delivered in the presence of:	Signed sealed and delivered by:	
[Witness]	[Seller]	[Seal]
[Witness]	[Seller]	[Seal]

(iii) The Seller hereby modifies this offer in the manner set out herein, which amendments are initialed, including any further amendments as follows (counteroffer):

____

____

____

This counteroffer shall be open for acceptance and irrevocable by the Seller until ________ [time — a.m. or p.m.] on ______________ [date], after which time, if not accepted by the Buyer, this counter offer shall be null and void and the deposit shall be returned to the Buyer without interest, penalty or deduction.

Signed at ______________ in the Province of Newfoundland & Labrador, at ________ [time — a.m. or p.m.] on ______________ [date].

Signed sealed and delivered in the presence of:	Signed sealed and delivered by:	
[Witness]	[Seller]	[Seal]
[Witness]	[Seller]	[Seal]

19. The Buyer accepts the modifications contained in this counteroffer together with the remaining terms and conditions set out in this Agreement.

Signed at ______________ in the Province of Newfoundland & Labrador, at ________ [time — a.m. or p.m.] on ______________ [date].

Signed sealed and delivered in the presence of:	Signed sealed and delivered by:	
[Witness]	[Buyer]	[Seal]
[Witness]	[Buyer]	[Seal]

All parties acknowledge having read and understood this Agreement as evidenced by their initials on this page 3 of 3

Date of Offer: MAY 12, 2003

Initials of Buyer: BS MS Witness: W1

Initials of Seller: JD JD Witness: W2

Yukon & Northwest Territories

Form of Agreement of Purchase & Sale (sample completed form)

CONTRACT OF PURCHASE AND SALE

For use in Yukon & Northwest Territories

THE BUYER, BOB SMITH & MARY SMITH (the "Buyer"), of

BUYER'S ADDRESS: 321 QUEEN ST., CENTREVILLE, B1B 2A2 PHONE: (H) (123) 987-6543 (W) (123) 987-1255

SUBMITS A DEPOSIT OF: FIFTEEN THOUSAND ($15,000.00) DOLLARS CASH ☐ CHEQUE ☑

LEGAL DESCRIPTION:	LOT(S) 1	BLOCK/QUAD/GROUP	AREA	PLAN 2

MUNICIPAL ADDRESS: 123 MAIN STREET, CENTREVILLE (the "Property")

PURCHASE PRICE OF: ONE HUNDRED & FIFTY THOUSAND DOLLARS $ 150,000.00

THE SELLER, JOHN DOE & JANE DOE (the "Seller"), of

SELLER'S ADDRESS: 123 MAIN ST., CENTREVILLE, 1A1 B2B PHONE: (H) (123) 345-6789 (W) N/A

PAYABLE on the following terms:

The deposit to be credited towards the purchase price, and, unless otherwise provided herein, the balance payable on the Closing Date by cash, lawyer's trust cheque, or certified cheque.

SCHEDULES ATTACHED HERETO YES ☑ NO ☐ Specify: "A" (SURVEY)

THE BUYER HEREBY OFFERS TO BUY THE PROPERTY FOR THE ABOVE STATED PRICE AND ON THE TERMS AND CONDITIONS SET OUT HEREIN.

1. **ITEMS INCLUDED/EXCLUDED:**
   a. The following items (chattels) are included: WASHER & DRYER IN BASEMENT. These chattels shall remain with the property on closing, free of any encumbrances or liens, and shall be in the same good working order and condition as they were at the time this Agreement was signed.
   b. All items attached to the property (fixtures) are included in the purchase price and shall remain with the property on closing, save and except the following fixtures which are not included: ANTIQUE LIGHT FIXTURE IN DINING ROOM.
   c. The following items are rented or leased, and the Buyer agrees to assume the rental contracts or leases in connection with same: HOT WATER TANK.

2. **CONDITION OF PROPERTY ON CLOSING:** On closing the property and all dwellings, structures and fences, and all included fixtures and chattels as set out above, shall be in substantially the same condition they were in on the date they were viewed by the Buyer – that date being MAY 12, 2003.

3. **CLOSING DATE:** This transaction shall be completed on JULY 14, 2003 (the "Closing Date").

4. **POSSESSION DATE:** The buyer shall be entitled to possession at 12:00 PM [am/pm] on JULY 14, 2003 (the "Possession Date"), at which time such possession shall be vacant unless otherwise provided for herein. Vacant possession requires that all persons, animals, chattels not included, and fixtures excluded must be removed from the Property, unless otherwise agreed to. If there are any items improperly left on the Property, the Buyer shall be entitled to keep such items, or may insist upon the removal of the items at the Seller's expense.

5. **ADJUSTMENTS:** The balance due on closing shall be subject to the usual adjustments consistent with the jurisdiction in which the Property is situate. Without limiting the generality of this statement, the following items shall be adjusted as of the Closing Date, unless expressly provided for elsewhere herein, the Closing Date itself to be apportioned to the Buyer: taxes, utilities, fuel, licenses, insurance, rents, deposits and chattel leases (if any). The adjustment date shall be the Closing Date, unless expressly set out otherwise in this Agreement.

6. **TITLE:** The property shall be conveyed free and clear of any mortgages, liens or encumbrances, save and except any reservations or exceptions contained in the original Crown Grant, or any easements in favor of utility or public authorities, and except as specifically allowed for elsewhere in this Agreement.

7. **RISK / INSURANCE:** The property and all fixtures and chattels contemplated under this Agreement shall remain at the risk of the Seller until 12:01 a.m. on the Closing Date. All related insurance policies held by the Seller, if any, as well as any proceeds paid under such policies, shall be held in trust for the benefit of the parties in relation to their respective interests under this Agreement. In the event of damage and subsequent payment under such policies, the Buyer shall have the option of terminating this Agreement or receiving the said payment and closing the transaction as scheduled with all other terms and conditions remaining the same. In the event that the Agreement is terminated pursuant to this section, the deposit shall be returned to the Buyer without interest, penalty or deduction. No insurance policies shall be transferred on closing unless otherwise provided herein.

8. **CONDITIONS:** *[stroke out any that do not apply]* The following conditions are for the benefit of the Buyer, and may be waived by the Buyer at the Buyer's sole discretion. The Seller shall not commit or omit any action that might reasonably prevent fulfillment of a condition. Unless expressly stated otherwise, the Buyer must notify the Seller in writing on or before the date specified that the condition cannot be satisfied. In the event that such notice is not given on or before the date specified, the condition shall be deemed fulfilled or waived and this Agreement shall, subject to any further outstanding conditions, be deemed to be firm and binding. In the event that such notice of non-satisfaction is given on or before the specified date, then the Agreement shall be considered null and void, and in such event the deposit shall be returned to the Buyer without interest, penalty or deduction.
   a) Financing – Notwithstanding the foregoing, notice that at least one of the following financing conditions have been satisfied or waived must be given to the Seller, in writing, on or before MAY 13, 2003 failing which the agreement shall be null and void, and the deposit shall be returned to the Buyer without interest, penalty or deduction.
      ~~(i) Buyer obtaining written approval to assume the existing mortgage, which is elsewhere described in full in this Agreement, or~~
      (ii) Buyer obtaining written approval of financing for the approx. amount of $112,000 – at an interest rate of not more than 7.0 %.
   b) Legal Status - Buyer confirming on or before JUNE 12, 2003 that the property complies with all local, provincial and municipal building, zoning fire department, and other relevant local authority requirements, that permits have been obtained for all structures or improvements requiring permits, or that the status is otherwise legal non-conforming

c) Other: NIL

9. **NOTICE:** Offer, acceptance or any notice or communication required under this Agreement shall be deemed delivered and received if given in writing by any of the following methods:
   a. by personal delivery to the addresses of the parties noted herein,
   b. by registered mail to the addresses of the parties noted herein (in which case receipt shall be deemed to be three days after mailing),
   c. by fax to the fax numbers noted by the parties herein, if any (Buyer's fax (NONE) / Seller's fax (NONE)), or
   d. by delivery or fax to either lawyer, if any, as noted herein or as otherwise reasonably established throughout the course of this transaction.

10. **RESIDENCY:** On closing the Seller shall furnish a certificate confirming that the Seller is not a "non-resident" within the meaning of the Income Tax Act, failing which the Buyer shall be entitled to hold-back funds in accordance with prudent legal practice sufficient to satisfy the Buyer's obligations under the Act.

11. **COSTS:** Each party shall bear their own costs. Specifically, and without limiting the foregoing, all costs relating to the conveyance and any new mortgage(s) or mortgage assumption shall be at the expense of the Buyer, and all costs related to the clearing of title shall be at the expense of the Seller.

12. **GST:** The Buyer and Seller agree that this transaction is not subject to Federal Goods and Services Tax [GST], and the Seller shall furnish a certificate confirming same on closing.

13. **TENDER:** Any tender of documents, keys or money may be effected by personal delivery upon the Buyer or Seller, as the case may be, or their lawyers, if any, on or before the closing date. The parties agree to instruct their lawyers to allow for reasonable undertakings as are traditionally necessary between lawyers to close successfully. Failing any agreement to the contrary, tender may also be effected at the local Land Titles Office on or before 5:00 PM [am or pm] on the Closing Date.

14. **ENFORCABILITY, ENTIRETY AND INTERPRETATION OF AGREEMENT:** Upon acceptance this Agreement shall constitute a binding agreement of purchase and sale. In the event that the Buyer defaults in the completion of this Agreement, the Buyer will forfeit the above deposit in addition to any other claims the Seller may have against the Buyer. This document, together with all listed Schedules, constitutes the entire Agreement between the parties and there shall be no collateral agreements, representations or warranties. This Agreement may only be amended or extended by mutual, written agreement between the parties, or between their lawyers, if any. Time shall be of the essence throughout this Agreement, including any extensions. This Agreement shall pass to the benefit of and be binding upon each of the parties' heirs, executors, administrators, successors and assigns. In the event of a discrepancy between the Schedules or added clauses in this Agreement and the pre-formatted form of Agreement, the Schedules or added clauses shall prevail to the extent of the discrepancy. Any references to gender or number of parties shall be read with the intended context applied. In the event that any specific provisions of this Agreement are declared illegal, invalid or unenforceable by a court of competent jurisdiction, then the offending provision(s) may be severed and shall not impair the validity or enforceability of the balance of the Agreement. This Agreement shall be interpreted and enforced in accordance with the laws of the jurisdiction in which the property is situate.

15. **LEGAL REPRESENTATION:** Each of the parties acknowledges having received a copy of this Agreement and having been advised to seek independent legal advice prior to signing. Each of the parties further acknowledges that they have either obtained such independent legal advice, or have declined to seek such advice and have otherwise entered into this Agreement with the knowledge that it creates firm and binding legal relations and in full comprehension of the terms and consequences set out herein. Notwithstanding the source of this document, the doctrine of "Contra Preferentem" shall not apply and the Agreement shall be interpreted and construed equally among the parties.

The Buyer's lawyer is:	The Seller's solicitor, until further notification, is:
Name: PENELOPE SOLICITOR	Name: ATTICUS LAWYER
Address: 245 BARRISTERS ROW, CENTREVILLE, C3C3B3	Address: 235 CHANCERY LANE, CENTREVILLE, C3C 3B4
Phone: (123) 246-1357	Phone: (123) 246-3579
Fax: (123) 246-1375	Fax: (123) 246-3597

16. **OFFER:** This offer, or counter-offer, shall be open for acceptance and irrevocable until 5:00 PM [am or pm] on MAY 13, 2003. and upon acceptance, and notification of same to the other party, there shall be a binding agreement of purchase and sale.

Dated: MAY 12, 2003.

X Witness One [Witness] X Bob Smith [Buyer] ● [Seal] BOB SMITH [Print Name]

X Witness One [Witness] X Mary Smith [Buyer] ● [Seal] MARY SMITH [Print Name]

17. **ACCEPTANCE:** The Seller accepts this offer on the terms and conditions set out herein.

Dated: MAY 13, 2003.

X Witness Two [Witness] X John Doe [Seller] ● [Seal] JOHN DOE [Print Name]

X Witness Two [Witness] X Jane Doe [Seller] ● [Seal] JANE DOE [Print Name]

Chapter 20

Blank Purchase Contracts

Purchase Agreement forms are included in this Chapter. Samples in Chapter 19 show you how to fill out the forms for:

British Columbia

Alberta

Saskatchewan

Manitoba

Ontario

Quebec

New Brunswick

Prince Edward Island

Nova Scotia

Newfoundland & Labrador

Yukon & Northwest Territories

British Columbia

Form of Agreement of Purchase & Sale (Blank)

CONTRACT
OF PURCHASE AND SALE (FOR USE IN BRITISH COLUMBIA)

INITIALS			

SELLER: ______________________ BUYER: ______________________

SELLER: ______________________ BUYER: ______________________

ADDRESS: ______________________ ADDRESS: ______________________

______________________ ______________________

______________ PC: ________ ______________ PC: ________

PHONE: ______________________ PHONE: ______________________

RESIDENT OF CANADA ☐ NON-RESIDENT OF CANADA ☐ OCCUPATION: ______________________
Pursuant to the Income Tax Act (Canada)

PROPERTY: Municipal Address: ______________________
Legal Description: ______________________
______________________ (the "Property") PID No. ______________

The Buyer agrees to buy the Property from the Seller on the following terms and conditions:

1. **PURCHASE PRICE:** The purchase price shall be

______________________ Dollars CDN $______________ (the "Purchase Price")
[written] [numerical]

2. **DEPOSIT:** A deposit of ______________________ Dollars CDN $______________
[written] [numerical]
(the "Deposit") shall be provided by the Buyer on the following terms: ______________________
____
The Deposit shall be delivered and made payable " in trust" to ______________ . The Deposit shall be held in trust in accordance with the *Real Estate Act* and shall be credited towards the Purchase Price on completion of this transaction. In the event that the Deposit is not received by the Seller or the Seller's authorized representative or solicitor in accordance with the terms, the Seller shall have the option of terminating this contract.

3. **TERMS & CONDITIONS:** This Contract shall be subject to the following terms and conditions: ______________________
____
____
____
____
The following provisions shall be deemed to apply to each stated condition, unless otherwise indicated: 1) each condition shall be deemed to be for the sole benefit of the party indicated, if so indicated, and 2) the benefiting party shall deliver to the other party a written notice that the condition has been waived or fulfilled, as the case may be, on or before the date specified, failing which this Contract shall become null and void and the Deposit shall be returned to the Buyer in accordance with the *Real Estate Act*.

4. **CLOSING:** This Contract shall be completed on ______________ (the "Closing Date") at the applicable Land Title Office.

5. **POSSESSION:** The Buyer shall have vacant possession of the Property at 12:00 p.m. (noon) on the Closing Date, unless another date is set out as follows: ______________; OR ALTERNATIVELY, the Buyer shall assume the existing tenancies set out as follows:
[alternate possession date, if any]
______________________.
[details of tenancy or tenancies, if any]

6. **ADJUSTMENTS:** As of ______________ (the "Adjustment Date") the Buyer shall assume and be responsible for all taxes, rates, local improvement assessments, fuel on the Property, and other charges applicable to the Property for the period subsequent to and including the Closing Date. All closing adjustments, whether to the credit of the Buyer or Seller, shall be made as of this date unless specified otherwise herein.

7. **INCLUDED/EXCLUDED ITEMS:** All fixtures shall be included in the Purchase Price, and without limiting the generality of the foregoing, such fixtures shall include: all buildings and ancillary structures on the Property, and improvements thereto, all affixed window dressings including blinds, awnings, curtain rods, tracks and valences, all affixed storm windows, screen doors, shelves, mirrors and carpeting, and all plumbing, electric, heating, ventilating, air conditioning and alarm fixtures; BUT EXCLUDING the following fixtures: ______________________.
The following items (chattels) shall also be included in the Purchase Price: ______________________
______________________.

8. **CONDITION & RISK:** The property and all fixtures and other items included under this Contract shall on closing be in the same condition as existed when viewed by the Buyer on ______________ , and shall remain at the risk of the Seller until closing.

9. **TITLE:** Title to the Property shall be free and clear of all liens, charges or encumbrances, save and except for: a) any conditions, restrictions or reservations, including any royalties, contained in the original grant or in any other grant or disposition from the Crown, b) any registered or pending restrictive covenants that run with the land, c) any easements or rights-of-way for utilities or public authorities, or d) any matters expressly allowed for elsewhere in this Contract.

10. **TENDER & DOCUMENTS:** Any tender of money from the Buyer to the Seller shall, unless otherwise expressly provided, be in the form of cash, Lawyer's or Notary's trust cheque, or certified cheque or bank draft drawn on a Canadian chartered bank, trust company or credit union. Any tender of documents, keys or money may be effected by personal delivery upon the Buyer or Seller, as the case may be, or their Lawyers or Notaries, if any, on or before the closing date, and any documents required to be registered shall be delivered in registrable form and shall be lodged for registration in the applicable Land Title Office on or before the Closing Date.

11. **TIME:** Time shall be of the essence throughout this Contract, including any extensions. The balance of the Purchase Price shall be paid on or before the Closing Date, and/or any formal agreement(s) regarding payment of the balance of the Purchase Price shall be entered into on or before the Closing Date, failing which the Seller may, at the Seller's option, terminate this Contract, and, without limiting any other claims or remedies available to the Seller, the Deposit shall be absolutely forfeited to the Seller in accordance with the *Real Estate Act*.

12.. **FINANCING:** If the Buyer is relying on any new mortgage financing for all or part the balance of the Purchase Price, the Buyer shall still be required to pay the Purchase Price on the Closing Date, however the Buyer may wait to pay the Purchase Price until after the transfer and new mortgage documents have been lodged for registration in the applicable Land Title Office, provided that, before such lodging, the Buyer has: a) tendered the balance of the Purchase Price not being financed by the new mortgage(s), b) satisfied all of the new mortgagee's conditions and requirements for funding except lodging the mortgage(s) for registration, and c) provided the Seller with a Lawyer's or Notary's undertaking to pay the balance of the Purchase Price upon the lodging of the transfer and new mortgage(s) and the advance by the mortgagee(s) of the mortgage proceeds.

13. **CLEARING TITLE:** If the Seller is required to clear any existing charges from title, the Seller shall still be required to clear the title, however the Seller may wait to pay and discharge such existing charges until immediately after receiving the Purchase Price, provided that the Buyer may insist that the Purchase Price be paid to a Lawyer or Notary in trust, on the Lawyer's or Notary's undertaking to pay and discharge the existing charges, and remit any balance to the Seller, the undertaking to be in the form approved by the Canadian Bar Association (BC Branch) (Real Property Section), as may be amended from time to time.

14. **COSTS:** Each party shall bear their own costs. Specifically, and without limiting the foregoing, all costs relating to the conveyance and any mortgage(s) shall be at the expense of the Buyer, and all costs related to the clearing of title shall be at the expense of the Seller.

15. **REPRESENTATIONS & WARRANTIES:** This document, together with all listed Schedules, and together with the Property Disclosure Statement if and only if included with and expressly incorporated as part of this Contract, shall constitute the entire agreement between the parties. There are no collateral agreements, representations, warranties, guarantees or promises unless expressly set out in this Contract. Any express warranties or guarantees shall survive and not merge on closing.

16. **ENFORCABILITY, ENTIRETY AND INTERPRETATION OF CONTRACT:** ***This is a legal document!*** This Contract may only be amended or extended by mutual, written agreement between the parties, or between their Lawyers or Notaries, if any. This Contract shall pass to the benefit of and be binding upon each of the parties' heirs, executors, administrators, successors and assigns. In the event of a discrepancy between the Schedules or added clauses in this Contract and the pre-formatted form of Contract, the Schedules or added clauses shall prevail to the extent of the discrepancy. Any references to gender or number of parties shall be read with the intended context applied. In the event that any specific provisions of this Contract are declared illegal, invalid or unenforceable by a court of competent jurisdiction, then the offending provision(s) may be severed and shall not impair the validity or enforceability of the balance of the Contract. This Contract shall be interpreted and enforced in accordance with the laws of the Province of British Columbia.

17. **LEGAL REPRESENTATION:** Each of the parties acknowledges: a) having read this Contract in its entirety, together with any relevant schedules, Property Disclosure Statements or information pages, b) having received a copy of this Contract, and c) having been advised to seek independent legal advice from a Lawyer or Notary prior to signing this Contract. Each of the parties further acknowledges that they have either obtained such independent advice, or have declined to seek such advice and have otherwise entered into this Contract with the knowledge that it creates firm and binding legal relations and in full comprehension of the terms and consequences set out herein. Notwithstanding the source of this document, the doctrine of "Contra Preferentem" shall not apply and the Contract shall be interpreted and construed equally among the parties.

18. **FURTHER SCHEDULES:** The following Schedules are attached to and form an integral part of this Contract: ______________________________
[applicable Schedules, if any]

19. **OFFER:** This offer, or counter-offer, shall be open for acceptance and irrevocable until ____________ on ______________________________.
[time – a.m. *or* p.m.] [date]

and upon acceptance, and notification of same to the other party, there shall be a binding agreement of purchase and sale.

Dated: ____________________________.

X ______________________ [Witness]	X ______________________ [Buyer]	[Seal]	______________ [Print Name]
X ______________________ [Witness]	X ______________________ [Buyer]	[Seal]	______________ [Print Name]

20. **ACCEPTANCE:** The Seller accepts this offer on the terms and conditions set out herein.

Dated: ____________________________.

X ______________________ [Witness]	X ______________________ [Seller]	[Seal]	______________ [Print Name]
X ______________________ [Witness]	X ______________________ [Seller]	[Seal]	______________ [Print Name]

Alberta

Form of Agreement of Purchase & Sale (Blank)

RESIDENTIAL REAL ESTATE PURCHASE CONTRACT

For use in the Province of Alberta

This Contract is hereby made between

SELLER	and	BUYER
Name ______________________		Name ______________________
Name ______________________		Name ______________________

1. PROPERTY

1.1 The Property is comprised of the Land, Buildings, and fixtures located at the following municipal address: ______________________

1.2 The legal description of the Property is as follows:
a) If freehold:
Plan __________ Block __________ Lot __________
or
b) If Condominium:
Condominium Plan ______ Unit ______ Parking Unit ______

Jurisdiction ______________________

Other______________________

1.3 All fixtures attached to the Property shall be included, save and except the following:______________________

1.4 The Following chattels shall be included and remain on the Property: ______________________

2. PURCHASE PRICE

2.1 The Purchase Price shall be paid in full on the Closing Date.

2.2 The balance due on closing set out below shall be paid by Lawyer's trust cheque, certified cheque or bank draft drawn on a Canadian chartered bank, trust company or credit union, or through such consideration as may be otherwise agreed upon herein.

2.3 The Purchase Price includes any applicable Goods and Services Tax (GST), unless otherwise agreed upon herein.

2.4 The Purchase Price shall be paid as follows:

$ ______________________ Deposit # 1

$ ______________________ Deposit # 2

$ ______________________ New Mortgage

$ ______________________ Mortgage to be assumed
[approx. principal on closing]

$ ______________________ Mortgage back to Seller

$ ______________________ Other

$ ______________________ Balance Due on Closing

$ ______________________ Purchase Price

3. DEPOSIT(S)

3.1 The Deposit(s) shall be made by cash or personal cheque payable to ______________________.

3.2 Deposit # 1 shall be delivered to the Seller within 2 days of acceptance and formation of this Contract.

3.3 Deposit # 2, if any, shall be delivered within 2 days of ______________________

3.4 The Deposit(s) shall be held in trust for the benefit of the Seller and the Buyer as their respective interests appear herein. No interest shall be payable on the deposit(s), unless otherwise agreed upon herein.

3.5 The Deposit(s) shall be subsequently:

a) applied towards the Purchase Price as set out in section 2,

b) returned to the Buyer in the event that this document in the form of an offer or counter offer is not accepted, or the transaction does not close due to any conditions not being satisfied or default on the part of the Seller, or

c) forfeited to the Seller in the event that the transaction does not close due to default on the part of the Buyer.

INITIALS

4. CLOSING DATE

4.1 This Contract shall be completed on

____ .
[Closing Date]

4.2 Possession of the Property shall be delivered by the Seller on or before 12:00 p.m. (noon) on the Closing Date, and such possession shall be vacant unless otherwise provided for herein.

4.3 If the Parties elect that the Closing Date shall occur on a day other than a day on which the Land Titles Office is open, then payment of the Purchase Price and all conveyancing matters shall occur on or before 12:00 p.m. (noon) on the last day on which the Land Titles Office is open immediately prior to the Closing Date, notwithstanding that possession shall be delivered on the Closing Date agreed upon above.

5. CONDITIONS

5.1 This Contract is conditional upon the Buyer...
(choose if applicable, stroke out if inapplicable)

❒ a) Financing:
obtaining written approval of mortgage financing
❒ (i) on terms acceptable to the Buyer at the Buyer's sole discretion

or

❒ (ii) on the following terms:
Principle amount $ ______________________
(plus high ratio mortgage insurance premiums, if applicable)
Interest Rate not greater than ________ %
Term not shorter than ______________________
Amortization not shorter than ________________
❒ Open ❒ Closed ❒ Limited Prepayment Options
Other material terms required by Buyer

____
____
____

This condition shall be satisfied on or before
__________ on ______________________ ,
[time – a.m. *or* p.m.] [date]

❒ b) Property Inspection Report:
obtaining an acceptable property inspection report prepared by a qualified home inspector,
❒ (i) the acceptability of which shall be at the sole discretion of the Buyer

or

❒ (ii) which shall not disclose any material deficiency that the Seller is unable or unwilling to remedy, at the Seller's option
This condition shall be satisfied on or before
__________ on ______________________ ,
[time – a.m. *or* p.m.] [date]

❒ c) Sale of Buyer's property:
entering into an unconditional and binding agreement of purchase and sale of the Buyer's property located at

____
This condition shall be satisfied on or before
__________ on ______________________ ,
[time – a.m. *or* p.m.] [date]

❒ d) Lawyer approval:
obtaining an acceptable lawyer's review and opinion on the form and content of this Contract, the acceptability of which shall be at the sole discretion of the Buyer.
This condition shall be satisfied on or before
__________ on ______________________ ,
[time – a.m. *or* p.m.] [date]

❒ e) Condominium Documents:
satisfying the Buyer's Condition re Condominium Documents as set out in the schedule attached.
This condition shall be satisfied on or before
__________ on ______________________ ,
[time – a.m. *or* p.m.] [date]

❒ f) Other Buyer conditions:

____
____
This condition shall be satisfied on or before
__________ on ______________________ ,
[time – a.m. *or* p.m.] [date]

____
____
This condition shall be satisfied on or before
__________ on ______________________ ,
[time – a.m. *or* p.m.] [date]

5.2 This Contract is conditional upon the Seller...
(choose if applicable, stroke out if inapplicable)

❒ a) Lawyer approval:
obtaining an acceptable lawyer's review and opinion on the form and content of this Contract, the acceptability of which shall be at the sole discretion of the Seller.
This condition shall be satisfied on or before
__________ on ______________________ ,
[time – a.m. *or* p.m.] [date]

❒ b) Other Seller conditions:
____
____
This condition shall be satisfied on or before
__________ on ______________________ ,
[time – a.m. *or* p.m.] [date]

____
____
This condition shall be satisfied on or before
__________ on ______________________ ,
[time – a.m. *or* p.m.] [date]

5.3 Purchaser's conditions shall be for the benefit of the Purchaser and Seller's conditions shall be for the benefit of the seller, and all conditions shall be deemed to be for the sole and exclusive benefit of the parties so stated, unless provided for otherwise.

5.4 Any Conditions may be waived at the sole option of the beneficial party, unless provided for otherwise.

5.5 Conditions shall be considered satisfied if, and only if, the beneficial party delivers written notice to the other party that the condition has been satisfied or otherwise waived.

5.6 If any condition is not satisfied within the required time limit, then this Contract shall be immediately terminated and the Deposit(s) returned in accordance with section 3.

6. TITLE

Title to the Property shall be free and clear of any liens, encumbrances, registrations or obligations, save and except any of the following:

a) registered or pending restrictive covenants that run with the land that do not materially affect the marketability of the Property,

INITIALS			

b) encumbrances or obligations imposed by law,
c) easements or right-of-way for utilities or public authorities that do not materially affect the marketability of the Property,
d) homeowner association agreements, restrictions, encumbrance or similar registrations that do not materially affect the marketability of the Property, or
e) matters expressly allowed for elsewhere in this Contract.

7. SURVEYOR'S REAL PROPERTY REPORT / TITLE INSURANCE

Seller shall furnish the Buyer with an up-to-date Surveyor's Real Property Report (RPR) at least 10 business days prior to the Closing Date. The RPR shall certify as to the current state of the property and shall be accompanied by written evidence regarding the status of municipal compliance. Alternatively, by acknowledging hereunder, the parties agree to obtain a title insurance policy in lieu of an RPR, provided that the policy shall be unqualified with respect to any losses that would have been addressed by obtaining the RPR and compliance report.

Buyer shall accept title insurance: ☐

8. CLOSING ARRANGEMENTS

8.1 The Buyer shall be provided with documents and shall have a reasonable period of time before the Closing Date to confirm registration of documents at the Land Titles Office and to obtain advances under any new mortgage(s).

8.2 If the Seller fails to deliver the required closing documents, then payment of the Purchase Price shall be delayed until the Buyer has received the documents and has had a reasonable period of time to register them and confirm registration in accordance with the above. In such event, any interest payable on the balance of the Purchase Price shall be waived pending the expiry of such reasonable time.

8.3 In the event that the Seller agrees to accept late payment of the whole or any part of the balance of Purchase Price, then interest shall be payable to the Seller on the amount so outstanding at 3% above the rate of the Province of Alberta Treasury Branches as published on the Closing Date, or alternatively the last business day prior to the Closing Date. Interest shall be calculated on a daily basis from and including the Closing Date, but excluding the date of subsequent payment. Payment tendered on any day after 12:00 p.m. (noon) shall be deemed paid on the following business day.

8.4 The Purchase Price may be used by the Seller's Lawyer to pay out any liens, charges or other obligations that affect title and that are the responsibility of the Seller to discharge and vacate. The Seller shall ensure that his/her lawyer provides the Buyer or the Buyer's lawyer with evidence of all discharges, including, where necessary, a certified copy of the certificate of title, within a reasonable time after the Closing Date.

9. COSTS

Each party shall bear their own costs. Specifically, and without limiting the foregoing, the costs shall be allocated as follows:

The Seller shall be responsible for: (i) the preparation of closing documents, (ii) the preparation, registration and discharge of any Seller's caveat(s) under this Contract, and(iii) the RPR and evidence of municipal status, or title insurance premium(s), pursuant to section 7.

The Buyer shall be responsible for: (i) the registration of the transfer, and (ii) the preparation, registration and discharge of any Buyer's caveat(s) under this Contract.

10. ADJUSTMENTS

10.1 The balance due on closing shall be subject to the usual adjustments, which shall include, without limitation and among other things expressly agreed upon: property taxes, amortized local improvement charges, utilities and any homeowner association fees.

10.2 In the case of condominiums such adjustments shall further include, without limitation, condominium fees and other amounts payable in the ordinary course of condominium ownership.

10.3 The Closing Date itself shall be apportioned to the Seller.

11. RISK & INSURANCE

11.1 On closing, the Property and all chattels included herein shall be in substantially the same condition they were in upon acceptance of this Contract.

11.2 The Property and all fixtures and chattels contemplated under this Contract shall remain at the risk of the Seller until closing.

11.3 All related insurance policies held by the Seller, if any, as well as any proceeds paid under such policies, shall be held in trust for the benefit of the parties in relation to their respective interests under this Contract. In the event of damage and subsequent payment under such policies the Buyer shall have the option of terminating this Contract or receiving the said payment and closing the transaction as scheduled with all other terms and conditions remaining the same. In the event that the Contract is terminated pursuant to this section, the deposit shall be returned to the Buyer in the same manner as if a condition had been unsatisfied under this Contract.

12. REPRESENTATIONS & WARRANTIES

12.1 The Seller represents and warrants that the following are, and as of the Closing Date shall be, true:

a) The Seller has the legal right to sell the Property,
b) The fixtures and chattels contemplated herein are in good working order,
c) The Seller is not a "non-resident" within the meaning of the *Income Tax Act (Canada)*,
d) The current use of the Land is in compliance with applicable zoning and land use by-laws,
e) The buildings, fences or other structures are located wholly within the lot lines of the Property, except where a continuing encroachment agreement exists with the adjoining property,
f) No buildings, fences or other structures are improperly located on any easements or utility Rights-of way, except where a continuing encroachment agreement.
g) The location of all buildings, fences and other structures on the Property does not violate any municipal regulations or by-laws, or alternatively that the locations of all buildings or other structures on the Property is legal non-conforming as that term is defined under the *Municipal Government Act (Alberta)*.

12.2 Any action or remedy in connection with any representation or warranty contained in this Contract, must be brought within 1 year of the Closing Date

12.3 This document, together with all listed Schedules, constitutes the entire Contract between the parties and there shall be no collateral agreements, representations or warranties.

12.4 All warranties contained herein shall survive and not merge on closing.

13. ADDITIONAL TERMS

13.1 Time shall be of the essence throughout this Contract, including any extensions, and all deadlines and date requirements shall be strictly construed and enforced. Stated times shall be interpreted as Alberta standard time.

13.2 This Contract shall enure to the benefit of and be binding upon each of the parties' heirs, executors, administrators, successors and assigns.

13.3 Any references to gender or number of parties shall be read with the intended context applied.

13.4 In the event that the contract is terminated, such portions shall remain enforceable as to give effect to the intent of the Contract and the reasonable equities between the parties.

13.5 In the event of a discrepancy between the Schedules or added clauses in this Contract and the pre-formatted form of Contract, the Schedules or added clauses shall prevail to the extent of the discrepancy.

13.6 In the event that any specific provisions of this Contract are declared illegal, invalid or unenforceable by a court of competent jurisdiction, then the offending provision(s) may be severed and shall not impair the validity or enforceability of the balance of the Contract.

13.7 The following Schedules are attached to and form an integral part of this Contract

13.8 This Contract shall be subject to the following additional terms and conditions:

____
____
____
____
____
____
____
____
____
____
____
____
____
____
____
____
____
____
____

14 ENFORCABILITY, ENTIRETY AND INTERPRETATION

14.1 Upon acceptance, this Contract shall constitute a binding agreement of purchase and sale.

14.2 The parties agree to act in good faith and to use reasonable effort and diligence in pursuing the satisfaction of conditions and carrying out the terms and intent of this Contract, and to instruct their Lawyers to act reasonably and in accordance with accepted practice in carrying out the terms and intent of this Contract.

14.3 This Contract may only be amended or collaterally agreed to by mutual, written agreement between the parties, or between their lawyers, if any, as such lawyers may be noted herein or as otherwise reasonably established during the course of this transaction.

14.4 This Contract shall be interpreted and enforced in accordance with the laws of the Province of Alberta.

15. LEGAL REPRESENTATION

15.1 Each of the parties acknowledges having received a copy of this Contract and having been advised to seek independent legal advice prior to signing. Each of the parties further acknowledges that they have either obtained such independent legal advice, or have declined to seek such advice and have otherwise entered into this Contract with the knowledge that it creates firm and binding legal relations and in full comprehension of the terms and consequences set out herein.

15.2 Notwithstanding the source of this document, the doctrine of "Contra Preferentem" shall not apply and the Contract shall be interpreted and construed equally among the parties.

16. NOTICE

16.1 Any notice given between the parties shall be deemed effected upon delivery and receipt through one of the following methods:

1) personal delivery to the addresses of the parties noted herein,

2) registered mail to the addresses of the parties noted herein (in which case receipt shall be deemed to be three days after mailing),

3) fax to the fax numbers noted by the parties herein, if any, or

4) delivery or fax to either party's lawyer, if any, as noted herein or as otherwise reasonably established during the course of the transaction.

16.2 Contacting the Buyer:

Address ______________________________
____
Phone (day) ______________ (night) ______________
Fax __________________________________

16.3 Contacting the Seller:

Address ______________________________
____
Phone (day) ______________ (night) ______________
Fax __________________________________

16.4 Buyer's lawyer, if any:

Name _________________________________
Firm _________________________________
Address ______________________________
____
Phone ________________________________
Fax __________________________________

16.5 Seller's lawyer, if any:

Name _________________________________
Firm _________________________________
Address ______________________________
____
Phone ________________________________
Fax __________________________________

INITIALS			

17. OFFER

This offer or counter offer shall be open for acceptance and irrevocable by the Buyer until

____________ on ______________________________________,
[time – a.m. *or* p.m.] [date]

Signed, sealed and delivered at the time of

____________ on ______________________________________
[time – a.m. *or* p.m.] [date]

in ______________________________________, Alberta
[jurisdiction]]

______________________ ______________________
[Buyer] [Witness]

______________________ ______________________
[Buyer] [Witness]

18. COUNTER OFFER(S)

18.1 The preceding offer or counter offer is hereby rejected and this counter offer shall now be open for acceptance and irrevocable by the

______________________________________ until
[Buyer *or* Seller]

____________ on ______________________________________,
[time – a.m. *or* p.m.] [date]

Signed, sealed and delivered at the time of

____________ on ______________________________________
[time – a.m. *or* p.m.] [date]

in ______________________________________, Alberta
[jurisdiction]]

______________________ ______________________
name: [Witness]

______________________ ______________________
name: [Witness]

18.2 The preceding counter offer is hereby rejected and this counter offer shall now be open for acceptance and irrevocable by the

______________________________________ until
[Buyer *or* Seller]

____________ on ______________________________________,
[time – a.m. *or* p.m.] [date]

Signed, sealed and delivered at the time of

____________ on ______________________________________
[time – a.m. *or* p.m.] [date]

in ______________________________________, Alberta
[jurisdiction]]

______________________ ______________________
name: [Witness]

______________________ ______________________
name: [Witness]

18.3 The preceding counter offer is hereby rejected and this counter offer shall now be open for acceptance and irrevocable by the

______________________________________ until
[Buyer *or* Seller]

____________ on ______________________________________,
[time – a.m. *or* p.m.] [date]

Signed, sealed and delivered at the time of

____________ on ______________________________________
[time – a.m. *or* p.m.] [date]

in ______________________________________, Alberta
[jurisdiction]]

______________________ ______________________
name: [Witness]

______________________ ______________________
name: [Witness]

18.4 The preceding counter offer is hereby rejected and this counter offer shall now be open for acceptance and irrevocable by the

______________________________________ until
[Buyer *or* Seller]

____________ on ______________________________________,
[time – a.m. *or* p.m.] [date]

Signed, sealed and delivered at the time of

____________ on ______________________________________
[time – a.m. *or* p.m.] [date]

in ______________________________________, Alberta
[jurisdiction]]

______________________ ______________________
name: [Witness]

______________________ ______________________
name: [Witness]

19. ACCEPTANCE

The preceding offer or counter offer is hereby accepted by the

________________ on the terms and conditions set out herein
.
[Buyer *or* Seller]

Signed, sealed and delivered at the time of

____________ on ______________________________________
[time – a.m. *or* p.m.] [date]

in ______________________________________, Alberta
[jurisdiction]]

______________________ ______________________
name: [Witness]

______________________ ______________________
name: [Witness]

INITIALS			

Saskatchewan

Form of Agreement of Purchase & Sale (Blank – 8.5" x 11")
Form of Agreement of Purchase & Sale (Blank – 8.5" x 14" reduced)

This form of Agreement is customarily presented on legal size paper (8.5" x 14".) While paper size does not affect the validity of the document, using legal size will put it in a more recognized format. A reduced version of the legal size form has been provided. It can be increased on most industrial photocopiers using the "enlarge" function from standard to legal size (121% increase.) Legal size paper is available at most stationers.

RESIDENTIAL CONTRACT OF PURCHASE AND SALE

For use in the Province of Saskatchewan

I / We____ the "Buyer" *[address]*

Business Phone: __________
Residence Phone: __________
Fax: __________

HEREBY OFFERS TO BUY

From ____ the "Seller" *[address]*

Business Phone: __________
Residence Phone: __________
Fax: __________

The property legally described as____

And municipally described as ____
(the "Property")

For the purchase price of ______________________________ dollars (CDN); $ ______________

To be paid in the following manner:

a) $ ____________ Deposit by cash or cheque, payable to ____________________, within ______ days after acceptance, to be held in trust pending completion or other termination of this Agreement, and to be credited towards the purchase price on closing.
b) $ ____________ New mortgage(s) on terms set out below and/or as may be set out in attached schedule
c) $ ____________ Assumed mortgage(s) on terms set out in attached schedule
d) $ ____________Other
e) $ ____________ Balance due on closing, subject to adjustments as provided for herein, by cash, lawyer's trust cheque or certified cheque drawn on a Canadian chartered bank, trust company or credit union, payable to the Seller or Seller's lawyer, in trust, or as may be redirected by them.

1. This offer is conditional upon the following *[complete as applicable or stroke out]*:
   a) The buyer shall, at the buyer's sole expense, use every reasonable effort to obtain approval of new mortgage financing on or before ____________ at the rate and on the terms as follows: ____.
   b) ____

2. The following schedules are attached hereto and shall form an integral part of this Agreement:____________________.

3. If any portion of the purchase price is not paid on the Closing Date (not including any assumed mortgage(s))pursuant to usual conveyancing practices, the Buyer shall pay the Seller interest at a rate of ________ % per annum on the amount so outstanding from the possession date up to and including the date of subsequent payment.

4. This transaction shall be completed on ____________________ (the "Closing Date"), at or before 12:00 p.m. (noon), at which time the Seller shall deliver vacant possession of the Property unless otherwise provided for herein

5. Except as otherwise provided for herein, title to the Property shall be conveyed free and clear of any mortgages, liens or encumbrances, save and except the reservations and exceptions appearing in the existing Certificate of Title.

6. The balance due on closing shall be subject to the usual adjustments as of the Closing Date for taxes and other incoming and outgoing amounts relating to the property.

7. a. The following items (chattels) are included: ______________________________ . These chattels shall remain with the property on closing, and the Seller warrants that they shall be free of any encumbrances or liens, and shall be in the same good working order and condition as they were at the time this Agreement was signed.
   b. All items attached to the property (fixtures) are included in the purchase price and shall remain with the property on closing, save and except the following fixtures which are not included:____________________.
   c. The following items are rented or leased, and the Buyer agrees to assume the rental contracts or leases in connection with same:______________.

8. The parties agree to execute all usual and reasonable documents required to complete this transaction. The Seller shall be responsible for the preparation of the Transfer of Title, and the Seller shall discharge all existing mortgages or encumbrances at the Seller's expense. The Buyer shall be responsible for the cost of registering the Transfer of Title under the *Land Titles Act*, and the Buyer shall be responsible for all costs associated with arranging and registering financing. Otherwise, each party shall bear their own costs, and the cost of any Agreement for Sale shall be borne equally by the Parties.

9. In the event that this offer or any counter-offer is not accepted, or in the event that any condition is not fulfilled or performed after the responsible party has made every reasonable effort to fulfill or perform same, then this Agreement shall be null and void and the deposit shall be returned to the Buyer without interest penalty or deduction. In the event that the Buyer defaults on the completion of this Agreement pursuant to its terms, the Buyer will forfeit the above deposit in addition to any other claims the Seller may have against the Buyer.

10. The Property and all fixtures and chattels contemplated under this Agreement shall remain at the risk of and insured by the Seller until closing. No insurance policies shall be transferred on closing unless otherwise provided herein.

11. The Seller warrants that the Seller is a resident of Canada as defined under the *Income Tax Act*, and the Seller shall furnish satisfactory evidence of same on closing.

12. Upon acceptance this Agreement shall constitute a binding agreement of purchase and sale. This document, together with all listed Schedules, constitutes the entire Agreement between the parties and there shall be no collateral agreements, representations or warranties. This Agreement may only be amended or extended by mutual, written agreement between the parties, or between their lawyers, if any. Time shall be of the essence throughout this offer and Agreement, including any extensions. This Agreement shall pass to the benefit of and be binding upon each of the parties' heirs, executors, administrators, successors and assigns. In the event of a discrepancy between the Schedules or added clauses in this Agreement and the pre-formatted form of Agreement, the Schedules or added clauses shall prevail to the extent of the discrepancy. Any references to gender or number of parties shall be read with the intended context applied. In the event that any specific provisions of this Agreement are declared illegal, invalid or unenforceable by a court of competent jurisdiction, then the offending provision(s) may be severed and shall not impair the validity or enforceability of the balance of the Agreement. This Agreement shall be interpreted and enforced in accordance with the laws of the Province of Saskatchewan.

13. Each of the parties acknowledges having received a copy of this Agreement and having been advised to seek independent legal advice prior to signing. Each of the parties further acknowledges that they have either obtained such independent legal advice, or have declined to seek such advice and have otherwise entered into this Agreement with the knowledge that it creates firm and binding legal relations and in full comprehension of the terms and consequences set out herein. Notwithstanding the source of this document, the doctrine of "Contra Preferentem" shall not apply and the Agreement shall be interpreted and construed equally among the parties.

14. Unless revoked sooner, this offer shall be open for acceptance by the seller until ____________ *[a.m. or p.m.]* on ____.

OFFER:

SIGNED, SEALED AND DELIVERED at ______________________________ on ______________________________, and in the presence of:

[place] *[date]*

______________________________ ______________________________

[Witness] *[Buyer]*

______________________________ ______________________________

[Witness] *[Buyer]*

ACCEPTANCE: This offer is hereby accepted on the terms and conditions set out herein.

SIGNED, SEALED AND DELIVERED at ______________________________ on ______________________________, and in the presence of:

[place] *[date]*

______________________________ ______________________________

[Witness] *[Seller]*

______________________________ ______________________________

[Witness] *[Seller]*

Buyer's Lawyer:______________________________ Seller's Lawyer: ______________________________

RESIDENTIAL CONTRACT OF PURCHASE AND SALE

For use in the Province of Saskatchewan

I / We ______________________________ [address] Business Phone: ______ Residence Phone: ______ Fax: ______
the "Buyer"

HEREBY OFFERS TO BUY

From ______________________________ [address] Business Phone: ______ Residence Phone: ______ Fax: ______
the "Seller"

The property legally described as ______________________________

And municipally described as ______________________________ (the "Property")

For the purchase price of ______________________________ dollars (CDN); $ ____________

To be paid in the following manner:

a) $ ____________ Deposit by cash or cheque, payable to ____________, within ______ days after acceptance, to be held in trust pending completion or other termination of this Agreement, and to be credited towards the purchase price on closing.

b) $ ____________ New mortgage(s) on terms set out below and/or as may be set out in attached schedule

c) $ ____________ Assumed mortgage(s) on terms set out in attached schedule

d) $ ____________ Other

e) $ ____________ Balance due on closing, subject to adjustments as provided for herein, by cash, lawyer's trust cheque or certified cheque drawn on a Canadian chartered bank, trust company or credit union, payable to the Seller or Seller's lawyer, in trust, or as may be redirected by them.

1. This offer is conditional upon the following *[complete as applicable or stroke out]*:
   a) The buyer shall, at the buyer's sole expense, use every reasonable effort to obtain approval of new mortgage financing on or before ____________ at the rate and on the terms as follows: ______________________________
   b) ______________________________
2. The following schedules are attached hereto and shall form an integral part of this Agreement: ____________.
3. If any portion of the purchase price is not paid on the Closing Date (not including any assumed mortgage(s))pursuant to usual conveyancing practices, the Buyer shall pay the Seller interest at a rate of ______ % per annum on the amount so outstanding from the possession date up to and including the date of subsequent payment.
4. This transaction shall be completed on ____________ (the "Closing Date"), at or before 12:00 p.m. (noon), at which time the Seller shall deliver vacant possession of the Property unless otherwise provided for herein
5. Except as otherwise provided for herein, title to the Property shall be conveyed free and clear of any mortgages, liens or encumbrances, save and except the reservations and exceptions appearing in the existing Certificate of Title.
6. The balance due on closing shall be subject to the usual adjustments as of the Closing Date for taxes and other incoming and outgoing amounts relating to the property.
7. a. The following items (chattels) are included: ____________. These chattels shall remain with the property on closing, and the Seller warrants that they shall be free of any encumbrances or liens, and shall be in the same good working order and condition as they were at the time this Agreement was signed.
   b. All items attached to the property (fixtures) are included in the purchase price and shall remain with the property on closing, save and except the following fixtures which are not included: ____________.
   c. The following items are rented or leased, and the Buyer agrees to assume the rental contracts or leases in connection with same: ____________.
8. The parties agree to execute all usual and reasonable documents required to complete this transaction. The Seller shall be responsible for the preparation of the Transfer of Title, and the Seller shall discharge all existing mortgages or encumbrances at the Seller's expense. The Buyer shall be responsible for the cost of registering the Transfer of Title under the *Land Titles Act*, and the Buyer shall be responsible for all costs associated with arranging and registering financing. Otherwise, each party shall bear their own costs, and the cost of any Agreement for Sale shall be borne equally by the Parties.
9. In the event that this offer or any counter-offer is not accepted, or in the event that any condition is not fulfilled or performed after the responsible party has made every reasonable effort to fulfill or perform same, then this Agreement shall be null and void and the deposit shall be returned to the Buyer without interest penalty or deduction. In the event that the Buyer defaults on the completion of this Agreement pursuant to its terms, the Buyer will forfeit the above deposit in addition to any other claims the Seller may have against the Buyer.
10. The Property and all fixtures and chattels contemplated under this Agreement shall remain at the risk of and insured by the Seller until closing. No insurance policies shall be transferred on closing unless otherwise provided herein.
11. The Seller warrants that the Seller is a resident of Canada as defined under the *Income Tax Act*, and the Seller shall furnish satisfactory evidence of same on closing.
12. Upon acceptance this Agreement shall constitute a binding agreement of purchase and sale. This document, together with all listed Schedules, constitutes the entire Agreement between the parties and there shall be no collateral agreements, representations or warranties. This Agreement may only be amended or extended by mutual, written agreement between the parties, or between their lawyers, if any. Time shall be of the essence throughout this offer and Agreement, including any extensions. This Agreement shall pass to the benefit of and be binding upon each of the parties' heirs, executors, administrators, successors and assigns. In the event of a discrepancy between the Schedules or added clauses in this Agreement and the pre-formatted form of Agreement, the Schedules or added clauses shall prevail to the extent of the discrepancy. Any references to gender or number of parties shall be read with the intended context applied. In the event that any specific provisions of this Agreement are declared illegal, invalid or unenforceable by a court of competent jurisdiction, then the offending provision(s) may be severed and shall not impair the validity or enforceability of the balance of the Agreement. This Agreement shall be interpreted and enforced in accordance with the laws of the Province of Saskatchewan.
13. Each of the parties acknowledges having received a copy of this Agreement and having been advised to seek independent legal advice prior to signing. Each of the parties further acknowledges that they have either obtained such independent legal advice, or have declined to seek such advice and have otherwise entered into this Agreement with the knowledge that it creates firm and binding legal relations and in full comprehension of the terms and consequences set out herein. Notwithstanding the source of this document, the doctrine of "Contra Preferentem" shall not apply and the Agreement shall be interpreted and construed equally among the parties.
14. Unless revoked sooner, this offer shall be open for acceptance by the seller until ________ *[a.m. or p.m.]* on ____________.

OFFER:

SIGNED, SEALED AND DELIVERED at ____________ [place] on ____________ [date], and in the presence of:

____________ [Witness] ____________ [Buyer]

____________ [Witness] ____________ [Buyer]

ACCEPTANCE: This offer is hereby accepted on the terms and conditions set out herein.

SIGNED, SEALED AND DELIVERED at ____________ [place] on ____________ [date], and in the presence of:

____________ [Witness] ____________ [Seller]

____________ [Witness] ____________ [Seller]

Buyer's Lawyer: ____________ Seller's Lawyer: ____________

Manitoba

Form of Agreement of Purchase & Sale (Blank)

CONTRACT
OF PURCHASE AND SALE (FOR USE IN MANITOBA)

To ____ (herein the "Vendor")

Vendor's Address for service ____
Phone ________________ Fax ________________

I / We ____ (herein the "Purchaser")

Purchaser's address for service ____
Phone ________________ Fax ________________

Hereby offers to purchase the Property set out below on the terms and conditions set out below:

SUBJECT PROPERTY

1. (a) The Property that is the subject matter of this Agreement is the land described as follows together with all structures and improvements thereon:

____
[civic address or legal description]

____ (herein the "Property")
[... continued]

(b) The Property shall include all items affixed to the Property (fixtures), including without limitation all of the following: light fixtures, HVAC and plumbing fixtures, built-in vacuum, fitted carpets, fixed shelves and mirrors, window dressing hardware such as curtain rods and drapery tracks, screens and storm windows and doors, imbedded plants and shrubs, fountains, T.V antennae or dishes, fixed basketball nets, and the like as are now on the Property; however the following fixtures are expressly excluded:

____

____

(c) All items not affixed to the Property (chattels) which are not fixtures shall be excluded; however the following chattels are expressly included:

____

____

(d) The following items are rented and are not included, and if assumable the Purchaser agrees to assume the rental contracts as of the Possession Date:

____

____

PURCHASE PRICE AND PAYMENT TERMS

2. (a) The Purchase Price to be paid on the Possession Date is $ ________________________________ (herein the "Purchase Price")

(b) The Purchase Price shall be arranged and paid on the following terms:

(i) Initial deposit
❐ presented with this offer
❐ to be provided within 48 hours after acceptance $ ______________

(ii) Additional deposit to be provided on or upon

____ $ ______________
[date or satisfaction of condition]

(iii) Proceeds of new mortgage(s)
❐ for which Purchaser has prior approval
❐ to be arranged pursuant to financing condition herein $ ______________

(iv) Assumption of existing mortgage(s) having a total balance outstanding on the Possession Date of not more than approximately $ ____________ $ ______________
(Mortgage Assumption Schedule attached hereto)

(v) Mortgage back to Vendor in __________ priority $ ______________
(Vendor Take-Back Mortgage Schedule attached hereto)

(vi) Other: ____ $ ______________

(vii) Balance Due on Possession Date $ ______________

TOTAL PURCHASE PRICE: $ ______________

(c) If the Purchaser will be relying on the proceeds of a new mortgage to satisfy part of the Purchase Price, payment of that amount may be postponed for such time as the Purchaser reasonably requires to register the mortgage at the Land Titles Office and to report same and obtain the proceeds from the mortgage lender. In such event the amount so outstanding shall bear interest at the same rate set out in the proposed new mortgage payable to the Vendor immediately upon and until the date of subsequent payment. Payment tendered on any day after 12:00 p.m. (noon) shall be deemed paid on the following business day. The Vendor shall have a lien on the Property for the unpaid portion of the Purchase Price as contemplated in this section, and the lien shall also have the benefit of interest as set out in this section.

(d) The Deposit(s) shall be made by cash or personal cheque payable to ____________________. The Deposit(s) shall be held in trust for the benefit of the Vendor and the Purchaser as their respective interests appear herein. The Deposit(s) shall be subsequently:

i. applied towards the Purchaser Price as set out in this section,

ii. returned to the Purchaser in the event that this offer or any counter offer is not accepted, or the transaction does not close due to any conditions not being satisfied or default on the part of the Vendor, or,

iii. forfeited to the Vendor in the event that the transaction does not close due to default on the part of the Purchaser.

(e) The Balance Due on the Possession Date shall be payable only by Lawyer's trust cheque, certified cheque or bank draft drawn on a Canadian chartered bank, trust company or credit union, or through such consideration as may be otherwise agreed upon in writing.

POSSESSION

3. (a) The Vendor shall provide possession of the Property at or before ____________ on ______________________________ (the "Possession Date")
[time – a.m. or p.m.] *[date]*

(b) On the Possession Date the property shall be vacant, unless otherwise provided for herein. Any chattels expressly included in this Agreement shall be left on the Property, and all other items, including those fixtures expressly excluded, shall be removed from the Property.

(c) Notwithstanding the foregoing, by acknowledging below, the Purchaser agrees to assume the existing tenancy(s) in connection with the Property (Tenancy Schedule attached hereto)

❒ Tenancy: ______________________________

TITLE

4. (a) Title to the Property, including all fixtures and chattels contemplated in this Agreement, shall be free and clear of all liens, mortgages, encumbrances or claims, whether registered or valid though unregistered, save and except any of the following:

i. Private or public restrictions, agreements or caveats relating to the buildings, structures or use of the Property, provided they have been complied with,

ii. Public utility easements or rights-of-way for services that supply the Property (and perhaps other properties),

iii. Easements, provided they were readily apparent at the time this initial offer was made,

iv. Existing mortgage(s) that is/are the responsibility of the Vendor to vacate and discharge, provided the requirements of section 2 have been met,

v. Matters which have been caused by, or are the responsibility of, the Purchaser, or

vi. Other liens, mortgages, encumbrances, claims or registrations listed as follows, or otherwise expressly agreed to herein:

____

(b) The Vendor shall, or shall have the right to, be in and convey personal and peaceable possession and occupation of the Property on the Possession Date, unless otherwise agreed to herein.

PROPERTY CONDITION

5. (a) On the Possession Date, the Property and all fixtures and included chattels shall be in substantially the same condition as they were in at the time this initial offer was made.

(b) The building(s), structures or improvements on the Property are located wholly within the lot lines of the Property.

(c) The building(s), structures or improvements on the Property do not illegally or without permission encroach onto any easements or rights-of-way located on the Property.

(d) The building(s), structures or improvements on any adjoining properties do not encroach onto the subject Property.

(e) Notwithstanding the foregoing, the Purchaser acknowledges and accepts the following encroachments and/or building or zoning non-compliance matters:

____

CONDITIONS

6. (a) This Agreement shall be conditional upon the following:

(i) Conditions for the benefit of the Purchaser *[check if applicable – stroke out provision entirely if not applicable]*

❒ 1. Financing

The Purchaser obtaining written approval of mortgage financing as set out in section 2.

This condition must be satisfied on or before __________ on __________________________,
[time – a.m. or p.m.] *[date]*

❒ 2. Lawyer Approval

Review and approval of the terms and content of this Agreement by the Purchaser's lawyer.

This condition must be satisfied on or before __________ on __________________________,
[time – a.m. or p.m.] *[date]*

❒ 3. Other

____

____

This condition must be satisfied on or before __________ on __________________________,
[time – a.m. or p.m.] *[date]*

(ii) Conditions for the benefit of the Vendor *[check if applicable – stroke out provision entirely if not applicable]*

❒ 1. Lawyer Approval

Review and approval of the terms and content of this Agreement by the Purchaser's lawyer.

This condition must be satisfied on or before __________ on __________________________,
[time – a.m. or p.m.] *[date]*

❒ 2. Other

____

____

This condition must be satisfied on or before __________ on ________________________,
[time – a.m. or p.m.] *[date]*

(b) Unless all of the foregoing conditions are satisfied, this agreement shall be null and void. A condition shall be deemed satisfied if, and only if, on or before the time specified, the party for whose benefit the condition exists delivers notice in writing to the other party that the condition has been satisfied or otherwise waived.

(c) The parties shall act in good faith and use reasonable efforts in fulfilling their conditions.

(d) Unless stated otherwise, each condition shall be for the sole and exclusive benefit of the party so stated, and may be waived by that party at their sole option.

GENERAL TERMS

7. (a) GST

The Vendor warrants that this transaction is not subject to Federal Goods and Services Tax [GST], and the Vendor shall furnish a certificate confirming same on closing.

(b) Closing Adjustments

The Balance Due on the Possession Date shall be subject to the usual adjustments, including, without limitation, taxes and any improvement levies for the current year. The Possession Date itself shall be the responsibility of the Purchaser.

(c) Risk & Insurance

The Property and all fixtures and chattels contemplated under this Agreement shall remain at the risk of the Vendor until closing. In the event of substantial damage to the Property, which the Vendor, acting in good faith, is unable or unwilling to put back into the same condition it was in prior to the damage, then this Agreement shall be null and void in the same manner as if a condition had been established as unsatisfied. No insurance policies shall be transferred on closing.

(d) Remedies

In addition to the agreed upon terms surrounding the deposit(s) set out in section 2, in the event of default by either party (herein the "Aggrieved Party) against the other party (herein the "Defaulting Party"), the Aggrieved Party shall have the benefit of any additional remedies available in law, and retainer or return of the deposit alone shall not constitute termination of this Agreement.

(e) Lawyers' Trust Conditions

The Vendor and Purchaser hereby agree and authorize their respective lawyers to enter into agreements whereby they impose and undertake certain trust conditions to fulfill the letter and intent of this Agreement, provided that the contractual obligations of the parties otherwise remain intact.

(f) Time

Time shall be of the essence throughout this Agreement. All times stated shall be deemed to be Manitoba time zone.

(g) Succession

This Agreement shall pass to the benefit of and be binding upon each of the party's successors, assigns and personal representatives.

(h) Enforceability, Entirety and Interpretation

Upon acceptance, **THIS AGREEMENT SHALL CONSTITUTE A BINDING AGREEMENT OF PURCHASE AND SALE. IT SHOULD BE READ IN ITS ENTIRETY!** This document, together with all listed Schedules, constitutes the entire Agreement between the parties and there shall be no collateral agreements, representations or warranties. This Agreement may only be amended by mutual, written agreement between the parties, or between their lawyers, if any, as set out herein or as may be have been reasonably established through the course of this transaction. Any references to gender or number of parties shall be read with the intended context applied. In the event that any specific provisions of this Agreement are declared illegal, invalid or unenforceable by a court of competent jurisdiction, then the offending provision(s) may be severed and shall not impair the validity or enforceability of the balance of the Agreement. Any representations or promises made by the Vendor shall survive closing only if expressly provided herein or if required by law. This Agreement shall be interpreted and enforced in accordance with the laws of the Province of Manitoba.

(i) Legal Representation

Each of the parties acknowledges having received a copy of this Agreement and having been advised to seek independent legal advice prior to signing. Each of the parties further acknowledges that they have either obtained such independent legal advice, or have declined to seek such advice and have otherwise entered into this Agreement with the knowledge that it creates firm and binding legal relations and in full comprehension of the terms and consequences set out herein. Notwithstanding the source of this document, the doctrine of "Contra Preferentem" shall not apply and the Agreement shall be interpreted and construed equally among the parties.

The Purchaser's lawyer, if any, is:

____

[name & address of lawyer]

Phone ________________ Fax ________________

The Vendor's lawyer, if any, is:

____

[name & address of lawyer]

Phone ________________ Fax ________________

(j) Notice

Any notice required under this Agreement shall be deemed effective if delivered to the receiving party or their respective lawyers, if any, as set out herein or as may be or have been reasonably established through the course of this transaction, by one of the following methods:

i. by personal delivery to the addresses of the parties noted herein,

ii. by registered mail to the addresses of the parties noted herein (in which case receipt shall be deemed to be three days after mailing),

iii. by fax to the fax numbers noted by the parties herein, if any.

(k) Tender

Any monies, keys, documents or other items required to be delivered pursuant to this Agreement may be or tendered by delivery of same to the respective lawyers, if any, as set out herein or as may be or have been reasonably established through the course of this transaction, or failing which upon the parties themselves.

(l) Schedules

The following Schedules are attached hereto and shall form an integral part of this Agreement

A. Homesteads Act Declaration　　　C. ______________________

B. ______________________　　　D. ______________________

In the event of a discrepancy between the Schedules or added clauses in this Agreement and the pre-formatted form of Agreement, the Schedules or added clauses shall prevail to the extent of the discrepancy.

ADDITIONAL TERMS

8. ____

____

____

____

OFFER

9. This offer from the Purchaser shall be open for acceptance and irrevocable, but shall expire completely at the following time and date:

______________ on ______________________________.
[time – a.m. or p.m.]　　　*[date]*

Signed at ______________ on ______________________________.
[time – a.m. or p.m.]　　　*[date]*

______________________　　　______________________
[Witness]　　　*[Purchaser]*

______________________　　　______________________
[Witness]　　　*[Purchaser]*

ACCEPTANCE of OFFER - or COUNTER-OFFER

10. This offer is hereby *[check if applicable – stroke out alternate provision entirely]*:

❒ accepted by the Vendor on the terms set out herein

or

❒ The Vendor submits a counteroffer on the terms set out herein as amended and initialed and/or as follows:

____

____

____

____

This counteroffer from the Vendor shall be open for acceptance and irrevocable, but shall expire completely at the following time and date:

_______________ on ______________________________.
[time – a.m. or p.m.] *[date]*

Signed at _______________ on ______________________________.
[time – a.m. or p.m.] *[date]*

____________________ ____________________
[Witness] *[Vendor]*

____________________ ____________________
[Witness] *[Vendor]*

ACCEPTANCE of COUNTEROFFER

11. This counteroffer is hereby accepted by the Purchaser on the terms set out herein.

Signed at _______________ on ______________________________.
[time – a.m. or p.m.] *[date]*

____________________ ____________________
[Witness] *[Purchaser]*

____________________ ____________________
[Witness] *[Purchaser]*

Schedule A

HOMESTEADS ACT DECLARATION

I / We, the Vendor(s) in the attached offer and final Agreement of Purchase and Sale (the "Agreement") do solemnly, and severally, if applicable, declare *[delete and initial all inapplicable statements]*:

1. The person who has signed the acceptance to the offer from the Purchaser is my spouse.
2. The person who has consented to the disposition of the homestead provided for by this Agreement is my spouse.
3. I am not a married person.
4. The land being bought and sold under this Agreement is not my homestead within the meaning of *The Homesteads Act*.

(SEVERALLY) DECLARED before me at)
)
)
)
)
this _______ day of __________________ , ______)

____

Commissioner for Oaths, A Notary Public, etc.

Ontario

Form of Agreement of Purchase & Sale (Blank - 8.5" x 11")
Form of Agreement of Purchase & Sale (Blank - 8.5" x 14" reduced)

This form of Agreement is customarily presented on legal size paper (8.5" x 14".) While paper size does not affect the validity of the document, using legal size will put it in a more recognized format. A reduced version of the legal size form has been provided. It can be increased on most industrial photocopiers using the "enlarge" function from standard to legal size (121% increase.) Legal size paper is available at most stationers.

AGREEMENT OF PURCHASE AND SALE

(FOR USE IN ONTARIO)

BUYER: .... (the "Buyer") hereby agrees to buy from
[legal name of Buyer]

SELLER: .... (the "Seller") the real property
[legal name of Seller]

PROPERTY: municipally described as: ....
[full street address]

fronting on the .... side of ....
[east, west, north, south] [street name]

with a total frontage of .... more or less, by a depth of .... more or less
[feet *or* metres] [feet *or* metres]

and legally described as .... (the "Property").
[legal description]

PRICE: The agreed upon price is .... Dollars (Canadian); $..........................
[written] [numerical]
payable as follows:

DEPOSIT: a Deposit of .... Dollars (Canadian); $..........................
[written] [numerical]
payable .... to ....,
[upon acceptance *or* herewith] [person to whom deposit is payable]
and, unless otherwise provided herein, the Balance payable on closing by cash or certified cheque, payable to the Seller or Seller's lawyer, or as they may redirect, and subject to the usual adjustments.

SCHEDULES: The following Schedules are attached to and form an integral part of this Agreement: ....
[applicable Schedules, if any]

1. ITEMS INCLUDED / EXCLUDED
The following items (chattels) are included: ....

The following items (fixtures) are excluded: ....

The following items are rented and are not included, and if assumable the Purchaser agrees to assume the rental contracts: ....

2. IRREVOCABILITY
This offer to reach Agreement shall be open for acceptance and irrevocable by the......................... until .... on ....
[Buyer *or* Seller] [time – a.m. *or* p.m.] [date]
failing which this offer shall become null and void and the deposit shall be returned to the Buyer without interest, bonus or deduction.

3. **CLOSING/POSSESSION DATE:** This Agreement shall be completed on .... between 9:00 am and 6:00 pm (the "Closing Date")
[closing date]
On the Closing Date the Seller shall provide the Buyer with vacant possession of the Property, unless otherwise provided herein.

4. **GST:** The Buyer and Seller agree that this transaction is not subject to Federal Goods and Services Tax [GST], and the Seller shall furnish a certificate confirming same on closing.

5. **DUE DILIGENCE:** The Buyer shall have until .... on .... (Requisition Date)
[time – a.m. *or* p.m.] [date]
to investigate title to the Property, and until the earlier of:

A) 30 days from the later of
(i) the Requisition Date, or (ii) the date on which any conditions of this Agreement are communicated as fulfilled or otherwise waived, or

B) 5 days before the Closing Date,

to satisfy him/herself(s) that the Property can be lawfully used for the purposes of ....,
[legally authorized use]
that there are no outstanding work orders, on-record violations or deficiency notices affecting the Property, and that the principle building(s) may be insured against risk of fire and other usual property casualties. Title to the Property shall be clear of any defects, liens, charges, registered restrictions or encumbrances, provided that title matters expressly allowed for and contemplated as acceptable shall include: A) registered restrictions or covenants that run with the land provided they are complied with, B) registered agreements with municipal authorities or public utilities, provided they are complied with or funds have been posted to secure compliance and the completion of same, C) minor easements for the supply of domestic utility, telephone or cable service to the Property or adjoining properties, D) easements for utility, telephone or cable lines, drainage, storm or sanitary sewers, or other services which do not have any material adverse affect on the use of the Property as contemplated herein, and E) any matters expressly allowed for elsewhere in this Agreement. If the Buyer makes a valid objection in writing to the matters contemplated in this section within the specified time periods, and if the Seller is unable or unwilling to remedy or satisfy the objection, and if the Buyer is then unwilling to waive the objection, then this Agreement shall be at an end and the deposit shall be returned to the Buyer without interest, bonus or deduction and without any further obligation for costs or damages between the parties. If the Buyer does not make a valid objection in writing within the specified time periods, or within any overriding limitation periods that may be otherwise prescribed by law, then the Buyer shall be deemed to have conclusively accepted the status of the Seller's title to the Property. All investigations shall be at the Buyer's own expense. Acceptance of this offer shall constitute the Seller's consent to the release of information by municipal, governmental or quasi governmental authorities concerning the legal status of the Property, and Seller agrees to provide such further written authorizations as may be reasonably required to give effect to the intent of this provision.

6. **CLOSING DETAILS:** If this transaction is to be completed by electronic registration, it is agreed that the exchange of closing funds, keys and ancillary documents or items shall be subject to the following: A) the exchange will not occur simultaneously with the registration of Deeds, Mortgages or other contemplated registered documentation, and B) the exchange will be governed by the terms of a Document Registration Agreement (DRA) between the lawyers retained by the parties, and the DRA shall provide that all deliveries shall be held in trust by the receiving lawyer and not released until all other terms of the DRA have been met. The exchange will occur at the applicable Land Registry Office, unless otherwise agreed.

7. **DISCLOSURE AND PRODUCTION OF DOCUMENTS:** In the event that the Seller is in possession or control of any deed, survey or other evidence of title, then, upon request, the Seller shall deliver such documentation to the Buyer as soon as possible and in any event prior to the Requisition Date.

8. **PREPARATION OF DOCUMENTS:** The Transfer/Deed shall be prepared in registrable form at the expense of the Seller. The Buyer shall be responsible for the Land Transfer Tax Affidavit and any ancillary documents that may be required pursuant to this Agreement, unless the Seller is expressly required to provide otherwise. If requested, the Seller agrees to execute statements on the Transfer/Deed relating to subdivision compliance pursuant to Section 50(22) of *The Planning Act, R.S.O. 1990*, and the Seller agrees to instruct his/her solicitor to execute such statements.

9. **DISCHARGE OF MORTGAGES:** In the event that the Seller will be discharging a mortgage or mortgages in favour of a Chartered Bank, Trust Company, Credit Union, Caisse Populaire, Insurance Company or a corporation under *The Trust And Loan Companies Act (Canada)*, then the Buyer shall be obligated to accept the Seller's lawyer's Undertaking, in a form acceptable to the Buyer's lawyer, to obtain and register a discharge within a reasonable period of time following the Closing Date, provided that the Seller shall also furnish the Buyer's lawyer with a copy of a Mortgage Discharge Statement from the mortgagee which sets out the balance required to discharge the mortgage as of the Closing Date, and the Seller shall execute a Direction instructing his/her lawyer to pay the closing proceeds in the required manner.

10. **INSPECTION:** The Buyer acknowledges having inspected the Property and the parties agree that the Property shall be delivered in the same condition as existed at the time of inspection.

11. **INSURANCE:** The Property and all fixtures and chattels contemplated under this Agreement shall remain at the risk of the Seller until the Closing Date. All related insurance policies held by the Seller, if any, as well as any proceeds paid under such policies, shall be held in trust for the benefit of the parties in relation to their respective interests under this Agreement. In the event of damage and subsequent payment under such policies the Buyer shall have the option of terminating this Agreement or receiving the said payment and closing the transaction as scheduled with all other terms and conditions remaining the same. In the event that the Agreement is terminated pursuant to this section the deposit shall be returned to the Buyer without interest, bonus or deduction. No insurance policies shall be transferred on closing.

12. **PLANNING ACT COMPLIANCE:** The Seller shall be obligated to obtain all consents and take all steps necessary to complete this transaction in compliance with *The Planning Act, R.S.O. 1990*. Such efforts, if necessary, shall be at the sole expense of the Vendor. In the event that such efforts are unsuccessful, this Agreement shall be at an end and the deposit shall be returned to the Buyer without interest, bonus or deduction.

13. **RESIDENCY STATUS:** On closing the Seller shall furnish a certificate confirming that the Seller is not a "non-resident" within the meaning of the *Income Tax Act*, failing which the Buyer shall be entitled to hold back funds in accordance with prudent legal practice sufficient to satisfy the Buyer's obligations under the Act.

14. **FAMILY LAW STATUS:** The Seller warrants that he/she is not a spouse and that no spousal consent is necessary to give full effect to this Agreement, or alternatively that the person executing the necessary consent below is the Seller's spouse.

15. **CLOSING ADJUSTMENTS:** The amount due on closing shall be adjusted and apportioned between the parties to reflect their obligations as of the Closing Date for the following items, as may be applicable: realty taxes, local improvement rates, unmetered utility charges and unmetered fuel costs. These amounts as they relate to the Closing Date itself shall be the responsibility of the Buyer.

16. **TIME CONSTRAINTS:** Time shall be of the essence throughout this Agreement. The Closing Date and any other deadlines may only be extended or amended by agreement in writing.

17. **TENDER:** Any tender of documents, keys or money may be made upon the Buyer or Seller, as the case may be, or their lawyers, if any, on or before the time specified on the Closing Date. Tender shall be validly effected if delivered personally upon the Buyer or Seller, as the case may be, or upon their respective lawyers, if any. Money tendered must be in the form of bank draft or certified cheque issued by a Chartered Bank, Trust Company, Credit Union, Caisse Populaire or Province of Ontario Savings Office.

18. **UFFI:** The Seller warrants that he/she has not caused or allowed any buildings on the Property to be insulated with ureaformaldehyde, and further that, to the best of the Seller's knowledge, none of the buildings on the Property have been insulated with ureaformaldehyde. This warranty shall survive and not merge on closing.
19. **NOTICE:** Offer, acceptance or any notice or communication required under this Agreement shall be deemed delivered and received if given in writing by any of the following methods: 1) by personal delivery to the addresses of the parties noted herein, 2) by registered mail to the addresses of the parties noted herein (in which case receipt shall be deemed to be three days after mailing), 3) by fax to the fax numbers noted by the parties herein, if any, or 4) by delivery or fax to either party's lawyer, if any, as noted herein or as otherwise reasonably established.
20. **SUCCESSORS AND ASSIGNS:** This Agreement shall pass to the benefit of and be binding upon each of the Parties' successors and assigns.
21. **ENFORCABILITY, ENTIRETY AND INTERPRETATION OF AGREEMENT:** Upon acceptance this Agreement shall constitute a binding agreement of purchase and sale. This document, together with all listed Schedules, constitutes the entire Agreement between the parties and there shall be no collateral agreements, representations or warranties. This Agreement may only be amended by mutual, written agreement between the parties, or between their lawyers, if any, as such lawyers may be noted herein or as otherwise reasonably established. In the event of a discrepancy between the Schedules or added clauses in this Agreement and the pre-formatted form of Agreement, the Schedules or added clauses shall prevail to the extent of the discrepancy. Any references to gender or number of parties shall be read with the intended context applied. In the event that any specific provisions of this Agreement are declared illegal, invalid or unenforceable by a court of competent jurisdiction, then the offending provision(s) may be severed and shall not impair the validity or enforceability of the balance of the Agreement. This Agreement shall be interpreted and enforced in accordance with the laws of the Province of Ontario.
22. **LEGAL REPRESENTATION:** Each of the parties acknowledges having received a copy of this Agreement and having been advised to seek independent legal advice prior to signing. Each of the parties further acknowledges that they have either obtained such independent legal advice, or have declined to seek such advice and have otherwise entered into this Agreement with the knowledge that it creates firm and binding legal relations and in full comprehension of the terms and consequences set out herein. Notwithstanding the source of this document, the doctrine of "Contra Preferentem" shall not apply and the Agreement shall be interpreted and construed equally among the parties.

Dated: ....

Signed sealed and delivered in the presence of: Signed sealed and delivered by:

.... [Witness]	.... [Buyer]	● [Seal]	Date: ....
.... [Witness]	.... [Buyer]	● [Seal]	Date: ....

Dated: ....

Signed sealed and delivered in the presence of: Signed sealed and delivered by:

.... [Witness]	.... [Seller]	● [Seal]	Date: ....
.... [Witness]	.... [Seller]	● [Seal]	Date: ....

SPOUSAL CONSENT: The person signing below is the spouse of the Seller and hereby consents to this transaction pursuant to *The Family Law Act, R.S.O. 1990*, and further agrees with the Buyer to execute any further assurances necessary to complete this transaction.

.... [Witness]	.... [Consenting Spouse]	● [Seal]	Date: ....

NOTICE

The Buyer's address for service is:	The Seller's address for service is:
Address:	Address: ....
Phone:	Phone: ....
Fax:	Fax: ....

LEGAL REPRESENTATION

The Buyer's solicitor, if any, until further notification, is:	The Seller's solicitor, if any, until further notification, is:
Name:	Name: ....
Address:	Address: ....
Phone:	Phone: ....
Fax:	Fax: ....

AGREEMENT OF PURCHASE AND SALE

(FOR USE IN ONTARIO)

BUYER: .... (the "Buyer") hereby agrees to buy from
[legal name of Buyer]

SELLER: .... (the "Seller") the real property
[legal name of Seller]

PROPERTY: municipally described as: ....
[full street address]

fronting on the .... side of ....
[east, west, north, south] [street name]

with a total frontage of .... more or less, by a depth of .... more or less
[feet or metres] [feet or metres]

and legally described as .... (the "Property").
[legal description]

PRICE: The agreed upon price is .... Dollars (Canadian); $..........................
[written] [numerical]

payable as follows:

DEPOSIT: a Deposit of .... Dollars (Canadian); $..........................
[written] [numerical]

payable .... to ....,
[upon acceptance or herewith] [person to whom deposit is payable]

and, unless otherwise provided herein, the Balance payable on closing by cash or certified cheque, payable to the Seller or Seller's lawyer, or as they may redirect, and subject to the usual adjustments.

SCHEDULES: The following Schedules are attached to and form an integral part of this Agreement: ....
[applicable Schedules, if any]

1. **ITEMS INCLUDED / EXCLUDED**

The following items (chattels) are included: ....

The following items (fixtures) are excluded: ....

The following items are rented and are not included, and if assumable the Purchaser agrees to assume the rental contracts: ....

2. **IRREVOCABILITY**

This offer to reach Agreement shall be open for acceptance and irrevocable by the......................... until .... on ....
[Buyer or Seller] [time – a.m. or p.m.] [date]

failing which this offer shall become null and void and the deposit shall be returned to the Buyer without interest, bonus or deduction.

3. **CLOSING/POSSESSION DATE:** This Agreement shall be completed on .... between 9:00 am and 6:00 pm (the "Closing Date")
[closing date]

On the Closing Date the Seller shall provide the Buyer with vacant possession of the Property, unless otherwise provided herein.

4. **GST:** The Buyer and Seller agree that this transaction is not subject to Federal Goods and Services Tax [GST], and the Seller shall furnish a certificate confirming same on closing.

5. **DUE DILIGENCE:** The Buyer shall have until .... on .... (Requisition Date)
[time – a.m. or p.m.] [date]

to investigate title to the Property, and until the earlier of:

A) 30 days from the later of
(i) the Requisition Date, or (ii) the date on which any conditions of this Agreement are communicated as fulfilled or otherwise waived, or

B) 5 days before the Closing Date,

to satisfy him/herself(s) that the Property can be lawfully used for the purposes of ....,
[legally authorized use]

that there are no outstanding work orders, on-record violations or deficiency notices affecting the Property, and that the principle building(s) may be insured against risk of fire and other usual property casualties. Title to the Property shall be clear of any defects, liens, charges, registered restrictions or encumbrances, provided that title matters expressly allowed for and contemplated as acceptable shall include: A) registered restrictions or covenants that run with the land provided they are complied with, B) registered agreements with municipal authorities or public utilities, provided they are complied with or funds have been posted to secure compliance and the completion of same, C) minor easements for the supply of domestic utility, telephone or cable service to the Property or adjoining properties, D) easements for utility, telephone or cable lines, drainage, storm or sanitary sewers, or other services which do not have any material adverse affect on the use of the Property as contemplated herein, and E) any matters expressly allowed for elsewhere in this Agreement. If the Buyer makes a valid objection in writing to the matters contemplated in this section within the specified time periods, and if the Seller is unable or unwilling to remedy or satisfy the objection, and if the Buyer is then unwilling to waive the objection, then this Agreement shall be at an end and the deposit shall be returned to the Buyer without interest, bonus or deduction and without any further obligation for costs or damages between the parties. If the Buyer does not make a valid objection in writing within the specified time periods, or within any overriding limitation periods that may be otherwise prescribed by law, then the Buyer shall be deemed to have conclusively accepted the status of the Seller's title to the Property. All investigations shall be at the Buyer's own expense. Acceptance of this offer shall constitute the Seller's consent to the release of information by municipal, governmental or quasi governmental authorities concerning the legal status of the Property, and Seller agrees to provide such further written authorizations as may be reasonably required to give effect to the intent of this provision.

6. **CLOSING DETAILS:** If this transaction is to be completed by electronic registration, it is agreed that the exchange of closing funds, keys and ancillary documents or items shall be subject to the following: A) the exchange will not occur simultaneously with the registration of Deeds, Mortgages or other contemplated registered documentation, and B) the exchange will be governed by the terms of a Document Registration Agreement (DRA) between the lawyers retained by the parties, and the DRA shall provide that all deliveries shall be held in trust by the receiving lawyer and not released until all other terms of the DRA have been met. The exchange will occur at the applicable Land Registry Office, unless otherwise agreed.

7. **DISCLOSURE AND PRODUCTION OF DOCUMENTS:** In the event that the Seller is in possession or control of any deed, survey or other evidence of title, then, upon request, the Seller shall deliver such documentation to the Buyer as soon as possible and in any event prior to the Requisition Date.

8. **PREPARATION OF DOCUMENTS:** The Transfer/Deed shall be prepared in registrable form at the expense of the Seller. The Buyer shall be responsible for the Land Transfer Tax Affidavit and any ancillary documents that may be required pursuant to this Agreement, unless the Seller is expressly required to provide otherwise. If requested, the Seller agrees to execute statements on the Transfer/Deed relating to subdivision compliance pursuant to Section 50(22) of *The Planning Act, R.S.O. 1990*, and the Seller agrees to instruct his/her solicitor to execute such statements.

9. **DISCHARGE OF MORTGAGES:** In the event that the Seller will be discharging a mortgage or mortgages in favour of a Chartered Bank, Trust Company, Credit Union, Caisse Populaire, Insurance Company or a corporation under *The Trust And Loan Companies Act (Canada)*, then the Buyer shall be obligated to accept the Seller's lawyer's Undertaking, in a form acceptable to the Buyer's lawyer, to obtain and register a discharge within a reasonable period of time following the Closing Date, provided that the Seller shall also furnish the Buyer's lawyer with a copy of a Mortgage Discharge Statement from the mortgagee which sets out the balance required to discharge the mortgage as of the Closing Date, and the Seller shall execute a Direction instructing his/her lawyer to pay the closing proceeds in the required manner.

10. **INSPECTION:** The Buyer acknowledges having inspected the Property and the parties agree that the Property shall be delivered in the same condition as existed at the time of inspection.

11. **INSURANCE:** The Property and all fixtures and chattels contemplated under this Agreement shall remain at the risk of the Seller until the Closing Date. All related insurance policies held by the Seller, if any, as well as any proceeds paid under such policies, shall be held in trust for the benefit of the parties in relation to their respective interests under this Agreement. In the event of damage and subsequent payment under such policies the Buyer shall have the option of terminating this Agreement or receiving the said payment and closing the transaction as scheduled with all other terms and conditions remaining the same. In the event that the Agreement is terminated pursuant to this section the deposit shall be returned to the Buyer without interest, bonus or deduction. No insurance policies shall be transferred on closing.

12. **PLANNING ACT COMPLIANCE:** The Seller shall be obligated to obtain all consents and take all steps necessary to complete this transaction in compliance with *The Planning Act, R.S.O. 1990*. Such efforts, if necessary, shall be at the sole expense of the Vendor. In the event that such efforts are unsuccessful, this Agreement shall be at an end and the deposit shall be returned to the Buyer without interest, bonus or deduction.

13. **RESIDENCY STATUS:** On closing the Seller shall furnish a certificate confirming that the Seller is not a "non-resident" within the meaning of the *Income Tax Act*, failing which the Buyer shall be entitled to hold back funds in accordance with prudent legal practice sufficient to satisfy the Buyer's obligations under the Act.

14. **FAMILY LAW STATUS:** The Seller warrants that he/she is not a spouse and that no spousal consent is necessary to give full effect to this Agreement, or alternatively that the person executing the necessary consent below is the Seller's spouse.

15. **CLOSING ADJUSTMENTS:** The amount due on closing shall be adjusted and apportioned between the parties to reflect their obligations as of the Closing Date for the following items, as may be applicable: realty taxes, local improvement rates, unmetered utility charges and unmetered fuel costs. These amounts as they relate to the Closing Date itself shall be the responsibility of the Buyer.

16. **TIME CONSTRAINTS:** Time shall be of the essence throughout this Agreement. The Closing Date and any other deadlines may only be extended or amended by agreement in writing.

17. **TENDER:** Any tender of documents, keys or money may be made upon the Buyer or Seller, as the case may be, or their lawyers, if any, on or before the time specified on the Closing Date. Tender shall be validly effected if delivered personally upon the Buyer or Seller, as the case may be, or upon their respective lawyers, if any. Money tendered must be in the form of bank draft or certified cheque issued by a Chartered Bank, Trust Company, Credit Union, Caisse Populaire or Province of Ontario Savings Office.

18. **UFFI:** The Seller warrants that he/she has not caused or allowed any buildings on the Property to be insulated with ureaformaldehyde, and further that, to the best of the Seller's knowledge, none of the buildings on the Property have been insulated with ureaformaldehyde. This warranty shall survive and not merge on closing.

19. **NOTICE:** Offer, acceptance or any notice or communication required under this Agreement shall be deemed delivered and received if given in writing by any of the following methods: 1) by personal delivery to the addresses of the parties noted herein, 2) by registered mail to the addresses of the parties noted herein (in which case receipt shall be deemed to be three days after mailing), 3) by fax to the fax numbers noted by the parties herein, if any, or 4) by delivery or fax to either party's lawyer, if any, as noted herein or as otherwise reasonably established.

20. **SUCCESSORS AND ASSIGNS:** This Agreement shall pass to the benefit of and be binding upon each of the parties' successors and assigns.

21. **ENFORCABILITY, ENTIRETY AND INTERPRETATION OF AGREEMENT:** Upon acceptance this Agreement shall constitute a binding agreement of purchase and sale. This document, together with all listed Schedules, constitutes the entire Agreement between the parties and there shall be no collateral agreements, representations or warranties. This Agreement may only be amended by mutual, written agreement between the parties, or between their lawyers, if any, as such lawyers may be noted herein or as otherwise reasonably established. In the event of a discrepancy between the Schedules or added clauses in this Agreement and the pre-formatted form of Agreement, the Schedules or added clauses shall prevail to the extent of the discrepancy. Any references to gender or number of parties shall be read with the intended context applied. In the event that any specific provisions of this Agreement are declared illegal, invalid or unenforceable by a court of competent jurisdiction, then the offending provision(s) may be severed and shall not impair the validity or enforceability of the balance of the Agreement. This Agreement shall be interpreted and enforced in accordance with the laws of the Province of Ontario.

22. **LEGAL REPRESENTATION:** Each of the parties acknowledges having received a copy of this Agreement and having been advised to seek independent legal advice prior to signing. Each of the parties further acknowledges that they have either obtained such independent legal advice, or have declined to seek such advice and have otherwise entered into this Agreement with the knowledge that it creates firm and binding legal relations and in full comprehension of the terms and consequences set out herein. Notwithstanding the source of this document, the doctrine of "Contra Preferentem" shall not apply and the Agreement shall be interpreted and construed equally among the parties.

Dated: ....

Signed sealed and delivered in the presence of:	Signed sealed and delivered by:		
.... [Witness]	.... [Buyer]	● [Seal]	Date: ....
.... [Witness]	.... [Buyer]	● [Seal]	Date: ....

Dated: ....

Signed sealed and delivered in the presence of:	Signed sealed and delivered by:		
.... [Witness]	.... [Seller]	● [Seal]	Date: ....
.... [Witness]	.... [Seller]	● [Seal]	Date: ....

SPOUSAL CONSENT: The person signing below is the spouse of the Seller and hereby consents to this transaction pursuant to *The Family Law Act, R.S.O. 1990*, and further agrees with the Buyer to execute any further assurances necessary to complete this transaction.

.... [Witness]	.... [Consenting Spouse]	● [Seal]	Date: ....

NOTICE

The Buyer's address for service is:	The Seller's address for service is:
Address:	Address: ....
Phone:	Phone: ....
Fax:	Fax: ....

LEGAL REPRESENTATION

The Buyer's solicitor, if any, until further notification, is:	The Seller's solicitor, if any, until further notification, is:
Name:	Name: ....
Address:	Address: ....
Phone:	Phone: ....
Fax:	Fax: ....

Quebec

Form of Agreement of Purchase & Sale (Blank – 8.5" x 11")
Form of Agreement of Purchase & Sale (Blank – 8.5" x 14" reduced)

This form of Agreement is customarily presented on legal size paper (8.5" x 14".) While paper size does not affect the validity of the document, using legal size will put it in a more recognized format. A reduced version of the legal size form has been provided. It can be increased on most industrial photocopiers using the "enlarge" function from standard to legal size (121% increase.) Legal size paper is available at most stationers.

OFFER TO PURCHASE
IMMOVABLE PROPERTY

For use in the Province of QUEBEC

I have requested that this contract be drafted in English. J'ai demandé que ce contrat soit rédigée en anglais

I/We, ... (the Buyer),
residing at the following address: ....,
hereby **offer to purchase** from.. (the Seller),
at the price and on the terms set out herein, the immovable land and buildings, which have been inspected and found to be satisfactory,
located at the following address:..(the Property).
The Property is designated in the Cadastre of ....
as Lot(s) Number(s) ....,
and having dimensions of ...., more or less.
In the case of a co-ownership, the Property is further described as set out in section 5.4

1. PURCHASE PRICE AND PAYMENT TERMS

The Price is .... dollars (the Purchase Price),
and shall be paid on the following terms:

1.1 DEPOSIT. The Buyer submits with this offer a deposit in the amount of: $ ....
The deposit shall be by cash or personal cheque payable to ...."in trust" and shall be held in trust, without interest unless otherwise provided for herein, by the trustee in accordance with the terms of this Agreement. The deposit shall be applied towards the purchase price at the signing of the Deed of Sale.

1.2 MORTGAGE ASSUMPTION. The Buyer shall assume an existing mortgage which, on the date of signing of the Deed of Sale, will have an approximate principle amount outstanding of: $ ....
The assumed mortgage shall be on the terms further set out in the attached schedule. This Agreement is conditional upon the mortgage being transferable to the Buyer, failing which this Agreement shall be at an end and the deposit shall be returned to the buyer without interest penalty or deduction

1.3 SELLER'S HYPOTHEC. The Buyer shall pay to the Seller the amount of: $ ....
which shall be secured by a vendor's privilege and a hypothec ranking in .... priority, and if there shall be any prior security it, shall not, in the aggregate, exceed $ ....
The Vendor's privilege and hypothec shall be on the terms further set out in the attached schedule.

1.4 BALANCE DUE. The Buyer shall, upon the signing of the Deed of Sale, and subject to the foregoing, remit the balance of the Purchase Price in the amount of: $ ....
This balance due shall be tendered by certified cheque(s) drawn to the order of the acting Notary "in trust". The Notary may hold back the sums owed to the Seller until the Deed of Sale has been registered and recorded in the Index of Immovables free and clear of any lien or encumbrance detrimental to the holder of the registered right and not otherwise contemplated herein. The balance due shall include any sums that must be obtained and secured through any new mortgage financing as contemplated in section 2.1 below.

1.5 OTHER. .... $ ....
....
....

TOTAL: $ ....

2. BUYER'S OBLIGATIONS

2.1 FINANCING. The Buyer shall, at the Buyer's sole expense, apply for new mortgage financing as soon as reasonably possible following acceptance of this offer to purchase. The financing shall be on the following terms:
principle amount $ .... *(including any high ratio mortgage insurance premiums, if applicable)*, interest rate not greater than .... % (*calculated semi-annually, not in advance*), term not shorter than ...., amortization not shorter than ...., ❒ Open *or* ❒ Closed *or* ❒ Limited Prepayment Options, priority ...., other material terms required by Buyer ....
The Buyer shall provide the Seller with a copy of a written approval of the foregoing, or otherwise waive the financing requirement, on or before ...., in which event this agreement shall be firm and binding. If such notice of approval or waiver is not received by the stated date, then the Seller shall have the option, upon written notice to the Buyer delivered within three days of the aforementioned date, of requiring the Buyer to resubmit the application on the same terms to a financing source of the Seller's choice. If all of the foregoing attempts to secure financing are unsuccessful and the financing requirement is not otherwise waived by the Buyer, then this offer to purchase shall be at an end and the deposit shall be returned to the Buyer without interest, penalty or deduction.

2.2 DEED OF SALE. The Buyer shall sign the Deed of Sale on or before ...., in the presence of the ....'s Notary.

2.3 CERTIFICATE OF LOCATION. The Buyer shall, if required or desired, bear the expense of a new Certificate of Location, unless it discloses additions or changes that have taken place subsequent to the date of the Certificate of Location being supplied by the Seller.

3. SELLER'S OBLIGATIONS

3.1 PROPERTY CONDITION. The Property and all included items shall be delivered in substantially the same condition they were in when inspected by the Buyer at the time this offer was presented.

3.2 TITLE. The Seller shall provide the Buyer with: (i) good and marketable title, free and clear of all liens, encumbrances and other real estate rights, save and except those expressly allowed for herein, (ii) any Title Deed that may be in the possession or control of the Seller, as soon as possible after acceptance of this offer, and (iii) an up-to-date Certificate of Location (unless the Property is a divided co-ownership) as soon as possible after acceptance of this offer.

3.3 DEED OF SALE. The Seller shall sign the notarized Deed of Sale within the time required herein, and shall be responsible for the full payment and discharge of any existing mortgage loans and the cancellation of any existing hypothecs.

4. SELLER'S DECLARATIONS

4.1 REAL RIGHTS AND ILLEGALITIES. The Property is not subject to any right, servitude or illegality, save and except any servitudes granted for public utilities, any liens, mortgages or encumbrances expressly contemplated elsewhere in this Agreement, or any of the following: ....

4.2 RESIDENCY STATUS. The Seller certifies that he/she is not a "non-resident" within the meaning of the *Income Tax Act (Canada)*, and the Seller agrees to provide an affidavit confirming same or include a statement to that effect in the notarized Deed of Sale, failing which the Buyer shall be entitled to hold back funds in accordance with prudent legal practice sufficient to satisfy the Buyer's obligations under the Act.

4.3 SPOUSAL STATUS. The Seller certifies that he/she is not a spouse; or alternatively that anyone with a spousal interest in the Property is named as a co-Seller in this Agreement; or alternatively that their spouse has consented below concurrent with acceptance of this offer; or alternatively that, as soon as reasonably possible after acceptance of this offer, the Seller shall deliver to the Buyer the required consent from the Seller's spouse together with their agreement to cooperate towards and to execute the notarized Deed of Sale, or a copy of a judgment authorizing the Seller to sell the Property without spousal consent. In the absence of any of the foregoing, the Buyer may, upon written notice, terminate this agreement in which event the deposit shall be returned to the Buyer without interest, penalty or deduction.

4.4 PROPERTY COMPLIANCE. The Seller certifies that, to the best of the Seller's knowledge, there are no existing or outstanding notices of non-compliance issued by any municipal or provincial government or other local authority, save and except as may be contemplated elsewhere in this Agreement or as follows: ....

4.5 UFFI. The Seller certifies that, to the best of the Seller's knowledge, the Property has not been insulated with urea-formaldehyde foam insulation.

5. OTHER TERMS AND CONDITIONS

5.1 CLOSING DATE. The Buyer shall become the owner of the Property upon the signing of the Deed of Sale and, subject to any tenancies expressly allowed for herein, the Buyer shall be entitled to occupancy of the Property on ....

5.2 ITEMS INCLUDED / EXCLUDED.

The following items are included: permanent electrical fixtures and heating, ventilating and air conditioning equipment, as well as ....

....

The following items are excluded: window dressings, curtain rods and blinds, as well as ....

....

The following items are rented and are not included, and if assumable the Buyer agrees to assume the rental contracts: ....

....

5.3 ADJUSTMENTS. Upon the signing of the Deed of Sale, adjustments shall be made as of .... between the Buyer and the Seller for their proportionate share of all general and special taxes, as well as, without limitation, any of the following as may be applicable to this transaction: fuel, co-ownership expenses, mortgage interest, rents and equipment leases.

5.4 CO-OWNERSHIPS. If the Property involves a co-ownership, the following shall apply: (i) type of ownership: ☐ divided, or ☐ undivided

(ii) parking space (if any) number(s) ....

(iii) storage space (if any) number(s) ....

(iv) other inclusions (if any) ....

The Buyer agrees to pay the Buyer's proportionate share of the ongoing co-ownership expenses, accept the reserve fund as of the date on which the Deed of Sale is signed, and respect the Declaration of Co-Ownership. The Seller certifies that the Seller is not aware of any pending increase in the co-ownership expenses, or any supplemental levy or special assessment pending or payable to the co-ownership, or any existing or pending legal actions against or initiated by the co-ownership, or any pending substantial change in the assets or liabilities of the co-ownership, or any upcoming special or general meetings of the co-ownership at which any of the foregoing will be addressed.

5.5 VACANT POSSESSION / TENANCIES. On the date of occupancy (above), the Buyer shall acquire vacant possession of the property unless tenancies are expressly agreed to as follows: ....

The details of the tenancy arrangement(s) are set out in the attached schedule. The Buyer agrees to respect any tenancy obligations assumed in connection with the foregoing.

5.6 COSTS. Each party shall bear their own costs in connection with this transaction. Specifically and without limitation, the Buyer shall bear the expense of the Deed of Sale, its registration and the production of any copies of same, as well as any applicable property transfer taxes, special taxes or church tax assessments that are the responsibility of the Buyer.

5.7 LANGUAGE. The Deed of Sale shall be drafted in French, or alternatively in English if expressly consented to as follows:

Initial if English desired ... ☐ ☐ ☐ ☐

Buyer's Initials *Seller's Initials*

5.8 ENFORCABILITY, ENTIRETY AND INTERPRETATION OF AGREEMENT. Upon acceptance, this Agreement shall constitute a binding agreement of purchase and sale. This document, together with all listed Schedules, constitutes the entire Agreement between the parties and there shall be no collateral agreements, representations or warranties. This Agreement may only be amended by mutual, written agreement between the parties, or between their Notaries, if any, as such Notaries may be set out herein or as otherwise reasonably established during the course of this transaction. In the event of a discrepancy between the Schedules or added clauses in this Agreement and the pre-formatted form of Agreement, the Schedules or added clauses shall prevail to the extent of the discrepancy. Time shall be of the essence throughout this Agreement and any deadlines or time limitations may only be extended or amended by agreement in writing. Any references to gender or number of parties shall be read with the intended context applied. In the event that any specific provisions of this Agreement are declared illegal, invalid or unenforceable by a court of competent jurisdiction, then the offending provision(s) may be severed and shall not impair the validity or enforceability of the balance of the Agreement. This Agreement shall be interpreted and enforced in accordance with the laws of the Province of Quebec.

5.9 LEGAL REPRESENTATION. Each of the parties acknowledges having read and understood this offer to purchase, and having received a copy of the Agreement, and having been advised to seek independent legal advice prior to signing. Each of the parties further acknowledges that they have either obtained such independent legal advice, or have declined to seek such advice and have otherwise entered into this Agreement with the knowledge that it creates firm and binding legal relations and in full comprehension of the terms and consequences set out herein. Notwithstanding which party drafted this Agreement, it shall be interpreted and construed equally among the parties.

5.10 ADDITIONAL TERMS OR CONDITIONS. ....
....
....
....

5.11 SCHEDULES. The following Schedules are attached to and form an integral part of this Agreement: ....

5.12 IRREVOCABILITY. This offer to purchase is open for acceptance and irrevocable by the Buyer until .... *[a.m. or p.m.]* on ...., after which time, if not accepted, this offer shall become null and void and the deposit shall be returned to the Buyer without interest, penalty or deduction. Any counteroffer shall also render the initial offer null and void to the same effect. Signed at *[location]* .... on *[date]* ...., at *[time]*........................ *[a.m. or p.m.]*

....	....	....
[Signature of Buyer]	*[Signature of Buyer]*	*[Signature of Witness]*

SELLER'S RESPONSE

I/We, ... (the Seller),
residing at the following address: ....,

[choose one – delete other]

❒ hereby **accept** this offer to purchase from the Buyer
❒ hereby **reject** this offer to purchase from the Buyer
❒ make the attached **counteroffer** to the Buyer

Signed at *[location]* .... on *[date]* ...., at *[time]*............................. *[a.m. or p.m.]*

....	....	....
[Signature of Seller]	*[Signature of Seller]*	*[Signature of Witness]*

SPOUSAL CONSENT ***[delete if not applicable]***

I, ...,
residing at the following address: ....,
declare that I am the spouse of the aforementioned Seller. I hereby consent to the acceptance of this offer on its terms and I agree to cooperate towards and to execute the notarized Deed of Sale.

Signed at *[location]* .... on *[date]* ...., at *[time]*............................. *[a.m. or p.m.]*

....	....	....
[Signature of Seller one's spouse]	*[Signature of Seller two's spouse]*	*[Signature of Witness]*

ACKNOWLEDGEMENT OF RECEIPT BY BUYER

I hereby acknowledge having received a copy of this executed response from the Seller.

Signed at *[location]* .... on *[date]* ...., at *[time]*............................. *[a.m. or p.m.]*

....	....	....
[Signature of Buyer]	*[Signature of Buyer]*	*[Signature of Witness]*

COUNTEROFFER

For use in the Province of QUEBEC

I have requested that this contract be drafted in English. J'ai demandé que ce contrat soit rédigée en anglais

I/We, ...,
residing at the following address: ....,
hereby **accept** the offer to purchase from the Buyer dated ...., at *[time]*.......................... *[a.m. or p.m.]*
on the terms as stated, but subject to the following amendments:

....
....
....
....
....
....
....
....
....
....
....
....
....
....
....
....
....
....

This counteroffer is open for acceptance and irrevocable by the Seller until .... [*a.m. or p.m.*] on ...., after which time, if not accepted, this counteroffer shall become null and void. Any further counteroffer from the Buyer shall also render this counteroffer null and void.
Signed at *[location]* .... on *[date]* ...., at *[time]*.......................... *[a.m. or p.m.]*

....	....	....
[Signature of Seller]	*[Signature of Seller]*	*[Signature of Witness]*

SPOUSAL CONSENT ***[delete if not applicable]***
I, ...,
residing at the following address: ....,
Declare that I am the spouse of the aforementioned Seller. I hereby consent to the terms of this counteroffer and I agree to cooperate towards and to execute the notarized Deed of Sale.
Signed at *[location]* .... on *[date]* ...., at *[time]*.......................... *[a.m. or p.m.]*

....	....	....
[Signature of Seller one's spouse]	*[Signature of Seller two's spouse]*	*[Signature of Witness]*

BUYER'S RESPONSE
I/We, ...,
residing at the following address: ....,

[choose one – delete other]
❒ hereby **accept** this counteroffer from the Seller
❒ hereby **reject** this counteroffer from the Seller
❒ make the attached **counteroffer** to the Seller
Signed at *[location]* .... on *[date]* ...., at *[time]*.......................... *[a.m. or p.m.]*

....	....	....
[Signature of Buyer]	*[Signature of Buyer]*	*[Signature of Witness]*

ACKNOWLEDGEMENT OF RECEIPT BY SELLER
I hereby acknowledge having received a copy of this executed response from the Buyer.
Signed at *[location]* .... on *[date]* ...., at *[time]*.......................... *[a.m. or p.m.]*

....	....	....
[Signature of Seller]	*[Signature of Seller]*	*[Signature of Witness]*

OFFER TO PURCHASE
IMMOVABLE PROPERTY

For use in the Province of QUEBEC

I have requested that this contract be drafted in English. J'ai demandé que ce contrat soit rédigée en anglais

I/We, ... (the Buyer),
residing at the following address: ....,
hereby **offer to purchase** from .... (the Seller),
at the price and on the terms set out herein, the immovable land and buildings, which have been inspected and found to be satisfactory,
located at the following address:..(the Property).
The Property is designated in the Cadastre of ....
as Lot(s) Number(s) ....,
and having dimensions of ...., more or less.
In the case of a co-ownership, the Property is further described as set out in section 5.4

1. PURCHASE PRICE AND PAYMENT TERMS

The Price is .... dollars (the Purchase Price),
and shall be paid on the following terms:

1.1 DEPOSIT. The Buyer submits with this offer a deposit in the amount of: $ ....
The deposit shall be by cash or personal cheque payable to ...."in trust" and shall be held in trust, without interest unless otherwise provided for herein, by the trustee in accordance with the terms of this Agreement. The deposit shall be applied towards the purchase price at the signing of the Deed of Sale.

1.2 MORTGAGE ASSUMPTION. The Buyer shall assume an existing mortgage which, on the date of signing of the Deed of Sale, will have an approximate principle amount outstanding of: $ ....
The assumed mortgage shall be on the terms further set out in the attached schedule. This Agreement is conditional upon the mortgage being transferable to the Buyer, failing which this Agreement shall be at an end and the deposit shall be returned to the buyer without interest penalty or deduction

1.3 SELLER'S HYPOTHEC. The Buyer shall pay to the Seller the amount of: $ ....
which shall be secured by a vendor's privilege and a hypothec ranking in .... priority, and if there shall be any prior security it, shall not, in the aggregate, exceed $ ....
The Vendor's privilege and hypothec shall be on the terms further set out in the attached schedule.

1.4 BALANCE DUE. The Buyer shall, upon the signing of the Deed of Sale, and subject to the foregoing, remit the balance of the Purchase Price in the amount of: $ ....
This balance due shall be tendered by certified cheque(s) drawn to the order of the acting Notary "in trust". The Notary may hold back the sums owed to the Seller until the Deed of Sale has been registered and recorded in the Index of Immovables free and clear of any lien or encumbrance detrimental to the holder of the registered right and not otherwise contemplated herein. The balance due shall include any sums that must be obtained and secured through any new mortgage financing as contemplated in section 2.1 below.

1.5 OTHER. .... $ ....
....
....

TOTAL: $ ....

2. BUYER'S OBLIGATIONS

2.1 FINANCING. The Buyer shall, at the Buyer's sole expense, apply for new mortgage financing as soon as reasonably possible following acceptance of this offer to purchase. The financing shall be on the following terms:
principle amount $ .... *(including any high ratio mortgage insurance premiums, if applicable)*, interest rate not greater than .... % *(calculated semi-annually, not in advance)*, term not shorter than ...., amortization not shorter than ...., ☐ Open or ☐ Closed or ☐ Limited Prepayment Options, priority ...., other material terms required by Buyer ....
The Buyer shall provide the Seller with a copy of a written approval of the foregoing, or otherwise waive the financing requirement, on or before ...., in which event this agreement shall be firm and binding. If such notice of approval or waiver is not received by the stated date, then the Seller shall have the option, upon written notice to the Buyer delivered within three days of the aforementioned date, of requiring the Buyer to resubmit the application on the same terms to a financing source of the Seller's choice. If all of the foregoing attempts to secure financing are unsuccessful and the financing requirement is not otherwise waived by the Buyer, then this offer to purchase shall be at an end and the deposit shall be returned to the Buyer without interest, penalty or deduction.

2.2 DEED OF SALE. The Buyer shall sign the Deed of Sale on or before ...., in the presence of the ....'s Notary.

2.3 CERTIFICATE OF LOCATION. The Buyer shall, if required or desired, bear the expense of a new Certificate of Location, unless it discloses additions or changes that have taken place subsequent to the date of the Certificate of Location being supplied by the Seller.

3. SELLER'S OBLIGATIONS

3.1 PROPERTY CONDITION. The Property and all included items shall be delivered in substantially the same condition they were in when inspected by the Buyer at the time this offer was presented.

3.2 TITLE. The Seller shall provide the Buyer with: (i) good and marketable title, free and clear of all liens, encumbrances and other real estate rights, save and except those expressly allowed for herein, (ii) any Title Deed that may be in the possession or control of the Seller, as soon as possible after acceptance of this offer, and (iii) an up-to-date Certificate of Location (unless the Property is a divided co-ownership) as soon as possible after acceptance of this offer.

3.3 DEED OF SALE. The Seller shall sign the notarized Deed of Sale within the time required herein, and shall be responsible for the full payment and discharge of any existing mortgage loans and the cancellation of any existing hypothecs.

4. SELLER'S DECLARATIONS

4.1 REAL RIGHTS AND ILLEGALITIES. The Property is not subject to any right, servitude or illegality, save and except any servitudes granted for public utilities, any liens, mortgages or encumbrances expressly contemplated elsewhere in this Agreement, or any of the following: ....

4.2 RESIDENCY STATUS. The Seller certifies that he/she is not a "non-resident" within the meaning of the *Income Tax Act (Canada)*, and the Seller agrees to provide an affidavit confirming same or include a statement to that effect in the notarized Deed of Sale, failing which the Buyer shall be entitled to hold back funds in accordance with prudent legal practice sufficient to satisfy the Buyer's obligations under the Act.

4.3 SPOUSAL STATUS. The Seller certifies that he/she is not a spouse; or alternatively that anyone with a spousal interest in the Property is named as a co-Seller in this Agreement; or alternatively that their spouse has consented below concurrent with acceptance of this offer; or alternatively that, as soon as reasonably possible after acceptance of this offer, the Seller shall deliver to the Buyer the required consent from the Seller's spouse together with their agreement to cooperate towards and to execute the notarized Deed of Sale, or a copy of a judgment authorizing the Seller to sell the Property without spousal consent. In the absence of any of the foregoing, the Buyer may, upon written notice, terminate this agreement in which event the deposit shall be returned to the Buyer without interest, penalty or deduction.

4.4 PROPERTY COMPLIANCE. The Seller certifies that, to the best of the Seller's knowledge, there are no existing or outstanding notices of non-compliance issued by any municipal or provincial government or other local authority, save and except as may be contemplated elsewhere in this Agreement or as follows: ....

4.5 UFFI. The Seller certifies that, to the best of the Seller's knowledge, the Property has not been insulated with urea-formaldehyde foam insulation.

5. OTHER TERMS AND CONDITIONS

5.1 CLOSING DATE. The Buyer shall become the owner of the Property upon the signing of the Deed of Sale and, subject to any tenancies expressly allowed for herein, the Buyer shall be entitled to occupancy of the Property on ....

5.2 ITEMS INCLUDED / EXCLUDED.

The following items are included: permanent electrical fixtures and heating, ventilating and air conditioning equipment, as well as ....

....

The following items are excluded: window dressings, curtain rods and blinds, as well as ....

....

The following items are rented and are not included, and if assumable the Buyer agrees to assume the rental contracts: ....

....

5.3 ADJUSTMENTS. Upon the signing of the Deed of Sale, adjustments shall be made as of .... between the Buyer and the Seller for their proportionate share of all general and special taxes, as well as, without limitation, any of the following as may be applicable to this transaction: fuel, co-ownership expenses, mortgage interest, rents and equipment leases.

5.4 CO-OWNERSHIPS. If the Property involves a co-ownership, the following shall apply: (i) type of ownership: ☐ divided, or ☐ undivided
(ii) parking space (if any) number(s) ....
(iii) storage space (if any) number(s) ....
(iv) other inclusions (if any) ....

The Buyer agrees to pay the Buyer's proportionate share of the ongoing co-ownership expenses, accept the reserve fund as of the date on which the Deed of Sale is signed, and respect the Declaration of Co-Ownership. The Seller certifies that the Seller is not aware of any pending increase in the co-ownership expenses, or any supplemental levy or special assessment pending or payable to the co-ownership, or any existing or pending legal actions against or initiated by the co-ownership, or any pending substantial change in the assets or liabilities of the co-ownership, or any upcoming special or general meetings of the co-ownership at which any of the foregoing will be addressed.

5.5 VACANT POSSESSION / TENANCIES. On the date of occupancy (above), the Buyer shall acquire vacant possession of the property unless tenancies are expressly agreed to as follows: ....
The details of the tenancy arrangement(s) are set out in the attached schedule. The Buyer agrees to respect any tenancy obligations assumed in connection with the foregoing.

5.6 COSTS. Each party shall bear their own costs in connection with this transaction. Specifically and without limitation, the Buyer shall bear the expense of the Deed of Sale, its registration and the production of any copies of same, as well as any applicable property transfer taxes, special taxes or church tax assessments that are the responsibility of the Buyer.

5.7 LANGUAGE. The Deed of Sale shall be drafted in French, or alternatively in English if expressly consented to as follows:

Initial if English desired ... ☐ ☐ *Buyer's Initials* ☐ ☐ *Seller's Initials*

5.8 ENFORCABILITY, ENTIRETY AND INTERPRETATION OF AGREEMENT. Upon acceptance, this Agreement shall constitute a binding agreement of purchase and sale. This document, together with all listed Schedules, constitutes the entire Agreement between the parties and there shall be no collateral agreements, representations or warranties. This Agreement may only be amended by mutual, written agreement between the parties, or between their Notaries, if any, as such Notaries may be set out herein or as otherwise reasonably established during the course of this transaction. In the event of a discrepancy between the Schedules or added clauses in this Agreement and the pre-formatted form of Agreement, the Schedules or added clauses shall prevail to the extent of the discrepancy. Time shall be of the essence throughout this Agreement and any deadlines or time limitations may only be extended or amended by agreement in writing. Any references to gender or number of parties shall be read with the intended context applied. In the event that any specific provisions of this Agreement are declared illegal, invalid or unenforceable by a court of competent jurisdiction, then the offending provision(s) may be severed and shall not impair the validity or enforceability of the balance of the Agreement. This Agreement shall be interpreted and enforced in accordance with the laws of the Province of Quebec.

5.9 LEGAL REPRESENTATION. Each of the parties acknowledges having read and understood this offer to purchase, and having received a copy of the Agreement, and having been advised to seek independent legal advice prior to signing. Each of the parties further acknowledges that they have either obtained such independent legal advice, or have declined to seek such advice and have otherwise entered into this Agreement with the knowledge that it creates firm and binding legal relations and in full comprehension of the terms and consequences set out herein. Notwithstanding which party drafted this Agreement, it shall be interpreted and construed equally among the parties.

5.10 ADDITIONAL TERMS OR CONDITIONS. ....

....

....

....

5.11 SCHEDULES. The following Schedules are attached to and form an integral part of this Agreement: ....

5.12 IRREVOCABILITY. This offer to purchase is open for acceptance and irrevocable by the Buyer until .... *[a.m. or p.m.]* on ...., after which time, if not accepted, this offer shall become null and void and the deposit shall be returned to the Buyer without interest, penalty or deduction. Any counteroffer shall also render the initial offer null and void to the same effect. Signed at *[location]* .... on *[date]* ...., at *[time]*.......... *[a.m. or p.m.]*

....	....	....
[Signature of Buyer]	*[Signature of Buyer]*	*[Signature of Witness]*

SELLER'S RESPONSE

I/We, ... (the Seller),
residing at the following address: ....,

[choose one – delete other]

☐ hereby **accept** this offer to purchase from the Buyer
☐ hereby **reject** this offer to purchase from the Buyer
☐ make the attached **counteroffer** to the Buyer

Signed at *[location]* .... on *[date]* ...., at *[time]*.......... *[a.m. or p.m.]*

....	....	....
[Signature of Seller]	*[Signature of Seller]*	*[Signature of Witness]*

SPOUSAL CONSENT ***[delete if not applicable]***

I, ...,
residing at the following address: ....,
declare that I am the spouse of the aforementioned Seller. I hereby consent to the acceptance of this offer on its terms and I agree to cooperate towards and to execute the notarized Deed of Sale.

Signed at *[location]* .... on *[date]* ...., at *[time]*.......... *[a.m. or p.m.]*

....	....	....
[Signature of Seller one's spouse]	*[Signature of Seller two's spouse]*	*[Signature of Witness]*

ACKNOWLEDGEMENT OF RECEIPT BY BUYER

I hereby acknowledge having received a copy of this executed response from the Seller.

Signed at *[location]* .... on *[date]* ...., at *[time]*.......... *[a.m. or p.m.]*

....	....	....
[Signature of Buyer]	*[Signature of Buyer]*	*[Signature of Witness]*

COUNTEROFFER

For use in the Province of QUEBEC

I have requested that this contract be drafted in English. J'ai demandé que ce contrat soit rédigée en anglais

I/We, ...,
residing at the following address: ....,
hereby **accept** the offer to purchase from the Buyer dated ...., at *[time]*........................ *[a.m. or p.m.]*
on the terms as stated, but subject to the following amendments:

....
....
....
....
....
....
....
....
....
....
....
....
....
....
....
....
....
....
....
....
....
....
....
....
....
....
....
....
....
....
....
....
....
....
....
....
....

This counteroffer is open for acceptance and irrevocable by the Seller until .... *[a.m. or p.m.]* on ...., after which time, if not accepted, this counteroffer shall become null and void. Any further counteroffer from the Buyer shall also render this counteroffer null and void.
Signed at *[location]* .... on *[date]* ...., at *[time]*........................ *[a.m. or p.m.]*

....	....	....
[Signature of Seller]	*[Signature of Seller]*	*[Signature of Witness]*

SPOUSAL CONSENT ***[delete if not applicable]***
I, ...,
residing at the following address: ....,
Declare that I am the spouse of the aforementioned Seller. I hereby consent to the terms of this counteroffer and I agree to cooperate towards and to execute the notarized Deed of Sale.
Signed at *[location]* .... on *[date]* ...., at *[time]*........................ *[a.m. or p.m.]*

....	....	....
[Signature of Seller one's spouse]	*[Signature of Seller two's spouse]*	*[Signature of Witness]*

BUYER'S RESPONSE
I/We, ...,
residing at the following address: ....,

[choose one – delete other]
❒ hereby **accept** this counteroffer from the Seller
❒ hereby **reject** this counteroffer from the Seller
❒ make the attached **counteroffer** to the Seller
Signed at *[location]* .... on *[date]* ...., at *[time]*........................ *[a.m. or p.m.]*

....	....	....
[Signature of Buyer]	*[Signature of Buyer]*	*[Signature of Witness]*

ACKNOWLEDGEMENT OF RECEIPT BY SELLER
I hereby acknowledge having received a copy of this executed response from the Buyer.
Signed at *[location]* .... on *[date]* ...., at *[time]*........................ *[a.m. or p.m.]*

....	....	....
[Signature of Seller]	*[Signature of Seller]*	*[Signature of Witness]*

New Brunswick

Form of Agreement of Purchase & Sale (Blank)

AGREEMENT OF PURCHASE AND SALE
(FOR USE IN NEW BRUNSWICK)

The BUYER, ____,
[legal name of Buyer(s)]

hereby offers to buy from the SELLER, ____,
[legal name of Seller(s)]

the real property located at ____,
[street address and legal description]

which comprises land the size of ____, more or less,
[feet *or* metres]

at a purchase price of ____ Dollars CDN ($______________________)
[written] [numerical]

on the following terms and conditions.

1. FINANCING & PROCEEDS

(a) The Buyer submits with this offer an initial deposit of ______________________________ Dollars CDN ($__________________)
[written] [numerical]

by cash or cheque payable to ____
[person to whom deposit is payable]

to be held in trust pending completion or other termination of this Agreement. On closing the deposit shall be credited towards the purchase price.

(b) This Agreement is conditional upon the Buyer obtaining written approval of financing, mortgage or otherwise, for the approximate amount of $ __________________, representing __________ % of the purchase price, at current interest rates. The Buyer shall provide the Seller with a written waiver of this financing condition on or before ______________________ on ______________________________,
[time – a.m. *or* p.m.] [date]

failing which this offer shall become null and void and the deposit shall be returned to the Buyer without interest, penalty or deduction.

(c) The Buyer agrees to increase the deposit to a total amount of ______________________________ Dollars CDN ($__________________),
[written] [numerical]

representing _______ % of the purchase price, within 24 hours of financing approval, to be held in trust and payable in the manner set out above.

(d) Unless otherwise provided herein, the balance of the purchase price shall be due on completion by cash, lawyer's trust cheque, or certified cheque drawn on a Chartered Canadian Bank, Trust Company or Credit Union, payable to the Seller or Seller's lawyer, or as they may redirect.

2. CLOSING & POSSESSION DATE This Agreement shall be completed on ______________________________ (Closing Date),
[date]

on which date the Seller shall provide the Buyer with vacant possession of the Property, unless otherwise provided herein.

3. PRE-CLOSING INSPECTION The Buyer shall have the right to conduct a pre-closing inspection of the property to ensure that the property is in the same condition as it was in at the time this Agreement was signed. Such inspection shall be performed on or before ______________________________, and at such time the property ______________________ be vacant.
[date] [shall *or* shall not]

4. ITEMS INCLUDED / EXCLUDED

(i) The following items (chattels) are included in the purchase price: ____ . Such chattels shall remain with the property on closing, free of any encumbrances or liens, and shall be in the same good working order and condition as they were at the time this Agreement was signed.

(i) All items attached to the property (fixtures) are included in the purchase price and shall remain with the property on closing, save and except the following fixtures which are not included: ____ .

(i) The following items are leased, and the Buyer agrees to assume the leases in connection with same:

Buyer(s)		Seller(s)	

[acknowledging initials required]

Hot Water Tank _____ Furnace/Heating System _____ Propane Tank _____

Other: ____

5. TITLE SEARCH & STATUS The seller shall provide the Buyer with the legal description of the subject property. The property is to be conveyed free and clear of any liens or encumbrances, unless otherwise specified herein. The Buyer shall have until ______________________________
[date]

to investigate title to the Property. If the Buyer makes a valid objection to the title in writing, and if the Seller is unable or unwilling to remedy or satisfy the objection, and if the Buyer is then unwilling to waive the objection, then this Agreement shall be null and void and the deposit shall be returned to the Buyer without interest, penalty or deduction and without any further obligation for costs or damages between the parties. If the Buyer does not make a valid objection in writing within the specified time periods, then the Buyer shall be deemed to have conclusively accepted the status of the Seller's title to the Property. All investigations shall be at the Buyer's own expense.

6. PREPARATION OF DOCUMENTS The Deed shall be prepared in registrable form at the expense of the Seller, and shall be tendered on closing in exchange for the purchase price. The Buyer shall be responsible for any ancillary documents that may be required pursuant to this Agreement, unless the Seller is expressly required to provide otherwise. If any survey work, permits or applications are required to put the conveyance in registrable form, such measures shall be taken at the Seller's expense.

7. INSURANCE The property and all fixtures and chattels contemplated under this Agreement shall remain at the risk of the Seller until closing. All related insurance policies held by the Seller, if any, as well as any proceeds paid under such policies, shall be held in trust for the benefit of the parties in relation to their respective interests under this Agreement. In the event of damage and subsequent payment under such policies the Buyer shall have the option of terminating this Agreement or receiving the said payment and closing the transaction as scheduled with all other terms and conditions remaining the same. In the event that the Agreement is terminated pursuant to this section, the deposit shall be returned to the Buyer without interest, penalty or deduction. No insurance policies shall be transferred on closing.

Acknowledgement of completion: *Buyer's initials* ________ ________ *Seller's initials* ________ ________

8. ADJUSTMENTS & TAXES

(i) The amount due on closing shall be adjusted and apportioned between the parties to reflect their obligations as of the closing date for the following items, as may be applicable: taxes, rates, assessments and fuel remaining on the property. These amounts as they relate to the closing date itself shall be the responsibility of the Buyer. Any charges for municipal improvements that have been completed as of the day this Agreement is signed – including, but without limitation, capital charges for municipal utilities or services, or betterment charges – unless otherwise provided in this Agreement shall be the responsibility of the Seller and shall be paid in full on or before closing. The Seller shall confirm that he/she is not a "non-resident" within the meaning of the Income Tax Act, failing which the Buyer shall be entitled to hold back funds in accordance with prudent legal practice sufficient to satisfy the Buyer's obligations under the Act.

(ii) If this transaction is subject to any applicable government taxes, then, unless otherwise provided in this Agreement, such taxes shall be in addition to and not included in the purchase price.

9. TENDER Any tender of documents, keys or money may be effected by personal delivery upon the Buyer or Seller, as the case may be, or their lawyers, if any, on or before the closing date.

10. UFFI The Seller warrants that he/she has not caused or allowed any buildings on the Property to be insulated with urea formaldehyde insulation, and further that, to the best of the Seller's knowledge, none of the buildings on the Property have been insulated with urea formaldehyde insulation. This warranty shall survive and not merge on closing.

11. SURVEYOR'S REAL PROPERTY REPORT The Seller shall deliver to the Buyer any Surveyor's Real Property Report(s) concerning the property that is/are in the Seller's possession or control; however, subject to any survey work required for a registrable conveyance, any new Surveyor's Real Property Report shall be the responsibility of the Buyers, unless otherwise agreed upon herein.

12. HOME INSPECTION The Buyer ____________________ require an inspection of the property on or before ________________________________
[does *or* does not] [date – must complete if inspection required]
by a qualified home inspector at the Buyer's expense. In the event that the report is not satisfactory to the Buyer, the Buyer shall have the option of terminating this Agreement upon written notice delivered to the Seller within _____ days following the date stated above, failing which this condition shall be deemed waived. In the event of such termination, the deposit shall be returned to the Buyer without interest, penalty or deduction. The Seller agrees to allow the inspector reasonable access to the property prior to the date stated above for the purpose of conducting the inspection.

13. ENVIRONMENTAL INSPECTION The Buyer ________________ require an inspection of the property on or before ______________________
[does *or* does not] [date – must complete if inspection required]
by a qualified environmental inspector at the Buyer's expense. In the event that the report is not satisfactory to the Buyer, the Buyer shall have the option of terminating this Agreement upon written notice delivered to the Seller within _____ days following the date stated above, failing which this condition shall be deemed waived. In the event of such termination, the deposit shall be returned to the Buyer without interest, penalty or deduction. The Seller agrees to allow the inspector reasonable access to the property prior to the date stated above for the purpose of conducting the inspection.

14. WATER TEST The Buyer _____________ require a water potability test regarding the water supply on or before _________________________.
[does *or* does not] [date – must complete if test required]
The test shall be conducted at the expense of the Buyer. In the event that the test discloses that the water supply of the property does not meet the requirements of the New Brunswick Department of Health, the Buyer shall have the option of terminating this Agreement upon written notice delivered to the Seller within _____ days following the date stated above, failing which this condition shall be deemed waived. In the event of such termination, the deposit shall be returned to the Buyer without interest, penalty or deduction. The Seller agrees to allow the buyer or their representative reasonable access to the property prior to the date stated above for the purpose of taking water samples.

15. PROPERTY DISCLOSURE STATEMENT The Seller _____________ provide a Property Condition Disclosure Statement to the Buyer within 36 hours
[shall *or* shall not]
of acceptance of this offer, and the Statement shall be acknowledged and signed by the Buyer on or before ________________________________.
[date - must complete if statement provided]

16. FURTHER TERMS & CONDITIONS This Agreement is subject to the following further terms and conditions: ____________________________
____
____
____
____
____
____.

17. FURTHER SCHEDULES: The following Schedules are attached to and form an integral part of this Agreement: ______________________
[applicable Schedules, if any]

18. ENFORCABILITY, ENTIRETY AND INTERPRETATION OF AGREEMENT: Upon acceptance this Agreement shall constitute a binding agreement of purchase and sale. In the event that the Buyer defaults in the completion of this Agreement, the Buyer will forfeit the above deposit in addition to any other claims the Seller may have against the Buyer. This document, together with all listed Schedules, constitutes the entire Agreement between the parties and there shall be no collateral agreements, representations or warranties. This Agreement may only be amended or extended by mutual, written agreement between the parties, or between their lawyers, if any. Time shall be of the essence throughout this Agreement, including any extensions. This Agreement shall pass to the benefit of and be binding upon each of the parties' heirs, executors, administrators, successors and assigns. In the event of a discrepancy between the Schedules or added clauses in this Agreement and the pre-formatted form of Agreement, the Schedules or added clauses shall prevail to the extent of the discrepancy. Any references to gender or number of parties shall be read with the intended context applied. In the event that any specific provisions of this Agreement are declared illegal, invalid or unenforceable by a court of competent jurisdiction, then the offending provision(s) may be severed and shall not impair the validity or enforceability of the balance of the Agreement. This Agreement shall be interpreted and enforced in accordance with the laws of the Province of New Brunswick.

19. LEGAL REPRESENTATION: Each of the parties acknowledges having received a copy of this Agreement and having been advised to seek independent legal advice prior to signing. Each of the parties further acknowledges that they have either obtained such independent legal advice, or have declined to seek such advice and have otherwise entered into this Agreement with the knowledge that it creates firm and binding legal relations and in full comprehension of the terms and consequences set out herein. Notwithstanding the source of this document, the doctrine of "Contra Preferentem" shall not apply and the Agreement shall be interpreted and construed equally among the parties.

Acknowledgement of completion: *Buyer's initials* ________ ________ *Seller's initials* ________ ________

20. OFFER This offer to purchase shall be open for acceptance and irrevocable by the Buyer until ___________ on ______________________________.
[time – a.m. *or* p.m.] [date]

Signed at ______________________________ in the Province of New Brunswick, at ___________ on ______________________________.
[time – a.m. *or* p.m.] [date]

Signed sealed and delivered in the presence of: Signed sealed and delivered by:

______________________________ [Witness] ______________________________ [Buyer] [Seal]

______________________________ [Witness] ______________________________ [Buyer] [Seal]

21. ACCEPTANCE

(i) The Seller accepts this offer on the terms and conditions set out herein.

Signed at ______________________________ in the Province of New Brunswick, at ___________ on ______________________________.
[time – a.m. *or* p.m.] [date]

Signed sealed and delivered in the presence of: Signed sealed and delivered by:

______________________________ [Witness] ______________________________ [Seller] [Seal]

______________________________ [Witness] ______________________________ [Seller] [Seal]

(ii) The Seller confirms that this offer was presented and not accepted, and returns herewith the deposit.

Signed at ______________________________ in the Province of New Brunswick, at ___________ on ______________________________.
[time – a.m. *or* p.m.] [date]

Signed sealed and delivered in the presence of: Signed sealed and delivered by:

______________________________ [Witness] ______________________________ [Seller] [Seal]

______________________________ [Witness] ______________________________ [Seller] [Seal]

22. COUNTEROFFER

(i) The undersigned confirms that they have read and understood this Agreement and have modified the offer as initialed herein and/or as follows:

____

____

____

____

(ii) This counteroffer shall be open for acceptance and irrevocable by the Seller until ___________ on ______________________________.
[time – a.m. *or* p.m.] [date]

after which time, if not accepted by the Buyer, this counteroffer shall be null and void and the deposit shall be returned to the Buyer without interest, penalty or deduction.

Signed at ______________________________ in the Province of New Brunswick, at ___________ on ______________________________.
[time – a.m. *or* p.m.] [date]

Signed sealed and delivered in the presence of: Signed sealed and delivered by:

______________________________ [Witness] ______________________________ [Seller] [Seal]

______________________________ [Witness] ______________________________ [Seller] [Seal]

(iii) The Buyer accepts the modifications contained in this counteroffer, having initialed same, together with the remaining terms and conditions set out in this Agreement.

Signed at ______________________________ in the Province of New Brunswick, at ___________ on ______________________________.
[time – a.m. *or* p.m.] [date]

Signed sealed and delivered in the presence of: Signed sealed and delivered by:

______________________________ [Witness] ______________________________ [Buyer] [Seal]

______________________________ [Witness] ______________________________ [Buyer] [Seal]

Acknowledgement of completion: *Buyer's initials* ________ ________ *Seller's initials* ________ ________

Prince Edward Island

Form of Agreement of Purchase & Sale (Blank - 8.5" x 11")
Form of Agreement of Purchase & Sale (Blank - 8.5" x 14" reduced)

This form of Agreement is customarily presented on legal size paper (8.5" x 14".) While paper size does not affect the validity of the document, using legal size will put it in a more recognized format. A reduced version of the legal size form has been provided. It can be increased on most industrial photocopiers using the "enlarge" function from standard to legal size (121% increase.) Legal size paper is available at most stationers.

AGREEMENT OF PURCHASE AND SALE
(FOR USE IN PRINCE EDWARD ISLAND)

The BUYER, ____, hereby offers to buy from
[legal name(s) of Buyer(s)]

the SELLER, ____, the real property described as
[legal name(s) of Seller(s)]

the PROPERTY: ____

____, at a purchase price of
[street address and legal description]

the PRICE: ________________________________ Dollars CDN ($________________)
[written] [numerical]

on the following terms and conditions.

1. a) The Buyer submits with this signed offer an initial deposit by cash or cheque payable to ________________
[person to whom deposit is payable]
in the amount of ________________________________ Dollars CDN ($________________)
[written] [numerical]
to be held in trust pending closing or other termination of this Agreement.

b) On closing the deposit shall be credited towards the purchase price. In the event that this transaction does not close, or the Agreement is otherwise terminated, other than due to default on the part of the Buyer, the deposit shall be returned to the Buyer without interest, penalty or deduction. In the event that the Buyer defaults in the completion of this Agreement, the Buyer will forfeit the above deposit in addition to any other claims the Seller may have against the Buyer.

c) Unless otherwise provided herein, the balance of the purchase price shall be due on completion by cash, lawyer's trust cheque, or certified cheque drawn on a Chartered Canadian Bank, Trust Company or Credit Union, payable to the Seller or Seller's lawyer, or as they may redirect.

2. This Agreement shall be completed on ________________________________ (the "Closing Date"),
[date]
on which date the Seller shall provide the Buyer with vacant possession of the Property, unless otherwise provided herein.

3. (i) The following items (chattels) are included in the purchase price: ________________________________

____

Such chattels shall remain with the property on closing, free of any encumbrances or liens, and shall be in the same condition and working order as they were at the time this Agreement was signed.
(i) All items attached to the property (fixtures) are included in the purchase price and shall remain with the property on closing, save and except the following fixtures which are not included: ________________________________

____

(i) The following items are leased, and the Buyer agrees to assume the leases in connection with same: ________________

____

4. The seller shall provide the Buyer, as soon as reasonably possible after acceptance, with a legal description of the subject property together with copies of any surveys or boundary plans of the Property that may be in the Seller's possession or control. After receipt of this information, the Buyer shall be allowed _______ days to investigate title to the Property. If the Buyer makes a valid objection to the title in writing within such time, and if the Seller is unable or unwilling to remedy or satisfy the objection, and if the Buyer is then unwilling to waive the objection, then this Agreement shall be null and void and the deposit shall be returned to the Buyer without interest, penalty or deduction and without any further obligation for costs or damages between the parties. If the Buyer does not make a valid objection in writing within the specified time period, then the Buyer shall be deemed to have conclusively accepted the status of the Seller's title to the Property. All investigations shall be at the Buyer's expense.

5. The conveyance of the subject property shall be by ________________ Deed prepared in registrable form at the expense of the Seller, and shall be tendered on closing in exchange for the purchase price. The Buyer shall be responsible for any ancillary documents that may be required pursuant to this Agreement, unless the Seller is expressly required to provide otherwise. The Seller shall obtain and register a discharge of all existing mortgages, and the property shall be conveyed free and clear of any mortgages, liens or encumbrances, save and except any easements, registered restrictions or covenants that affect the property but do not materially affect the enjoyment or marketability of the property, and except as specifically allowed for elsewhere in this Agreement. The conveyance shall be in compliance with any provincial family law legislation.

Date of Offer: ________________________

All parties acknowledge having read and understood this Agreement as evidenced by their initials on this page 1 of 4

Initials of Buyer:_______ _______ Witness: _______

Initials of Seller:_______ _______ Witness: _______

6. The property and all fixtures and chattels contemplated under this Agreement shall remain at the risk of the Seller until closing. All related insurance policies held by the Seller, if any, as well as any proceeds paid under such policies, shall be held in trust for the benefit of the parties in relation to their respective interests under this Agreement. In the event of damage and subsequent payment under such policies, the Buyer shall have the option of terminating this Agreement or receiving the said payment and closing the transaction as scheduled with all other terms and conditions remaining the same. In the event that the Agreement is terminated pursuant to this section, the deposit shall be returned to the Buyer without interest, penalty or deduction. No insurance policies shall be transferred on closing unless otherwise provided herein.

7. The balance due on closing shall be subject to the usual adjustments for property related expenses and receipts, including, without limitation, all property taxes, rates and assessments. The closing date itself shall be the responsibility of the Buyer. Any charges for municipal improvements that have been completed as of the day this Agreement is signed – including, but without limitation, capital charges for municipal utilities or services, or betterment charges – whether billed or not, unless otherwise provided in this Agreement, shall be the responsibility of the Seller and shall be paid in full on or before closing.

8. Any Harmonized Sales Tax (HST) payable pursuant to the *Excise Tax Act* shall be [choose one and initial]

Seller(s)	Buyer(s)		
		☐	included in the purchase price
			OR
[initials required]		☐	in addition to the purchase price

If there is no HST payable, the Seller agrees to provide a Certificate in a form satisfactory to the buyer's lawyer certifying that there is no HST payable.

9. On closing the Seller shall furnish a certificate confirming that the Seller is not a "non-resident" within the meaning of the Income Tax Act, failing which the Buyer shall be entitled to hold-back funds in accordance with prudent legal practice sufficient to satisfy the Buyer's obligations under the Act.

10. Any tender of documents, keys or money may be effected by personal delivery upon the Buyer or Seller, as the case may be, or their lawyers, if any, on or before the closing date.

11. All representations and warranties contained in this Agreement shall survive closing unless otherwise stated herein. The Seller represents and warrants as follows *[attach additional schedules if necessary]*:

a) The Seller has not caused or allowed any buildings on the Property to be insulated with urea formaldehyde insulation, and further, to the best of the Seller's knowledge, none of the buildings on the Property have been insulated with urea formaldehyde insulation.

b) ____

c) ____

d) ____

12. This Agreement is further conditional upon the following *[attach additional schedules if necessary]*:

(a) This Agreement is conditional upon the Buyer obtaining written approval of financing on terms satisfactory to the Buyer or as otherwise specified in this Agreement. The Buyer must notify the Seller in writing on or before ____________ [time – a.m. or p.m.] on ________________________ [date] that the financing is unavailable and that the condition cannot be satisfied. In the event that such notice is not given on or before the specified date, the condition shall be deemed fulfilled or waived and this Agreement shall, subject to any further outstanding conditions, be deemed to be firm and binding. In the event that such notice is given on or before the specified date, the this Agreement shall be null and void and the deposit shall be returned to the Buyer without interest, penalty or deduction. This condition is for the sole benefit of the Buyer and may be waived by the Buyer on or before the specified time.

(b) ____

(c) ____

Date of Offer: ________________________

All parties acknowledge having read and understood this Agreement as evidenced by their initials on this page 2 of 4

Initials of Buyer:_______ _______ Witness: _______

Initials of Seller:_______ _______ Witness: _______

13. The following Schedules are attached to and form an integral part of this Agreement: ______________________________.
[applicable Schedules, if any]

14. Upon acceptance, this Agreement shall constitute a binding agreement of purchase and sale. This document, together with all listed Schedules, constitutes the entire Agreement between the parties and there shall be no collateral agreements, representations or warranties. This Agreement may only be amended or extended by mutual, written agreement between the parties, or between their lawyers, if any. Time shall be of the essence throughout this Agreement, including any extensions. This Agreement shall pass to the benefit of and be binding upon each of the parties' heirs, executors, administrators, successors and assigns. In the event of a discrepancy between the Schedules or added clauses in this Agreement and the pre-formatted form of Agreement, the Schedules or added clauses shall prevail to the extent of the discrepancy. Any references to gender or number of parties shall be read with the intended context applied. In the event that any specific provisions of this Agreement are declared illegal, invalid or unenforceable by a court of competent jurisdiction, then the offending provision(s) may be severed and shall not impair the validity or enforceability of the balance of the Agreement. This Agreement shall be interpreted and enforced in accordance with the laws of the Province of Prince Edward Island.

15. Each of the parties acknowledges having received a copy of this Agreement and having been advised to seek independent legal advice prior to signing. Each of the parties further acknowledges that they have either obtained such independent legal advice, or have declined to seek such advice and have otherwise entered into this Agreement with the knowledge that it creates firm and binding legal relations and in full comprehension of the terms and consequences set out herein. Notwithstanding the source of this document, the doctrine of "Contra Preferentem" shall not apply and the Agreement shall be interpreted and construed equally among the parties.

16. Offer, acceptance or any notice or communication required under this Agreement shall be deemed delivered and received if given in writing by any of the following methods: 1) by personal delivery to the addresses of the parties noted herein, 2) by registered mail to the addresses of the parties noted herein (in which case receipt shall be deemed to be three days after mailing), 3) by fax to the fax numbers noted by the parties herein, if any, or 4) by delivery or fax to either party's lawyer, if any, as noted herein or as otherwise reasonably established during the course of this transaction.

Buyer's address: ______________________________

Phone: ________________ Fax: ________________

Lawyer name: ______________________________

address: ______________________________

Phone: ________________ Fax: ________________

Seller's address: ______________________________

Phone: ________________ Fax: ________________

Lawyer name: ______________________________

address: ______________________________

Phone: ________________ Fax: ________________

17. This offer to purchase shall be open for acceptance and irrevocable by the Buyer until ____________ on ______________________.
[time – a.m. *or* p.m.] [date]

Signed at ______________________ in the Province of Prince Edward Island, at ____________ on ______________________.
[time – a.m. *or* p.m.] [date]

Signed sealed and delivered in the presence of: Signed sealed and delivered by:

______________________________ [Witness] ______________________________ [Buyer] [Seal]

______________________________ [Witness] ______________________________ [Buyer] [Seal]

All parties acknowledge having read and understood this Agreement as evidenced by their initials on this page 3 of 4

Date of Offer: ______________________

Initials of Buyer: _______ _______ Witness: _______

Initials of Seller: _______ _______ Witness: _______

18. *[choose one – delete others]*

(i) The Seller hereby accepts this offer on the terms and conditions set out herein.

Signed at ______________________________ in the Province of Prince Edward Island, at ____________ on ____________________________.
[time – a.m. *or* p.m.] [date]

Signed sealed and delivered in the presence of: Signed sealed and delivered by:

______________________________ [Witness] ______________________________ [Seller] [Seal]

______________________________ [Witness] ______________________________ [Seller] [Seal]

(ii) The Seller confirms that this offer was presented and not accepted, and returns herewith the deposit.

Signed at ______________________________ in the Province of Prince Edward Island, at ____________ on ____________________________.
[time – a.m. *or* p.m.] [date]

Signed sealed and delivered in the presence of: Signed sealed and delivered by:

______________________________ [Witness] ______________________________ [Seller] [Seal]

______________________________ [Witness] ______________________________ [Seller] [Seal]

(iii) The Seller hereby modifies this offer in the manner set out herein, which amendments are initialed, including any further amendments as follows (counteroffer):

____

____

____

____

This counteroffer shall be open for acceptance and irrevocable by the Seller until ____________ on ____________________________.
[time – a.m. *or* p.m.] [date]

after which time, if not accepted by the Buyer, this counter offer shall be null and void and the deposit shall be returned to the Buyer without interest, penalty or deduction.

Signed at ______________________________ in the Province of Prince Edward Island, at ____________ on ____________________________.
[time – a.m. *or* p.m.] [date]

Signed sealed and delivered in the presence of: Signed sealed and delivered by:

______________________________ [Witness] ______________________________ [Seller] [Seal]

______________________________ [Witness] ______________________________ [Seller] [Seal]

19. The Buyer accepts the modifications contained in this counteroffer together with the remaining terms and conditions set out in this Agreement.

Signed at ______________________________ in the Province of Prince Edward Island, at ____________ on ____________________________.
[time – a.m. *or* p.m.] [date]

Signed sealed and delivered in the presence of: Signed sealed and delivered by:

______________________________ [Witness] ______________________________ [Buyer] [Seal]

______________________________ [Witness] ______________________________ [Buyer] [Seal]

Date of Offer: ______________________________

All parties acknowledge having read and understood this Agreement as evidenced by their initials on this page 4 of 4

Initials of Buyer: _______ _______ Witness: _______

Initials of Seller: _______ _______ Witness: _______

AGREEMENT OF PURCHASE AND SALE

(FOR USE IN PRINCE EDWARD ISLAND)

The BUYER, ____, hereby offers to buy from
[legal name(s) of Buyer(s)]

the SELLER, ____, the real property described as
[legal name(s) of Seller(s)]

the PROPERTY: ____

____, at a purchase price of
[street address and legal description]

the PRICE: ______________________________ Dollars CDN ($______________)
[written] [numerical]

on the following terms and conditions.

1. a) The Buyer submits with this signed offer an initial deposit by cash or cheque payable to ______________________
[person to whom deposit is payable]
in the amount of ______________________________ Dollars CDN ($______________)
[written] [numerical]
to be held in trust pending closing or other termination of this Agreement.

b) On closing the deposit shall be credited towards the purchase price. In the event that this transaction does not close, or the Agreement is otherwise terminated, other than due to default on the part of the Buyer, the deposit shall be returned to the Buyer without interest, penalty or deduction. In the event that the Buyer defaults in the completion of this Agreement, the Buyer will forfeit the above deposit in addition to any other claims the Seller may have against the Buyer.

c) Unless otherwise provided herein, the balance of the purchase price shall be due on completion by cash, lawyer's trust cheque, or certified cheque drawn on a Chartered Canadian Bank, Trust Company or Credit Union, payable to the Seller or Seller's lawyer, or as they may redirect.

2. This Agreement shall be completed on ______________________________ (the "Closing Date"),
[date]
on which date the Seller shall provide the Buyer with vacant possession of the Property, unless otherwise provided herein.

3. (i) The following items (chattels) are included in the purchase price: ______________________________

____

Such chattels shall remain with the property on closing, free of any encumbrances or liens, and shall be in the same condition and working order as they were at the time this Agreement was signed.
(i) All items attached to the property (fixtures) are included in the purchase price and shall remain with the property on closing, save and except the following fixtures which are not included: ______________________________

____

(i) The following items are leased, and the Buyer agrees to assume the leases in connection with same: ______________________

____

4. The seller shall provide the Buyer, as soon as reasonably possible after acceptance, with a legal description of the subject property together with copies of any surveys or boundary plans of the Property that may be in the Seller's possession or control. After receipt of this information, the Buyer shall be allowed _______ days to investigate title to the Property. If the Buyer makes a valid objection to the title in writing within such time, and if the Seller is unable or unwilling to remedy or satisfy the objection, and if the Buyer is then unwilling to waive the objection, then this Agreement shall be null and void and the deposit shall be returned to the Buyer without interest, penalty or deduction and without any further obligation for costs or damages between the parties. If the Buyer does not make a valid objection in writing within the specified time period, then the Buyer shall be deemed to have conclusively accepted the status of the Seller's title to the Property. All investigations shall be at the Buyer's expense.

5. The conveyance of the subject property shall be by ______________________ Deed prepared in registrable form at the expense of the Seller, and shall be tendered on closing in exchange for the purchase price. The Buyer shall be responsible for any ancillary documents that may be required pursuant to this Agreement, unless the Seller is expressly required to provide otherwise. The Seller shall obtain and register a discharge of all existing mortgages, and the property shall be conveyed free and clear of any mortgages, liens or encumbrances, save and except any easements, registered restrictions or covenants that affect the property but do not materially affect the enjoyment or marketability of the property, and except as specifically allowed for elsewhere in this Agreement. The conveyance shall be in compliance with any provincial family law legislation.

6. The property and all fixtures and chattels contemplated under this Agreement shall remain at the risk of the Seller until closing. All related insurance policies held by the Seller, if any, as well as any proceeds paid under such policies, shall be held in trust for the benefit of the parties in relation to their respective interests under this Agreement. In the event of damage and subsequent payment under such policies, the Buyer shall have the option of terminating this Agreement or receiving the said payment and closing the transaction as scheduled with all other terms and conditions remaining the same. In the event that the Agreement is terminated pursuant to this section, the deposit shall be returned to the Buyer without interest, penalty or deduction. No insurance policies shall be transferred on closing unless otherwise provided herein.

7. The balance due on closing shall be subject to the usual adjustments for property related expenses and receipts, including, without limitation, all property taxes, rates and assessments. The closing date itself shall be the responsibility of the Buyer. Any charges for municipal improvements that have been completed as of the day this Agreement is signed – including, but without limitation, capital charges for municipal utilities or services, or betterment charges – whether billed or not, unless otherwise provided in this Agreement, shall be the responsibility of the Seller and shall be paid in full on or before closing.

8. Any Harmonized Sales Tax (HST) payable pursuant to the *Excise Tax Act* shall be [choose one and initial]

Seller(s)	Buyer(s)

[initials required]

☐ included in the purchase price

OR

☐ in addition to the purchase price

If there is no HST payable, the Seller agrees to provide a Certificate in a form satisfactory to the buyer's lawyer certifying that there is no HST payable.

Date of Offer: ______________________

Initials of Buyer: _______ _______ Witness: _______

Initials of Seller: _______ _______ Witness: _______

9. On closing the Seller shall furnish a certificate confirming that the Seller is not a "non-resident" within the meaning of the Income Tax Act, failing which the Buyer shall be entitled to hold-back funds in accordance with prudent legal practice sufficient to satisfy the Buyer's obligations under the Act.

10. Any tender of documents, keys or money may be effected by personal delivery upon the Buyer or Seller, as the case may be, or their lawyers, if any, on or before the closing date.

11. All representations and warranties contained in this Agreement shall survive closing unless otherwise stated herein. The Seller represents and warrants as follows *[attach additional schedules if necessary]*:

a) The Seller has not caused or allowed any buildings on the Property to be insulated with urea formaldehyde insulation, and further, to the best of the Seller's knowledge, none of the buildings on the Property have been insulated with urea formaldehyde insulation.

b) ____________________

c) ____________________

d) ____________________

12. This Agreement is further conditional upon the following *[attach additional schedules if necessary]*:

(a) This Agreement is conditional upon the Buyer obtaining written approval of financing on terms satisfactory to the Buyer or as otherwise specified in this Agreement. The Buyer must notify the Seller in writing on or before __________ [time – a.m. or p.m.] on __________ [date] that the financing is unavailable and that the condition cannot be satisfied. In the event that such notice is not given on or before the specified date, the condition shall be deemed fulfilled or waived and this Agreement shall, subject to any further outstanding conditions, be deemed to be firm and binding. In the event that such notice is given on or before the specified date, the this Agreement shall be null and void and the deposit shall be returned to the Buyer without interest, penalty or deduction. This condition is for the sole benefit of the Buyer and may be waived by the Buyer on or before the specified time.

(b) ____________________

(c) ____________________

13. The following Schedules are attached to and form an integral part of this Agreement: __________ [applicable Schedules, if any].

14. Upon acceptance, this Agreement shall constitute a binding agreement of purchase and sale. This document, together with all listed Schedules, constitutes the entire Agreement between the parties and there shall be no collateral agreements, representations or warranties. This Agreement may only be amended or extended by mutual, written agreement between the parties, or between their lawyers, if any. Time shall be of the essence throughout this Agreement, including any extensions. This Agreement shall pass to the benefit of and be binding upon each of the parties' heirs, executors, administrators, successors and assigns. In the event of a discrepancy between the Schedules or added clauses in this Agreement and the pre-formatted form of Agreement, the Schedules or added clauses shall prevail to the extent of the discrepancy. Any references to gender or number of parties shall be read with the intended context applied. In the event that any specific provisions of this Agreement are declared illegal, invalid or unenforceable by a court of competent jurisdiction, then the offending provision(s) may be severed and shall not impair the validity or enforceability of the balance of the Agreement. This Agreement shall be interpreted and enforced in accordance with the laws of the Province of Prince Edward Island.

15. Each of the parties acknowledges having received a copy of this Agreement and having been advised to seek independent legal advice prior to signing. Each of the parties further acknowledges that they have either obtained such independent legal advice, or have declined to seek such advice and have otherwise entered into this Agreement with the knowledge that it creates firm and binding legal relations and in full comprehension of the terms and consequences set out herein. Notwithstanding the source of this document, the doctrine of "Contra Preferentem" shall not apply and the Agreement shall be interpreted and construed equally among the parties.

16. Offer, acceptance or any notice or communication required under this Agreement shall be deemed delivered and received if given in writing by any of the following methods: 1) by personal delivery to the addresses of the parties noted herein, 2) by registered mail to the addresses of the parties noted herein (in which case receipt shall be deemed to be three days after mailing), 3) by fax to the fax numbers noted by the parties herein, if any, or 4) by delivery or fax to either party's lawyer, if any, as noted herein or as otherwise reasonably established during the course of this transaction.

Buyer's address: __________	Seller's address: __________
Phone: __________ Fax: __________	Phone: __________ Fax: __________
Lawyer name: __________	Lawyer name: __________
address: __________	address: __________
Phone: __________ Fax: __________	Phone: __________ Fax: __________

Date of Offer: __________

All parties acknowledge having read and understood this Agreement as evidenced by their initials on this page 2 of 3

Initials of Buyer: ______ ______ Witness: ______

Initials of Seller: ______ ______ Witness: ______

17. This offer to purchase shall be open for acceptance and irrevocable by the Buyer until ___________ on _______________________.
[time – a.m. or p.m.] [date]

Signed at _______________________ in the Province of Prince Edward Island, at ___________ on _______________________.
[time – a.m. or p.m.] [date]

Signed sealed and delivered in the presence of: Signed sealed and delivered by:

_______________________ [Witness] _______________________ [Buyer] [Seal]

_______________________ [Witness] _______________________ [Buyer] [Seal]

18. ***[choose one – delete others]***

(i) The Seller hereby accepts this offer on the terms and conditions set out herein.

Signed at _______________________ in the Province of Prince Edward Island, at ___________ on _______________________.
[time – a.m. or p.m.] [date]

Signed sealed and delivered in the presence of: Signed sealed and delivered by:

_______________________ [Witness] _______________________ [Seller] [Seal]

_______________________ [Witness] _______________________ [Seller] [Seal]

(ii) The Seller confirms that this offer was presented and not accepted, and returns herewith the deposit.

Signed at _______________________ in the Province of Prince Edward Island, at ___________ on _______________________.
[time – a.m. or p.m.] [date]

Signed sealed and delivered in the presence of: Signed sealed and delivered by:

_______________________ [Witness] _______________________ [Seller] [Seal]

_______________________ [Witness] _______________________ [Seller] [Seal]

(iii) The Seller hereby modifies this offer in the manner set out herein, which amendments are initialed, including any further amendments as follows (counteroffer):

____

____

____

____

This counteroffer shall be open for acceptance and irrevocable by the Seller until ___________ on _______________________.
[time – a.m. or p.m.] [date]

after which time, if not accepted by the Buyer, this counter offer shall be null and void and the deposit shall be returned to the Buyer without interest, penalty or deduction.

Signed at _______________________ in the Province of Prince Edward Island, at ___________ on _______________________.
[time – a.m. or p.m.] [date]

Signed sealed and delivered in the presence of: Signed sealed and delivered by:

_______________________ [Witness] _______________________ [Seller] [Seal]

_______________________ [Witness] _______________________ [Seller] [Seal]

19. The Buyer accepts the modifications contained in this counteroffer together with the remaining terms and conditions set out in this Agreement.

Signed at _______________________ in the Province of Prince Edward Island, at ___________ on _______________________.
[time – a.m. or p.m.] [date]

Signed sealed and delivered in the presence of: Signed sealed and delivered by:

_______________________ [Witness] _______________________ [Buyer] [Seal]

_______________________ [Witness] _______________________ [Buyer] [Seal]

All parties acknowledge having read and understood this Agreement as evidenced by their initials on this page 3 of 3

Date of Offer: _______________

Initials of Buyer: ______ ______ Witness: ______

Initials of Seller: ______ ______ Witness: ______

Nova Scotia

Form of Agreement of Purchase & Sale (Blank - 8.5" x 11")
Form of Agreement of Purchase & Sale (Blank - 8.5" x 14" reduced)

This form of Agreement is customarily presented on legal size paper (8.5" x 14".) While paper size does not affect the validity of the document, using legal size will put it in a more recognized format. A reduced version of the legal size form has been provided. It can be increased on most industrial photocopiers using the "enlarge" function from standard to legal size (121% increase.) Legal size paper is available at most stationers.

AGREEMENT OF PURCHASE AND SALE
(FOR USE IN NOVA SCOTIA)

The BUYER, ____,
[legal name of Buyer(s)]

of ____, has inspected and hereby offers to buy from
[address of Buyer(s)]

the SELLER, ____,
[legal name of Seller(s)]

of ____, the real property described as
[address of Seller(s)]

____

____,
[street address and legal description]

at a purchase price of ______________________________ Dollars CDN ($__________)
[written] [numerical]

on the following terms and conditions.

1. a) The Buyer submits, on execution of this offer, an initial deposit by cash or cheque payable to ______________________
[person to whom deposit is payable]
in the amount of ______________________________ Dollars CDN ($__________)
[written] [numerical]
to be held in trust pending closing or other termination of this Agreement. On closing the deposit shall be credited towards the purchase price.

(b) This Agreement is conditional upon the Buyer obtaining written approval of financing for the approximate amount of $__________, representing ______ % of the purchase price, at an interest rate of not more than ______ %. The Buyer must notify the Seller in writing on or before ______________ on ______________________ that the financing is unavailable and that
[time – a.m. or p.m.] [date]
the condition cannot be satisfied. In the event that such notice is not given on or before the specified date, the condition shall be deemed fulfilled or waived and this Agreement shall, subject to any further outstanding conditions, be deemed to be firm and binding. In the event that such notice is given on or before the specified date, then either party may declare the Agreement null and void and in such event the deposit shall be returned to the Buyer without interest, penalty or deduction.

(c) Unless otherwise provided herein, the balance of the purchase price shall be due on completion by cash, lawyer's trust cheque, or certified cheque drawn on a Chartered Canadian Bank, Trust Company or Credit Union, payable to the Seller or Seller's lawyer, or as they may redirect.

2. This Agreement shall be completed on ______________________________ (the "Closing Date"),
[date]
on which date the Seller shall provide the Buyer with vacant possession of the Property, unless otherwise provided herein.

3. (i) The following items (chattels) are included in the purchase price: ______________________________

____

Such chattels shall remain with the property on closing, free of any encumbrances or liens, and shall be in the same good working order and condition as they were at the time this Agreement was signed.

(i) All items attached to the property (fixtures) are included in the purchase price and shall remain with the property on closing, save and except the following fixtures which are not included: ______________________________

____

(i) The following items are leased, and the Buyer agrees to assume the leases in connection with same:

Seller(s)	Buyer(s)

[initials required]

____

____

All parties acknowledge having read and understood this Agreement as evidenced by their initials on this page 1 of 4

Date of Offer: ______________________

Initials of Buyer: ________ ________ Witness: ________

Initials of Seller: ________ ________ Witness: ________

4. The seller shall provide the Buyer with a metes & bounds description of the subject property. After receipt of the description the Buyer shall be allowed ________ days to investigate title to the Property. If the Buyer makes a valid objection to the title in writing within such time, and if the Seller is unable or unwilling to remedy or satisfy the objection, and if the Buyer is then unwilling to waive the objection, then this Agreement shall be null and void and the deposit shall be returned to the Buyer without interest, penalty or deduction and without any further obligation for costs or damages between the parties. If the Buyer does not make a valid objection in writing within the specified time periods, then the Buyer shall be deemed to have conclusively accepted the status of the Seller's title to the Property. All investigations shall be at the Buyer's own expense.

5. The conveyance of the subject property shall be by ________________________ Deed prepared in registrable form at the expense of the Seller, and shall be tendered on closing in exchange for the purchase price. The Buyer shall be responsible for any ancillary documents that may be required pursuant to this Agreement, unless the Seller is expressly required to provide otherwise. The Seller shall obtain and register a discharge of all existing mortgages, and the property shall be conveyed free and clear of any mortgages, liens or encumbrances, save and except any easements, registered restrictions or covenants that affect the property but do not materially affect the enjoyment of the property, and except as specifically allowed for elsewhere in this Agreement. The conveyance shall be in compliance with the provisions of the *Matrimonial Property Act.*

6. The property and all fixtures and chattels contemplated under this Agreement shall remain at the risk of the Seller until closing. All related insurance policies held by the Seller, if any, as well as any proceeds paid under such policies, shall be held in trust for the benefit of the parties in relation to their respective interests under this Agreement. In the event of damage and subsequent payment under such policies, the Buyer shall have the option of terminating this Agreement or receiving the said payment and closing the transaction as scheduled with all other terms and conditions remaining the same. In the event that the Agreement is terminated pursuant to this section, the deposit shall be returned to the Buyer without interest, penalty or deduction. No insurance policies shall be transferred on closing unless otherwise provided herein.

7. a) All taxes, rates and Assessments shall be adjusted to the Closing Date, as well as any of the usual adjustments, including the following as may be applicable: interest, rents, security deposits and insurance premiums. The closing date itself shall be the responsibility of the Buyer. Any charges for municipal improvements that have been completed as of the day this Agreement is signed – including, but without limitation, capital charges for municipal utilities or services, or betterment charges – whether billed or not, unless otherwise provided in this Agreement, shall be the responsibility of the Seller and shall be paid in full on or before closing.

b) Any Harmonized Sales Tax (HST) payable pursuant to the *Excise Tax Act* shall be [choose one and initial]

Seller(s)	Buyer(s)

[initials required]

☐ included in the purchase price

OR

☐ in addition to the purchase price

c) If there is no HST payable, the Seller agrees to provide a Certificate in a form satisfactory to the buyer's lawyer certifying that there is no HST payable.

8. Any tender of documents, keys or money may be effected by personal delivery upon the Buyer or Seller, as the case may be, or their lawyers, if any, on or before the closing date.

9. The Buyer shall have the right to conduct a pre-closing inspection of the property to ensure that the property is in the same condition as it was in at the time this Agreement was signed. Such inspection shall be performed on or before ____, and only upon reasonable advance notice to the Seller. [date]

10. All representations and warranties contained in this Agreement shall survive closing unless otherwise stated herein. The Seller represents and warrants as follows:

a) The Seller has not caused or allowed any buildings on the Property to be insulated with urea formaldehyde insulation, and further, to the best of the Seller's knowledge, none of the buildings on the Property have been insulated with urea formaldehyde insulation.

b) ____
____

c) ____
____

d) ____
____

11. This Agreement is further conditional upon the following [initial clauses that apply, or stroke them out]:

___ ___ a) The Buyer shall obtain a satisfactory report from a qualified home inspector of the Buyer's choice, at the Buyer's expense. This condition is for the benefit of the Buyer and in the event that the report is not satisfactory to the Buyer, the Buyer shall have the option of terminating this Agreement upon written notice delivered to the Seller on or before [date] ______________________________, failing which this condition shall be deemed waived. In the event of such termination, the deposit shall be returned to the Buyer without interest, penalty or deduction. The Seller agrees to allow the inspector reasonable access to the property, upon giving the Seller reasonable advanced notice for the purpose of conducting the inspection.

___ ___ b) The Seller shall provide the Buyer with a Property Condition Disclosure Statement within _______ hours of acceptance of this Agreement. In the event that the information disclosed by the Statement is not satisfactory to the Buyer, the Buyer shall have the option of terminating this Agreement upon written notice delivered to the Seller on or before [date] ______________________________, failing which this condition shall be deemed waived. In the event of such termination, the deposit shall be returned to the Buyer without interest, penalty or deduction. This condition is for the benefit of the Buyer. If a Statement is provided pursuant to this section, the Seller warrants that the Statement shall be current and accurate to the best of the Seller's knowledge, and the Seller agrees to advise the buyer of any change pending closing.

___ ___ c) The Buyer shall have this Agreement reviewed by a lawyer of the Buyer's choice, at the Buyer's expense. This condition is for the benefit of the Buyer and in the event that the lawyer is not satisfied with the form or content of this Agreement, the Buyer shall have the option of terminating this Agreement upon written notice delivered to the Seller on or before [date] ______________________________, failing which this condition shall be deemed waived. In the event of such termination, the deposit shall be returned to the Buyer without interest, penalty or deduction.

___ ___ d) The Seller shall have this Agreement reviewed by a lawyer of the Seller's choice, at the Seller's expense. This condition is for the benefit of the Seller and in the event that the lawyer is not satisfied with the form or content of this Agreement, the Seller shall have the option of terminating this Agreement upon written notice delivered to the Buyer on or before [date] ______________________________, failing which this condition shall be deemed waived. In the event of such termination, the deposit shall be returned to the Buyer without interest, penalty or deduction.

___ ___ e) ____

___ ___ f) ____

12. The Seller shall deliver to the Buyer any Surveyor's Real Property Report(s) or plot plan(s) concerning the property that are in the Seller's possession; however, any new Surveys or plans shall be the responsibility of the Buyers, unless otherwise required or agreed upon herein.

13. The following Schedules are attached to and form an integral part of this Agreement: ______________________________.
[applicable Schedules, if any]

14. Upon acceptance this Agreement shall constitute a binding agreement of purchase and sale. In the event that the Buyer defaults in the completion of this Agreement, the Buyer will forfeit the above deposit in addition to any other claims the Seller may have against the Buyer. This document, together with all listed Schedules, constitutes the entire Agreement between the parties and there shall be no collateral agreements, representations or warranties. This Agreement may only be amended or extended by mutual, written agreement between the parties, or between their lawyers, if any. Time shall be of the essence throughout this Agreement, including any extensions. This Agreement shall pass to the benefit of and be binding upon each of the parties' heirs, executors, administrators, successors and assigns. In the event of a discrepancy between the Schedules or added clauses in this Agreement and the pre-formatted form of Agreement, the Schedules or added clauses shall prevail to the extent of the discrepancy. Any references to gender or number of parties shall be read with the intended context applied. In the event that any specific provisions of this Agreement are declared illegal, invalid or unenforceable by a court of competent jurisdiction, then the offending provision(s) may be severed and shall not impair the validity or enforceability of the balance of the Agreement. This Agreement shall be interpreted and enforced in accordance with the laws of the Province of Nova Scotia.

15. Each of the parties acknowledges having received a copy of this Agreement and having been advised to seek independent legal advice prior to signing. Each of the parties further acknowledges that they have either obtained such independent legal advice, or have declined to seek such advice and have otherwise entered into this Agreement with the knowledge that it creates firm and binding legal relations and in full comprehension of the terms and consequences set out herein. Notwithstanding the source of this document, the doctrine of "Contra Preferentem" shall not apply and the Agreement shall be interpreted and construed equally among the parties.

All parties acknowledge having read and understood this Agreement as evidenced by their initials on this page 3 of 4

Date of Offer: ______________________

Initials of Buyer: ________ ________ Witness: ________

Initials of Seller: ________ ________ Witness: ________

16. This offer to purchase shall be open for acceptance and irrevocable by the Buyer until ____________ on ______________________________.
[time – a.m. *or* p.m.] [date]

Signed at ______________________________ in the Province of Nova Scotia, at ____________ on ______________________________.
[time – a.m. *or* p.m.] [date]

Signed sealed and delivered in the presence of: Signed sealed and delivered by:

______________________________ [Witness] ______________________________ [Buyer] [Seal]

______________________________ [Witness] ______________________________ [Buyer] [Seal]

17. ***[choose one – delete others]***

(i) The Seller hereby accepts this offer on the terms and conditions set out herein.

Signed at ______________________________ in the Province of Nova Scotia, at ____________ on ______________________________.
[time – a.m. *or* p.m.] [date]

Signed sealed and delivered in the presence of: Signed sealed and delivered by:

______________________________ [Witness] ______________________________ [Seller] [Seal]

______________________________ [Witness] ______________________________ [Seller] [Seal]

(ii) The Seller confirms that this offer was presented and not accepted, and returns herewith the deposit.

Signed at ______________________________ in the Province of Nova Scotia, at ____________ on ______________________________.
[time – a.m. *or* p.m.] [date]

Signed sealed and delivered in the presence of: Signed sealed and delivered by:

______________________________ [Witness] ______________________________ [Seller] [Seal]

______________________________ [Witness] ______________________________ [Seller] [Seal]

(iii) The Seller hereby modifies this offer in the manner set out herein, which amendments are initialed, including any further amendments as follows (counteroffer): ______________________________

____

____

____

This counteroffer shall be open for acceptance and irrevocable by the Seller until ____________ on ______________________________.
[time – a.m. *or* p.m.] [date]

after which time, if not accepted by the Buyer, this counteroffer shall be null and void and the deposit shall be returned to the Buyer without interest, penalty or deduction.

Signed at ______________________________ in the Province of Nova Scotia, at ____________ on ______________________________.
[time – a.m. *or* p.m.] [date]

Signed sealed and delivered in the presence of: Signed sealed and delivered by:

______________________________ [Witness] ______________________________ [Seller] [Seal]

______________________________ [Witness] ______________________________ [Seller] [Seal]

18. The Buyer accepts the modifications contained in this counteroffer together with the remaining terms and conditions set out in this Agreement.

Signed at ______________________________ in the Province of Nova Scotia, at ____________ on ______________________________.
[time – a.m. *or* p.m.] [date]

Signed sealed and delivered in the presence of: Signed sealed and delivered by:

______________________________ [Witness] ______________________________ [Buyer] [Seal]

______________________________ [Witness] ______________________________ [Buyer] [Seal]

AGREEMENT OF PURCHASE AND SALE

(FOR USE IN NOVA SCOTIA)

The BUYER, ____,
[legal name of Buyer(s)]

of ____ , has inspected and hereby offers to buy from
[address of Buyer(s)]

the SELLER, ____,
[legal name of Seller(s)]

of ____ , the real property described as
[address of Seller(s)]

____

____,
[street address and legal description]

at a purchase price of ______________________________________ Dollars CDN ($__________________)
[written] [numerical]

on the following terms and conditions.

1. a) The Buyer submits, on execution of this offer, an initial deposit by cash or cheque payable to ______________________
[person to whom deposit is payable]

in the amount of ______________________________________ Dollars CDN ($__________________)
[written] [numerical]

to be held in trust pending closing or other termination of this Agreement. On closing the deposit shall be credited towards the purchase price.

(b) This Agreement is conditional upon the Buyer obtaining written approval of financing for the approximate amount of $______________, representing ______ % of the purchase price, at an interest rate of not more than ______ %. The Buyer must notify the Seller in writing on or before ______________ on ______________________________ that the financing is unavailable and that
[time – a.m. or p.m.] [date]
the condition cannot be satisfied. In the event that such notice is not given on or before the specified date, the condition shall be deemed fulfilled or waived and this Agreement shall, subject to any further outstanding conditions, be deemed to be firm and binding. In the event that such notice is given on or before the specified date, then either party may declare the Agreement null and void and in such event the deposit shall be returned to the Buyer without interest, penalty or deduction.

(c) Unless otherwise provided herein, the balance of the purchase price shall be due on completion by cash, lawyer's trust cheque, or certified cheque drawn on a Chartered Canadian Bank, Trust Company or Credit Union, payable to the Seller or Seller's lawyer, or as they may redirect.

2. This Agreement shall be completed on ______________________________________ (the "Closing Date"),
[date]
on which date the Seller shall provide the Buyer with vacant possession of the Property, unless otherwise provided herein.

3. (i) The following items (chattels) are included in the purchase price: ______________________________

____

Such chattels shall remain with the property on closing, free of any encumbrances or liens, and shall be in the same good working order and condition as they were at the time this Agreement was signed.

(i) All items attached to the property (fixtures) are included in the purchase price and shall remain with the property on closing, save and except the following fixtures which are not included: ______________________________

____

(i) The following items are leased, and the Buyer agrees to assume the leases in connection with same:

Seller(s)	Buyer(s)	
		______________________________
		______________________________

[initials required]

4. The seller shall provide the Buyer with a metes & bounds description of the subject property. After receipt of the description the Buyer shall be allowed _______ days to investigate title to the Property. If the Buyer makes a valid objection to the title in writing within such time, and if the Seller is unable or unwilling to remedy or satisfy the objection, and if the Buyer is then unwilling to waive the objection, then this Agreement shall be null and void and the deposit shall be returned to the Buyer without interest, penalty or deduction and without any further obligation for costs or damages between the parties. If the Buyer does not make a valid objection in writing within the specified time periods, then the Buyer shall be deemed to have conclusively accepted the status of the Seller's title to the Property. All investigations shall be at the Buyer's own expense.

5. The conveyance of the subject property shall be by ______________________ Deed prepared in registrable form at the expense of the Seller, and shall be tendered on closing in exchange for the purchase price. The Buyer shall be responsible for any ancillary documents that may be required pursuant to this Agreement, unless the Seller is expressly required to provide otherwise. The Seller shall obtain and register a discharge of all existing mortgages, and the property shall be conveyed free and clear of any mortgages, liens or encumbrances, save and except any easements, registered restrictions or covenants that affect the property but do not materially affect the enjoyment of the property, and except as specifically allowed for elsewhere in this Agreement. The conveyance shall be in compliance with the provisions of the *Matrimonial Property Act*.

6. The property and all fixtures and chattels contemplated under this Agreement shall remain at the risk of the Seller until closing. All related insurance policies held by the Seller, if any, as well as any proceeds paid under such policies, shall be held in trust for the benefit of the parties in relation to their respective interests under this Agreement. In the event of damage and subsequent payment under such policies, the Buyer shall have the option of terminating this Agreement or receiving the said payment and closing the transaction as scheduled with all other terms and conditions remaining the same. In the event that the Agreement is terminated pursuant to this section, the deposit shall be returned to the Buyer without interest, penalty or deduction. No insurance policies shall be transferred on closing unless otherwise provided herein.

Date of Offer: ______________________

Initials of Buyer: _______ _______ Witness: _______

Initials of Seller: _______ _______ Witness: _______

All parties acknowledge having read and understood this Agreement as evidenced by their initials on this page 1 of 3

7. a) All taxes, rates and Assessments shall be adjusted to the Closing Date, as well as any of the usual adjustments, including the following as may be applicable: interest, rents, security deposits and insurance premiums. The closing date itself shall be the responsibility of the Buyer. Any charges for municipal improvements that have been completed as of the day this Agreement is signed – including, but without limitation, capital charges for municipal utilities or services, or betterment charges – whether billed or not, unless otherwise provided in this Agreement, shall be the responsibility of the Seller and shall be paid in full on or before closing.

b) Any Harmonized Sales Tax (HST) payable pursuant to the *Excise Tax Act* shall be [choose one and initial]

Seller(s)	Buyer(s)	
		☐ included in the purchase price
		OR
[initials required]		☐ in addition to the purchase price

c) If there is no HST payable, the Seller agrees to provide a Certificate in a form satisfactory to the buyer's lawyer certifying that there is no HST payable.

8. Any tender of documents, keys or money may be effected by personal delivery upon the Buyer or Seller, as the case may be, or their lawyers, if any, on or before the closing date.

9. The Buyer shall have the right to conduct a pre-closing inspection of the property to ensure that the property is in the same condition as it was in at the time this Agreement was signed. Such inspection shall be performed on or before ______________________ [date], and only upon reasonable advance notice to the Seller.

10. All representations and warranties contained in this Agreement shall survive closing unless otherwise stated herein. The Seller represents and warrants as follows:

a) The Seller has not caused or allowed any buildings on the Property to be insulated with urea formaldehyde insulation, and further, to the best of the Seller's knowledge, none of the buildings on the Property have been insulated with urea formaldehyde insulation.

b) ____

c) ____

d) ____

11. This Agreement is further conditional upon the following [initial clauses that apply, or stroke them out]:

___ ___ a) The Buyer shall obtain a satisfactory report from a qualified home inspector of the Buyer's choice, at the Buyer's expense. This condition is for the benefit of the Buyer and in the event that the report is not satisfactory to the Buyer, the Buyer shall have the option of terminating this Agreement upon written notice delivered to the Seller on or before [date] ______________________, failing which this condition shall be deemed waived. In the event of such termination, the deposit shall be returned to the Buyer without interest, penalty or deduction. The Seller agrees to allow the inspector reasonable access to the property, upon giving the Seller reasonable advanced notice for the purpose of conducting the inspection.

___ ___ b) The Seller shall provide the Buyer with a Property Condition Disclosure Statement within ______ hours of acceptance of this Agreement. In the event that the information disclosed by the Statement is not satisfactory to the Buyer, the Buyer shall have the option of terminating this Agreement upon written notice delivered to the Seller on or before [date] ______________________, failing which this condition shall be deemed waived. In the event of such termination, the deposit shall be returned to the Buyer without interest, penalty or deduction. This condition is for the benefit of the Buyer. If a Statement is provided pursuant to this section, the Seller warrants that the Statement shall be current and accurate to the best of the Seller's knowledge, and the Seller agrees to advise the buyer of any change pending closing.

___ ___ c) The Buyer shall have this Agreement reviewed by a lawyer of the Buyer's choice, at the Buyer's expense. This condition is for the benefit of the Buyer and in the event that the lawyer is not satisfied with the form or content of this Agreement, the Buyer shall have the option of terminating this Agreement upon written notice delivered to the Seller on or before [date] ______________________, failing which this condition shall be deemed waived. In the event of such termination, the deposit shall be returned to the Buyer without interest, penalty or deduction.

___ ___ d) The Seller shall have this Agreement reviewed by a lawyer of the Seller's choice, at the Seller's expense. This condition is for the benefit of the Seller and in the event that the lawyer is not satisfied with the form or content of this Agreement, the Seller shall have the option of terminating this Agreement upon written notice delivered to the Buyer on or before [date] ______________________, failing which this condition shall be deemed waived. In the event of such termination, the deposit shall be returned to the Buyer without interest, penalty or deduction.

___ ___ e) ____

___ ___ f) ____

12. The Seller shall deliver to the Buyer any Surveyor's Real Property Report(s) or plot plan(s) concerning the property that are in the Seller's possession; however, any new Surveys or plans shall be the responsibility of the Buyers, unless otherwise required or agreed upon herein.

13. The following Schedules are attached to and form an integral part of this Agreement: ______________________ [applicable Schedules, if any].

Date of Offer: ______________________

All parties acknowledge having read and understood this Agreement as evidenced by their initials on this page 2 of 3

Initials of Buyer: ________ ________ Witness: ________

Initials of Seller: ________ ________ Witness: ________

14. Upon acceptance this Agreement shall constitute a binding agreement of purchase and sale. In the event that the Buyer defaults in the completion of this Agreement, the Buyer will forfeit the above deposit in addition to any other claims the Seller may have against the Buyer. This document, together with all listed Schedules, constitutes the entire Agreement between the parties and there shall be no collateral agreements, representations or warranties. This Agreement may only be amended or extended by mutual, written agreement between the parties, or between their lawyers, if any. Time shall be of the essence throughout this Agreement, including any extensions. This Agreement shall pass to the benefit of and be binding upon each of the parties' heirs, executors, administrators, successors and assigns. In the event of a discrepancy between the Schedules or added clauses in this Agreement and the pre-formatted form of Agreement, the Schedules or added clauses shall prevail to the extent of the discrepancy. Any references to gender or number of parties shall be read with the intended context applied. In the event that any specific provisions of this Agreement are declared illegal, invalid or unenforceable by a court of competent jurisdiction, then the offending provision(s) may be severed and shall not impair the validity or enforceability of the balance of the Agreement. This Agreement shall be interpreted and enforced in accordance with the laws of the Province of Nova Scotia.

15. Each of the parties acknowledges having received a copy of this Agreement and having been advised to seek independent legal advice prior to signing. Each of the parties further acknowledges that they have either obtained such independent legal advice, or have declined to seek such advice and have otherwise entered into this Agreement with the knowledge that it creates firm and binding legal relations and in full comprehension of the terms and consequences set out herein. Notwithstanding the source of this document, the doctrine of "Contra Preferentem" shall not apply and the Agreement shall be interpreted and construed equally among the parties.

16. This offer to purchase shall be open for acceptance and irrevocable by the Buyer until ____________ on ______________________________.
[time – a.m. *or* p.m.] [date]

Signed at ________________________________ in the Province of Nova Scotia, at ____________ on ______________________________.
[time – a.m. *or* p.m.] [date]

Signed sealed and delivered in the presence of: Signed sealed and delivered by:

________________________ [Witness] ________________________ [Buyer] ● [Seal]

________________________ [Witness] ________________________ [Buyer] ● [Seal]

17. ***[choose one – delete others]***
(i) The Seller hereby accepts this offer on the terms and conditions set out herein.

Signed at ________________________________ in the Province of Nova Scotia, at ____________ on ______________________________.
[time – a.m. *or* p.m.] [date]

Signed sealed and delivered in the presence of: Signed sealed and delivered by:

________________________ [Witness] ________________________ [Seller] ● [Seal]

________________________ [Witness] ________________________ [Seller] ● [Seal]

(ii) The Seller confirms that this offer was presented and not accepted, and returns herewith the deposit.

Signed at ________________________________ in the Province of Nova Scotia, at ____________ on ______________________________.
[time – a.m. *or* p.m.] [date]

Signed sealed and delivered in the presence of: Signed sealed and delivered by:

________________________ [Witness] ________________________ [Seller] ● [Seal]

________________________ [Witness] ________________________ [Seller] ● [Seal]

(iii) The Seller hereby modifies this offer in the manner set out herein, which amendments are initialed, including any further amendments as follows (counteroffer): ____
____
____
____

This counteroffer shall be open for acceptance and irrevocable by the Seller until ____________ on ______________________________.
[time – a.m. *or* p.m.] [date]
after which time, if not accepted by the Buyer, this counteroffer shall be null and void and the deposit shall be returned to the Buyer without interest, penalty or deduction.

Signed at ________________________________ in the Province of Nova Scotia, at ____________ on ______________________________.
[time – a.m. *or* p.m.] [date]

Signed sealed and delivered in the presence of: Signed sealed and delivered by:

________________________ [Witness] ________________________ [Seller] ● [Seal]

________________________ [Witness] ________________________ [Seller] ● [Seal]

18. The Buyer accepts the modifications contained in this counteroffer together with the remaining terms and conditions set out in this Agreement.

Signed at ________________________________ in the Province of Nova Scotia, at ____________ on ______________________________.
[time – a.m. *or* p.m.] [date]

Signed sealed and delivered in the presence of: Signed sealed and delivered by:

________________________ [Witness] ________________________ [Buyer] ● [Seal]

________________________ [Witness] ________________________ [Buyer] ● [Seal]

Date of Offer: ____________________

All parties acknowledge having read and understood this Agreement as evidenced by their initials on this page 3 of 3

Initials of Buyer: ______ ______ Witness: ______

Initials of Seller: ______ ______ Witness: ______

Newfoundland & Labrador

Form of Agreement of Purchase & Sale (Blank – 8.5" x 11")
Form of Agreement of Purchase & Sale (Blank – 8.5 x 14" reduced)

This form of Agreement is customarily presented on legal size paper (8.5" x 14".) While paper size does not affect the validity of the document, using legal size will put it in a more recognized format. A reduced version of the legal size form has been provided. It can be increased on most industrial photocopiers using the "enlarge" function from standard to legal size (121% increase.) Legal size paper is available at most stationers.

AGREEMENT OF PURCHASE AND SALE
(FOR USE IN NEWFOUNDLAND & LABRADOR)

The BUYER, ______________________________, hereby offers to buy from
[legal name(s) of Buyer(s)]

the SELLER, ______________________________, the real property described as
[legal name(s) of Seller(s)]

the PROPERTY: ______________________________

______________________________, at a purchase price of
[street address and legal description]

the PRICE: ______________________________ Dollars CDN ($______________)
[written] [numerical]

on the following terms and conditions.

1. a) The Buyer submits with this signed offer an initial deposit by cash or cheque payable to ______________________________
[person to whom deposit is payable]
in the amount of ______________________________ Dollars CDN ($______________)
[written] [numerical]
to be held in trust pending closing or other termination of this Agreement.

b) On closing the deposit shall be credited towards the purchase price. In the event that this transaction does not close, or the Agreement is otherwise terminated, other than due to default on the part of the Buyer, the deposit shall be returned to the Buyer without interest, penalty or deduction. In the event that the Buyer defaults in the completion of this Agreement, the Buyer will forfeit the above deposit in addition to any other claims the Seller may have against the Buyer.

c) Unless otherwise provided herein, the balance of the purchase price shall be due on completion by cash, lawyer's trust cheque, or certified cheque drawn on a Chartered Canadian Bank, Trust Company or Credit Union, payable to the Seller or Seller's lawyer, or as they may redirect.

2. This Agreement shall be completed on ______________________________ (the "Closing Date"),
[date]
on which date the Seller shall provide the Buyer with vacant possession of the Property, unless otherwise provided herein.

3. (i) The following items (chattels) are included in the purchase price: ______________________________
____
____
Such chattels shall remain with the property on closing, free of any encumbrances or liens, and shall be in the same condition and working order as they were at the time this Agreement was signed.
(i) All items attached to the property (fixtures) are included in the purchase price and shall remain with the property on closing, save and except the following fixtures which are not included: ______________________________
____
(i) The following items are leased, and the Buyer agrees to assume the leases in connection with same: ______________________________
____

4. The seller shall provide the Buyer, as soon as reasonably possible after acceptance, with a legal description of the subject property together with copies of any surveys or boundary plans of the Property that may be in the Seller's possession or control. After receipt of this information, the Buyer shall be allowed ________ days to investigate title to the Property. If the Buyer makes a valid objection to the title in writing within such time, and if the Seller is unable or unwilling to remedy or satisfy the objection, and if the Buyer is then unwilling to waive the objection, then this Agreement shall be null and void and the deposit shall be returned to the Buyer without interest, penalty or deduction and without any further obligation for costs or damages between the parties. If the Buyer does not make a valid objection in writing within the specified time period, then the Buyer shall be deemed to have conclusively accepted the status of the Seller's title to the Property. All investigations shall be at the Buyer's expense.

5. The conveyance of the subject property shall be by ______________________ Deed prepared in registrable form at the expense of the Seller, and shall be tendered on closing in exchange for the purchase price. The Buyer shall be responsible for any ancillary documents that may be required pursuant to this Agreement, unless the Seller is expressly required to provide otherwise. The Seller shall obtain and register a discharge of all existing mortgages, and the property shall be conveyed free and clear of any mortgages, liens or encumbrances, save and except any easements, registered restrictions or covenants that affect the property but do not materially affect the enjoyment or marketability of the property, and except as specifically allowed for elsewhere in this Agreement. The conveyance shall be in compliance with any provincial family law legislation.

Date of Offer: ______________________________

All parties acknowledge having read and understood this Agreement as evidenced by their initials on this page 1 of 4

Initials of Buyer: ________ ________ Witness: ________

Initials of Seller: ________ ________ Witness: ________

6. The property and all fixtures and chattels contemplated under this Agreement shall remain at the risk of the Seller until closing. All related insurance policies held by the Seller, if any, as well as any proceeds paid under such policies, shall be held in trust for the benefit of the parties in relation to their respective interests under this Agreement. In the event of damage and subsequent payment under such policies, the Buyer shall have the option of terminating this Agreement or receiving the said payment and closing the transaction as scheduled with all other terms and conditions remaining the same. In the event that the Agreement is terminated pursuant to this section, the deposit shall be returned to the Buyer without interest, penalty or deduction. No insurance policies shall be transferred on closing unless otherwise provided herein.

7. The balance due on closing shall be subject to the usual adjustments for property related expenses and receipts, including, without limitation, all property taxes, rates and assessments. The closing date itself shall be the responsibility of the Buyer. Any charges for municipal improvements that have been completed as of the day this Agreement is signed – including, but without limitation, capital charges for municipal utilities or services, or betterment charges – whether billed or not, unless otherwise provided in this Agreement, shall be the responsibility of the Seller and shall be paid in full on or before closing.

8. Any Harmonized Sales Tax (HST) payable pursuant to the *Excise Tax Act* shall be [choose one and initial]

Seller(s)	Buyer(s)

[initials required]

☐ included in the purchase price

OR

☐ in addition to the purchase price

If there is no HST payable, the Seller agrees to provide a Certificate in a form satisfactory to the buyer's lawyer certifying that there is no HST payable.

9. On closing the Seller shall furnish a certificate confirming that the Seller is not a "non-resident" within the meaning of the Income Tax Act, failing which the Buyer shall be entitled to hold-back funds in accordance with prudent legal practice sufficient to satisfy the Buyer's obligations under the Act.

10. Any tender of documents, keys or money may be effected by personal delivery upon the Buyer or Seller, as the case may be, or their lawyers, if any, on or before the closing date.

11. All representations and warranties contained in this Agreement shall survive closing unless otherwise stated herein. The Seller represents and warrants as follows *[attach additional schedules if necessary]*:

a) The Seller has not caused or allowed any buildings on the Property to be insulated with urea formaldehyde insulation, and further, to the best of the Seller's knowledge, none of the buildings on the Property have been insulated with urea formaldehyde insulation.

b) ______________________________

c) ______________________________

d) ______________________________

12. This Agreement is further conditional upon the following *[attach additional schedules if necessary]*:

(a) This Agreement is conditional upon the Buyer obtaining written approval of financing on terms satisfactory to the Buyer or as otherwise specified in this Agreement. The Buyer must notify the Seller in writing on or before ____________ [time – a.m. or p.m.] on ____________________ [date] that the financing is unavailable and that the condition cannot be satisfied. In the event that such notice is not given on or before the specified date, the condition shall be deemed fulfilled or waived and this Agreement shall, subject to any further outstanding conditions, be deemed to be firm and binding. In the event that such notice is given on or before the specified date, the this Agreement shall be null and void and the deposit shall be returned to the Buyer without interest, penalty or deduction. This condition is for the sole benefit of the Buyer and may be waived by the Buyer on or before the specified time.

(b) ______________________________

(c) ______________________________

Date of Offer: ____________________

All parties acknowledge having read and understood this Agreement as evidenced by their initials on this page 2 of 4

Initials of Buyer:_______ _______ Witness: _______

Initials of Seller:_______ _______ Witness: _______

13. The following Schedules are attached to and form an integral part of this Agreement: ______________________.
[applicable Schedules, if any]

14. Upon acceptance, this Agreement shall constitute a binding agreement of purchase and sale. This document, together with all listed Schedules, constitutes the entire Agreement between the parties and there shall be no collateral agreements, representations or warranties. This Agreement may only be amended or extended by mutual, written agreement between the parties, or between their lawyers, if any. Time shall be of the essence throughout this Agreement, including any extensions. This Agreement shall pass to the benefit of and be binding upon each of the parties' heirs, executors, administrators, successors and assigns. In the event of a discrepancy between the Schedules or added clauses in this Agreement and the pre-formatted form of Agreement, the Schedules or added clauses shall prevail to the extent of the discrepancy. Any references to gender or number of parties shall be read with the intended context applied. In the event that any specific provisions of this Agreement are declared illegal, invalid or unenforceable by a court of competent jurisdiction, then the offending provision(s) may be severed and shall not impair the validity or enforceability of the balance of the Agreement. This Agreement shall be interpreted and enforced in accordance with the laws of the Province of Newfoundland & Labrador.

15. Each of the parties acknowledges having received a copy of this Agreement and having been advised to seek independent legal advice prior to signing. Each of the parties further acknowledges that they have either obtained such independent legal advice, or have declined to seek such advice and have otherwise entered into this Agreement with the knowledge that it creates firm and binding legal relations and in full comprehension of the terms and consequences set out herein. Notwithstanding the source of this document, the doctrine of "Contra Preferentem" shall not apply and the Agreement shall be interpreted and construed equally among the parties.

16. Offer, acceptance or any notice or communication required under this Agreement shall be deemed delivered and received if given in writing by any of the following methods: 1) by personal delivery to the addresses of the parties noted herein, 2) by registered mail to the addresses of the parties noted herein (in which case receipt shall be deemed to be three days after mailing), 3) by fax to the fax numbers noted by the parties herein, if any, or 4) by delivery or fax to either party's lawyer, if any, as noted herein or as otherwise reasonably established during the course of this transaction.

Buyer's address: ______________________

Phone: ______________ Fax: ______________

Lawyer name: ______________________

address: ______________________

Phone: ______________ Fax: ______________

Seller's address: ______________________

Phone: ______________ Fax: ______________

Lawyer name: ______________________

address: ______________________

Phone: ______________ Fax: ______________

17. This offer to purchase shall be open for acceptance and irrevocable by the Buyer until __________ on ______________________.
[time – a.m. *or* p.m.] [date]

Signed at ______________ in the Province of Newfoundland & Labrador, at __________ on ______________.
[time – a.m. *or* p.m.] [date]

Signed sealed and delivered in the presence of: Signed sealed and delivered by:

______________________ [Witness] ______________________ [Buyer] [Seal]

______________________ [Witness] ______________________ [Buyer] [Seal]

All parties acknowledge having read and understood this Agreement as evidenced by their initials on this page 3 of 4

Date of Offer: ______________________

Initials of Buyer: ______ ______ Witness: ______

Initials of Seller: ______ ______ Witness: ______

18. *[choose one – delete others]*

(i) The Seller hereby accepts this offer on the terms and conditions set out herein.

Signed at ______________________________ in the Province of Newfoundland & Labrador, at ____________ on __________________________.
[time – a.m. *or* p.m.] [date]

Signed sealed and delivered in the presence of: Signed sealed and delivered by:

______________________________ ______________________________
[Witness] [Seller] [Seal]

______________________________ ______________________________
[Witness] [Seller] [Seal]

(ii) The Seller confirms that this offer was presented and not accepted, and returns herewith the deposit.

Signed at ______________________________ in the Province of Newfoundland & Labrador, at ____________ on __________________________.
[time – a.m. *or* p.m.] [date]

Signed sealed and delivered in the presence of: Signed sealed and delivered by:

______________________________ ______________________________
[Witness] [Seller] [Seal]

______________________________ ______________________________
[Witness] [Seller] [Seal]

(iii) The Seller hereby modifies this offer in the manner set out herein, which amendments are initialed, including any further amendments as follows (counteroffer):

____
____
____
____

This counteroffer shall be open for acceptance and irrevocable by the Seller until ______________ on ______________________________.
[time – a.m. *or* p.m.] [date]

after which time, if not accepted by the Buyer, this counter offer shall be null and void and the deposit shall be returned to the Buyer without interest, penalty or deduction.

Signed at ______________________________ in the Province of Newfoundland & Labrador, at ____________ on __________________________.
[time – a.m. *or* p.m.] [date]

Signed sealed and delivered in the presence of: Signed sealed and delivered by:

______________________________ ______________________________
[Witness] [Seller] [Seal]

______________________________ ______________________________
[Witness] [Seller] [Seal]

19. The Buyer accepts the modifications contained in this counteroffer together with the remaining terms and conditions set out in this Agreement.

Signed at ______________________________ in the Province of Newfoundland & Labrador, at ____________ on __________________________.
[time – a.m. *or* p.m.] [date]

Signed sealed and delivered in the presence of: Signed sealed and delivered by:

______________________________ ______________________________
[Witness] [Buyer] [Seal]

______________________________ ______________________________
[Witness] [Buyer] [Seal]

All parties acknowledge having read and understood this Agreement as evidenced by their initials on this page 4 of 4

Date of Offer: ______________________________

Initials of Buyer:_______ _______ Witness: _______

Initials of Seller:_______ _______ Witness: _______

AGREEMENT OF PURCHASE AND SALE
(FOR USE IN NEWFOUNDLAND & LABRADOR)

The BUYER, ______________________________, hereby offers to buy from
[legal name(s) of Buyer(s)]

the SELLER, ______________________________, the real property described as
[legal name(s) of Seller(s)]

the PROPERTY: ______________________________

______________________________, at a purchase price of
[street address and legal description]

the PRICE: ______________________________ Dollars CDN ($______________)
[written] [numerical]

on the following terms and conditions.

1. a) The Buyer submits with this signed offer an initial deposit by cash or cheque payable to ______________________________
[person to whom deposit is payable]

in the amount of ______________________________ Dollars CDN ($______________)
[written] [numerical]

to be held in trust pending closing or other termination of this Agreement.

b) On closing the deposit shall be credited towards the purchase price. In the event that this transaction does not close, or the Agreement is otherwise terminated, other than due to default on the part of the Buyer, the deposit shall be returned to the Buyer without interest, penalty or deduction. In the event that the Buyer defaults in the completion of this Agreement, the Buyer will forfeit the above deposit in addition to any other claims the Seller may have against the Buyer.

c) Unless otherwise provided herein, the balance of the purchase price shall be due on completion by cash, lawyer's trust cheque, or certified cheque drawn on a Chartered Canadian Bank, Trust Company or Credit Union, payable to the Seller or Seller's lawyer, or as they may redirect.

2. This Agreement shall be completed on ______________________________ (the "Closing Date"),
[date]

on which date the Seller shall provide the Buyer with vacant possession of the Property, unless otherwise provided herein.

3. (i) The following items (chattels) are included in the purchase price: ______________________________

____

____

Such chattels shall remain with the property on closing, free of any encumbrances or liens, and shall be in the same condition and working order as they were at the time this Agreement was signed.

(i) All items attached to the property (fixtures) are included in the purchase price and shall remain with the property on closing, save and except the following fixtures which are not included: ______________________________

____

(i) The following items are leased, and the Buyer agrees to assume the leases in connection with same: ______________________________

____

4. The seller shall provide the Buyer, as soon as reasonably possible after acceptance, with a legal description of the subject property together with copies of any surveys or boundary plans of the Property that may be in the Seller's possession or control. After receipt of this information, the Buyer shall be allowed ________ days to investigate title to the Property. If the Buyer makes a valid objection to the title in writing within such time, and if the Seller is unable or unwilling to remedy or satisfy the objection, and if the Buyer is then unwilling to waive the objection, then this Agreement shall be null and void and the deposit shall be returned to the Buyer without interest, penalty or deduction and without any further obligation for costs or damages between the parties. If the Buyer does not make a valid objection in writing within the specified time period, then the Buyer shall be deemed to have conclusively accepted the status of the Seller's title to the Property. All investigations shall be at the Buyer's expense.

5. The conveyance of the subject property shall be by ______________________ Deed prepared in registrable form at the expense of the Seller, and shall be tendered on closing in exchange for the purchase price. The Buyer shall be responsible for any ancillary documents that may be required pursuant to this Agreement, unless the Seller is expressly required to provide otherwise. The Seller shall obtain and register a discharge of all existing mortgages, and the property shall be conveyed free and clear of any mortgages, liens or encumbrances, save and except any easements, registered restrictions or covenants that affect the property but do not materially affect the enjoyment or marketability of the property, and except as specifically allowed for elsewhere in this Agreement. The conveyance shall be in compliance with any provincial family law legislation.

6. The property and all fixtures and chattels contemplated under this Agreement shall remain at the risk of the Seller until closing. All related insurance policies held by the Seller, if any, as well as any proceeds paid under such policies, shall be held in trust for the benefit of the parties in relation to their respective interests under this Agreement. In the event of damage and subsequent payment under such policies, the Buyer shall have the option of terminating this Agreement or receiving the said payment and closing the transaction as scheduled with all other terms and conditions remaining the same. In the event that the Agreement is terminated pursuant to this section, the deposit shall be returned to the Buyer without interest, penalty or deduction. No insurance policies shall be transferred on closing unless otherwise provided herein.

7. The balance due on closing shall be subject to the usual adjustments for property related expenses and receipts, including, without limitation, all property taxes, rates and assessments. The closing date itself shall be the responsibility of the Buyer. Any charges for municipal improvements that have been completed as of the day this Agreement is signed – including, but without limitation, capital charges for municipal utilities or services, or betterment charges – whether billed or not, unless otherwise provided in this Agreement, shall be the responsibility of the Seller and shall be paid in full on or before closing.

8. Any Harmonized Sales Tax (HST) payable pursuant to the *Excise Tax Act* shall be [choose one and initial]

Seller(s)	Buyer(s)

[initials required]

☐ included in the purchase price

OR

☐ in addition to the purchase price

If there is no HST payable, the Seller agrees to provide a Certificate in a form satisfactory to the buyer's lawyer certifying that there is no HST payable.

Date of Offer: ______________________

All parties acknowledge having read and understood this Agreement as evidenced by their initials on this page 1 of 3

Initials of Buyer: ________ ________ Witness: ________

Initials of Seller: ________ ________ Witness: ________

9. On closing the Seller shall furnish a certificate confirming that the Seller is not a "non-resident" within the meaning of the Income Tax Act, failing which the Buyer shall be entitled to hold-back funds in accordance with prudent legal practice sufficient to satisfy the Buyer's obligations under the Act.

10. Any tender of documents, keys or money may be effected by personal delivery upon the Buyer or Seller, as the case may be, or their lawyers, if any, on or before the closing date.

11. All representations and warranties contained in this Agreement shall survive closing unless otherwise stated herein. The Seller represents and warrants as follows *[attach additional schedules if necessary]*:

a) The Seller has not caused or allowed any buildings on the Property to be insulated with urea formaldehyde insulation, and further, to the best of the Seller's knowledge, none of the buildings on the Property have been insulated with urea formaldehyde insulation.

b) ____________________

c) ____________________

d) ____________________

12. This Agreement is further conditional upon the following *[attach additional schedules if necessary]*:

(a) This Agreement is conditional upon the Buyer obtaining written approval of financing on terms satisfactory to the Buyer or as otherwise specified in this Agreement. The Buyer must notify the Seller in writing on or before ________ [time – a.m. or p.m.] on ____________ [date] that the financing is unavailable and that the condition cannot be satisfied. In the event that such notice is not given on or before the specified date, the condition shall be deemed fulfilled or waived and this Agreement shall, subject to any further outstanding conditions, be deemed to be firm and binding. In the event that such notice is given on or before the specified date, the this Agreement shall be null and void and the deposit shall be returned to the Buyer without interest, penalty or deduction. This condition is for the sole benefit of the Buyer and may be waived by the Buyer on or before the specified time.

(b) ____________________

(c) ____________________

13. The following Schedules are attached to and form an integral part of this Agreement: ____________________ [applicable Schedules, if any].

14. Upon acceptance, this Agreement shall constitute a binding agreement of purchase and sale. This document, together with all listed Schedules, constitutes the entire Agreement between the parties and there shall be no collateral agreements, representations or warranties. This Agreement may only be amended or extended by mutual, written agreement between the parties, or between their lawyers, if any. Time shall be of the essence throughout this Agreement, including any extensions. This Agreement shall pass to the benefit of and be binding upon each of the **parties'** heirs, executors, administrators, successors and assigns. In the event of a discrepancy between the Schedules or added clauses in this Agreement and the pre-formatted form of Agreement, the Schedules or added clauses shall prevail to the extent of the discrepancy. Any references to gender or number of parties shall be read with the intended context applied. In the event that any specific provisions of this Agreement are declared illegal, invalid or unenforceable by a court of competent jurisdiction, then the offending provision(s) may be severed and shall not impair the validity or enforceability of the balance of the Agreement. This Agreement shall be interpreted and enforced in accordance with the laws of the Province of Newfoundland & Labrador.

15. Each of the parties acknowledges having received a copy of this Agreement and having been advised to seek independent legal advice prior to signing. Each of the parties further acknowledges that they have either obtained such independent legal advice, or have declined to seek such advice and have otherwise entered into this Agreement with the knowledge that it creates firm and binding legal relations and in full comprehension of the terms and consequences set out herein. Notwithstanding the source of this document, the doctrine of "Contra Preferentem" shall not apply and the Agreement shall be interpreted and construed equally among the parties.

16. Offer, acceptance or any notice or communication required under this Agreement shall be deemed delivered and received if given in writing by any of the following methods: 1) by personal delivery to the addresses of the parties noted herein, 2) by registered mail to the addresses of the parties noted herein (in which case receipt shall be deemed to be three days after mailing), 3) by fax to the fax numbers noted by the parties herein, if any, or 4) by delivery or fax to either party's lawyer, if any, as noted herein or as otherwise reasonably established during the course of this transaction.

Buyer's address: ____________________

Phone: __________ Fax: __________

Lawyer name: ____________________

address: ____________________

Phone: __________ Fax: __________

Seller's address: ____________________

Phone: __________ Fax: __________

Lawyer name: ____________________

address: ____________________

Phone: __________ Fax: __________

Date of Offer: ____________________

Initials of Buyer: ______ ______ Witness: ______

Initials of Seller: ______ ______ Witness: ______

17. This offer to purchase shall be open for acceptance and irrevocable by the Buyer until ____________ [time – a.m. or p.m.] on ______________________________ [date].

Signed at ____________________________ in the Province of Newfoundland & Labrador, at ____________ [time – a.m. or p.m.] on ________________________ [date].

Signed sealed and delivered in the presence of: Signed sealed and delivered by:

______________________ [Witness] ______________________ [Buyer] ● [Seal]

______________________ [Witness] ______________________ [Buyer] ● [Seal]

18. ***[choose one – delete others]***

(i) The Seller hereby accepts this offer on the terms and conditions set out herein.

Signed at ____________________________ in the Province of Newfoundland & Labrador, at ____________ [time – a.m. or p.m.] on ________________________ [date].

Signed sealed and delivered in the presence of: Signed sealed and delivered by:

______________________ [Witness] ______________________ [Seller] ● [Seal]

______________________ [Witness] ______________________ [Seller] ● [Seal]

(ii) The Seller confirms that this offer was presented and not accepted, and returns herewith the deposit.

Signed at ____________________________ in the Province of Newfoundland & Labrador, at ____________ [time – a.m. or p.m.] on ________________________ [date].

Signed sealed and delivered in the presence of: Signed sealed and delivered by:

______________________ [Witness] ______________________ [Seller] ● [Seal]

______________________ [Witness] ______________________ [Seller] ● [Seal]

(iii) The Seller hereby modifies this offer in the manner set out herein, which amendments are initialed, including any further amendments as follows (counteroffer):

____

____

____

____

This counteroffer shall be open for acceptance and irrevocable by the Seller until ______________ [time – a.m. or p.m.] on ________________________ [date]. after which time, if not accepted by the Buyer, this counter offer shall be null and void and the deposit shall be returned to the Buyer without interest, penalty or deduction.

Signed at ____________________________ in the Province of Newfoundland & Labrador, at ____________ [time – a.m. or p.m.] on ________________________ [date].

Signed sealed and delivered in the presence of: Signed sealed and delivered by:

______________________ [Witness] ______________________ [Seller] ● [Seal]

______________________ [Witness] ______________________ [Seller] ● [Seal]

19. The Buyer accepts the modifications contained in this counteroffer together with the remaining terms and conditions set out in this Agreement.

Signed at ____________________________ in the Province of Newfoundland & Labrador, at ____________ [time – a.m. or p.m.] on ________________________ [date].

Signed sealed and delivered in the presence of: Signed sealed and delivered by:

______________________ [Witness] ______________________ [Buyer] ● [Seal]

______________________ [Witness] ______________________ [Buyer] ● [Seal]

Yukon & Northwest Territories

Form of Agreement of Purchase & Sale (Blank - 8.5" x 11")
Form of Agreement of Purchase & Sale (Blank - 8.5" x 14" reduced)

This form of Agreement is customarily presented on legal size paper (8.5" x 14".) While paper size does not affect the validity of the document, using legal size will put it in a more recognized format. A reduced version of the legal size form has been provided. It can be increased on most industrial photocopiers using the "enlarge" function from standard to legal size (121% increase.) Legal size paper is available at most stationers.

CONTRACT OF PURCHASE AND SALE

For use in Yukon & Northwest Territories

THE BUYER, ______________________________ (the "Buyer"), of

BUYER'S ADDRESS: ______________________________ PHONE: (H) (W)

SUBMITS A DEPOSIT OF: ______________________________ DOLLARS | CASH ☐ CHEQUE ☐

LEGAL DESCRIPTION:	LOT(S)	BLOCK/QUAD/GROUP	AREA	PLAN

MUNICIPAL ADDRESS: (the "Property")

PURCHASE PRICE OF:	$

THE SELLER, ______________________________ (the "Seller"), of

SELLER'S ADDRESS: ______________________________ PHONE: (H) (W)

PAYABLE on the following terms:

The deposit to be credited towards the purchase price, and, unless otherwise provided herein, the balance payable on the Closing Date by cash, lawyer's trust cheque, or certified cheque.

SCHEDULES ATTACHED HERETO YES ☐ NO ☐ Specify: ______________________________

THE BUYER HEREBY OFFERS TO BUY THE PROPERTY FOR THE ABOVE STATED PRICE AND ON THE TERMS AND CONDITIONS SET OUT HEREIN.

1. ITEMS INCLUDED/EXCLUDED:
   a. The following items (chattels) are included: ______________________________ . These chattels shall remain with the property on closing, free of any encumbrances or liens, and shall be in the same good working order and condition as they were at the time this Agreement was signed.
   b. All items attached to the property (fixtures) are included in the purchase price and shall remain with the property on closing, save and except the following fixtures which are not included: ______________________________ .
   c. The following items are rented or leased, and the Buyer agrees to assume the rental contracts or leases in connection with same: ______________________________ .

2. CONDITION OF PROPERTY ON CLOSING: On closing the property and all dwellings, structures and fences, and all included fixtures and chattels as set out above, shall be in substantially the same condition they were in on the date they were viewed by the Buyer – that date being ______________________________ .

3. CLOSING DATE: This transaction shall be completed on ______________________________ (the "Closing Date").

4. POSSESSION DATE: The buyer shall be entitled to possession at ________ [am/pm] on ______________________ (the "Possession Date"), at which time such possession shall be vacant unless otherwise provided for herein. Vacant possession requires that all persons, animals, chattels not included, and fixtures excluded must be removed from the Property, unless otherwise agreed to. If there are any items improperly left on the Property, the Buyer shall be entitled to keep such items, or may insist upon the removal of the items at the Seller's expense.

5. ADJUSTMENTS: The balance due on closing shall be subject to the usual adjustments consistent with the jurisdiction in which the Property is situate. Without limiting the generality of this statement, the following items shall be adjusted as of the Closing Date, unless expressly provided for elsewhere herein, the Closing Date itself to be apportioned to the Buyer: taxes, utilities, fuel, licenses, insurance, rents, deposits and chattel leases (if any). The adjustment date shall be the Closing Date, unless expressly set out otherwise in this Agreement.

6. TITLE: The property shall be conveyed free and clear of any mortgages, liens or encumbrances, save and except any reservations or exceptions contained in the original Crown Grant, or any easements in favor of utility or public authorities , and except as specifically allowed for elsewhere in this Agreement.

7. RISK / INSURANCE: The property and all fixtures and chattels contemplated under this Agreement shall remain at the risk of the Seller until 12:01 a.m. on the Closing Date. All related insurance policies held by the Seller, if any, as well as any proceeds paid under such policies, shall be held in trust for the benefit of the parties in relation to their respective interests under this Agreement. In the event of damage and subsequent payment under such policies, the Buyer shall have the option of terminating this Agreement or receiving the said payment and closing the transaction as scheduled with all other terms and conditions remaining the same. In the event that the Agreement is terminated pursuant to this section, the deposit shall be returned to the Buyer without interest, penalty or deduction. No insurance policies shall be transferred on closing unless otherwise provided herein.

8. **CONDITIONS:** *[stroke out any that do not apply]* The following conditions are for the benefit of the Buyer, and may be waived by the Buyer at the Buyer's sole discretion. The Seller shall not commit or omit any action that might reasonably prevent fulfillment of a condition. Unless expressly stated otherwise, the Buyer must notify the Seller in writing on or before the date specified that the condition cannot be satisfied. In the event that such notice is not given on or before the date specified, the condition shall be deemed fulfilled or waived and this Agreement shall, subject to any further outstanding conditions, be deemed to be firm and binding. In the event that such notice of non-satisfaction is given on or before the specified date, then the Agreement shall be considered null and void, and in such event the deposit shall be returned to the Buyer without interest, penalty or deduction.

a) Financing – Notwithstanding the foregoing, notice that at least one of the following financing conditions have been satisfied or waived must be given to the Seller, in writing, on or before ______________________________ failing which the agreement shall be null and void, and the deposit shall be returned to the Buyer without interest, penalty or deduction.
   (i) Buyer obtaining written approval to assume the existing mortgage, which is elsewhere described in full in this Agreement, or
   (ii) Buyer obtaining written approval of financing for the approx. amount of $__________, at an interest rate of not more than ____ %.

b) Legal Status - Buyer confirming on or before ______________________________________ that the property complies with all local, provincial and municipal building, zoning fire department, and other relevant local authority requirements, that permits have been obtained for all structures or improvements requiring permits, or that the status is otherwise legal non-conforming

c) Other: ____
____
____
____
____

9. **NOTICE:** Offer, acceptance or any notice or communication required under this Agreement shall be deemed delivered and received if given in writing by any of the following methods:

a. by personal delivery to the addresses of the parties noted herein,
b. by registered mail to the addresses of the parties noted herein (in which case receipt shall be deemed to be three days after mailing),
c. by fax to the fax numbers noted by the parties herein, if any (Buyer's fax ________________ / Seller's fax ________________), or
d. by delivery or fax to either lawyer, if any, as noted herein or as otherwise reasonably established throughout the course of this transaction.

10. **RESIDENCY:** On closing the Seller shall furnish a certificate confirming that the Seller is not a "non-resident" within the meaning of the Income Tax Act, failing which the Buyer shall be entitled to hold-back funds in accordance with prudent legal practice sufficient to satisfy the Buyer's obligations under the Act.

11. **COSTS:** Each party shall bear their own costs. Specifically, and without limiting the foregoing, all costs relating to the conveyance and any new mortgage(s) or mortgage assumption shall be at the expense of the Buyer, and all costs related to the clearing of title shall be at the expense of the Seller.

12. **GST:** The Buyer and Seller agree that this transaction is not subject to Federal Goods and Services Tax [GST], and the Seller shall furnish a certificate confirming same on closing.

13. **TENDER:** Any tender of documents, keys or money may be effected by personal delivery upon the Buyer or Seller, as the case may be, or their lawyers, if any, on or before the closing date. The parties agree to instruct their lawyers to allow for reasonable undertakings as are traditionally necessary between lawyers to close successfully. Failing any agreement to the contrary, tender may also be effected at the local Land Titles Office on or before _________ [am or pm] on the Closing Date.

14. **ENFORCABILITY, ENTIRETY AND INTERPRETATION OF AGREEMENT:** Upon acceptance this Agreement shall constitute a binding agreement of purchase and sale. In the event that the Buyer defaults in the completion of this Agreement, the Buyer will forfeit the above deposit in addition to any other claims the Seller may have against the Buyer. This document, together with all listed Schedules, constitutes the entire Agreement between the parties and there shall be no collateral agreements, representations or warranties. This Agreement may only be amended or extended by mutual, written agreement between the parties, or between their lawyers, if any. Time shall be of the essence throughout this Agreement, including any extensions. This Agreement shall pass to the benefit of and be binding upon each of the parties' heirs, executors, administrators, successors and assigns. In the event of a discrepancy between the Schedules or added clauses in this Agreement and the pre-formatted form of Agreement, the Schedules or added clauses shall prevail to the extent of the discrepancy. Any references to gender or number of parties shall be read with the intended context applied. In the event that any specific provisions of this Agreement are declared illegal, invalid or unenforceable by a court of competent jurisdiction, then the offending provision(s) may be severed and shall not impair the validity or enforceability of the balance of the Agreement. This Agreement shall be interpreted and enforced in accordance with the laws of the jurisdiction in which the property is situate.

15. **LEGAL REPRESENTATION:** Each of the parties acknowledges having received a copy of this Agreement and having been advised to seek independent legal advice prior to signing. Each of the parties further acknowledges that they have either obtained such independent legal advice, or have declined to seek such advice and have otherwise entered into this Agreement with the knowledge that it creates firm and binding legal relations and in full comprehension of the terms and consequences set out herein. Notwithstanding the source of this document, the doctrine of "Contra Preferentem" shall not apply and the Agreement shall be interpreted and construed equally among the parties.

The Buyer's lawyer is:
Name:
Address:
Phone:
Fax:

The Seller's solicitor, until further notification, is:
Name:
Address:
Phone:
Fax:

16. **OFFER:** This offer, or counter-offer, shall be open for acceptance and irrevocable until ________ [am or pm] on ____________________________.
and upon acceptance, and notification of same to the other party, there shall be a binding agreement of purchase and sale.

Dated: ______________________________.

X ______________________ [Witness]	X ______________________ [Buyer]	[Seal]	______________________ [Print Name]
X ______________________ [Witness]	X ______________________ [Buyer]	[Seal]	______________________ [Print Name]

17. **ACCEPTANCE:** The Seller accepts this offer on the terms and conditions set out herein.

Dated: ______________________________.

X ______________________ [Witness]	X ______________________ [Seller]	[Seal]	______________________ [Print Name]
X ______________________ [Witness]	X ______________________ [Seller]	[Seal]	______________________ [Print Name]

CONTRACT OF PURCHASE AND SALE

For use in Yukon & Northwest Territories

THE BUYER, ______________________________ (the "Buyer"), of

BUYER'S ADDRESS: ______________________________ PHONE: (H) (W)

SUBMITS A DEPOSIT OF: ______________________________ DOLLARS | CASH ☐ | CHEQUE ☐

LEGAL DESCRIPTION:	LOT(S)	BLOCK/QUAD/GROUP	AREA	PLAN

MUNICIPAL ADDRESS: (the "Property")

PURCHASE PRICE OF: $

THE SELLER, ______________________________ (the "Seller"), of

SELLER'S ADDRESS: ______________________________ PHONE: (H) (W)

PAYABLE on the following terms:

The deposit to be credited towards the purchase price, and, unless otherwise provided herein, the balance payable on the Closing Date by cash, lawyer's trust cheque, or certified cheque.

SCHEDULES ATTACHED HERETO YES ☐ NO ☐ Specify: ______________________________

THE BUYER HEREBY OFFERS TO BUY THE PROPERTY FOR THE ABOVE STATED PRICE AND ON THE TERMS AND CONDITIONS SET OUT HEREIN.

1. **ITEMS INCLUDED/EXCLUDED:**
   a. The following items (chattels) are included: ______________________________. These chattels shall remain with the property on closing, free of any encumbrances or liens, and shall be in the same good working order and condition as they were at the time this Agreement was signed.
   b. All items attached to the property (fixtures) are included in the purchase price and shall remain with the property on closing, save and except the following fixtures which are not included: ______________________________.
   c. The following items are rented or leased, and the Buyer agrees to assume the rental contracts or leases in connection with same: ______________________________.

2. **CONDITION OF PROPERTY ON CLOSING:** On closing the property and all dwellings, structures and fences, and all included fixtures and chattels as set out above, shall be in substantially the same condition they were in on the date they were viewed by the Buyer – that date being ______________________________.

3. **CLOSING DATE:** This transaction shall be completed on ______________________________ (the "Closing Date").

4. **POSSESSION DATE:** The buyer shall be entitled to possession at ________ [am/pm] on ______________________ (the "Possession Date"), at which time such possession shall be vacant unless otherwise provided for herein. Vacant possession requires that all persons, animals, chattels not included, and fixtures excluded must be removed from the Property, unless otherwise agreed to. If there are any items improperly left on the Property, the Buyer shall be entitled to keep such items, or may insist upon the removal of the items at the Seller's expense.

5. **ADJUSTMENTS:** The balance due on closing shall be subject to the usual adjustments consistent with the jurisdiction in which the Property is situate. Without limiting the generality of this statement, the following items shall be adjusted as of the Closing Date, unless expressly provided for elsewhere herein, the Closing Date itself to be apportioned to the Buyer: taxes, utilities, fuel, licenses, insurance, rents, deposits and chattel leases (if any). The adjustment date shall be the Closing Date, unless expressly set out otherwise in this Agreement.

6. **TITLE:** The property shall be conveyed free and clear of any mortgages, liens or encumbrances, save and except any reservations or exceptions contained in the original Crown Grant, or any easements in favor of utility or public authorities , and except as specifically allowed for elsewhere in this Agreement.

7. **RISK / INSURANCE:** The property and all fixtures and chattels contemplated under this Agreement shall remain at the risk of the Seller until 12:01 a.m. on the Closing Date. All related insurance policies held by the Seller, if any, as well as any proceeds paid under such policies, shall be held in trust for the benefit of the parties in relation to their respective interests under this Agreement. In the event of damage and subsequent payment under such policies, the Buyer shall have the option of terminating this Agreement or receiving the said payment and closing the transaction as scheduled with all other terms and conditions remaining the same. In the event that the Agreement is terminated pursuant to this section, the deposit shall be returned to the Buyer without interest, penalty or deduction. No insurance policies shall be transferred on closing unless otherwise provided herein.

8. **CONDITIONS:** ***[stroke out any that do not apply]*** The following conditions are for the benefit of the Buyer, and may be waived by the Buyer at the Buyer's sole discretion. The Seller shall not commit or omit any action that might reasonably prevent fulfillment of a condition. Unless expressly stated otherwise, the Buyer must notify the Seller in writing on or before the date specified that the condition cannot be satisfied. In the event that such notice is not given on or before the date specified, the condition shall be deemed fulfilled or waived and this Agreement shall, subject to any further outstanding conditions, be deemed to be firm and binding. In the event that such notice of non-satisfaction is given on or before the specified date, then the Agreement shall be considered null and void, and in such event the deposit shall be returned to the Buyer without interest, penalty or deduction.
   a) Financing – Notwithstanding the foregoing, notice that at least one of the following financing conditions have been satisfied or waived must be given to the Seller, in writing, on or before ______________________ failing which the agreement shall be null and void, and the deposit shall be returned to the Buyer without interest, penalty or deduction.
      (i) Buyer obtaining written approval to assume the existing mortgage, which is elsewhere described in full in this Agreement, or
      (ii) Buyer obtaining written approval of financing for the approx. amount of $____________, at an interest rate of not more than ____ %.
   b) Legal Status - Buyer confirming on or before ______________________ that the property complies with all local, provincial and municipal building, zoning fire department, and other relevant local authority requirements, that permits have been obtained for all structures or improvements requiring permits, or that the status is otherwise legal non-conforming

c) Other: ____
____
____
____
____

9. **NOTICE:** Offer, acceptance or any notice or communication required under this Agreement shall be deemed delivered and received if given in writing by any of the following methods:
   a. by personal delivery to the addresses of the parties noted herein,
   b. by registered mail to the addresses of the parties noted herein (in which case receipt shall be deemed to be three days after mailing),
   c. by fax to the fax numbers noted by the parties herein, if any (Buyer's fax __________________ / Seller's fax __________________), or
   d. by delivery or fax to either lawyer, if any, as noted herein or as otherwise reasonably established throughout the course of this transaction.

10. **RESIDENCY:** On closing the Seller shall furnish a certificate confirming that the Seller is not a "non-resident" within the meaning of the Income Tax Act, failing which the Buyer shall be entitled to hold-back funds in accordance with prudent legal practice sufficient to satisfy the Buyer's obligations under the Act.

11. **COSTS:** Each party shall bear their own costs. Specifically, and without limiting the foregoing, all costs relating to the conveyance and any new mortgage(s) or mortgage assumption shall be at the expense of the Buyer, and all costs related to the clearing of title shall be at the expense of the Seller.

12. **GST:** The Buyer and Seller agree that this transaction is not subject to Federal Goods and Services Tax [GST], and the Seller shall furnish a certificate confirming same on closing.

13. **TENDER:** Any tender of documents, keys or money may be effected by personal delivery upon the Buyer or Seller, as the case may be, or their lawyers, if any, on or before the closing date. The parties agree to instruct their lawyers to allow for reasonable undertakings as are traditionally necessary between lawyers to close successfully. Failing any agreement to the contrary, tender may also be effected at the local Land Titles Office on or before _________ [am or pm] on the Closing Date.

14. **ENFORCABILITY, ENTIRETY AND INTERPRETATION OF AGREEMENT:** Upon acceptance this Agreement shall constitute a binding agreement of purchase and sale. In the event that the Buyer defaults in the completion of this Agreement, the Buyer will forfeit the above deposit in addition to any other claims the Seller may have against the Buyer. This document, together with all listed Schedules, constitutes the entire Agreement between the parties and there shall be no collateral agreements, representations or warranties. This Agreement may only be amended or extended by mutual, written agreement between the parties, or between their lawyers, if any. Time shall be of the essence throughout this Agreement, including any extensions. This Agreement shall pass to the benefit of and be binding upon each of the parties' heirs, executors, administrators, successors and assigns. In the event of a discrepancy between the Schedules or added clauses in this Agreement and the pre-formatted form of Agreement, the Schedules or added clauses shall prevail to the extent of the discrepancy. Any references to gender or number of parties shall be read with the intended context applied. In the event that any specific provisions of this Agreement are declared illegal, invalid or unenforceable by a court of competent jurisdiction, then the offending provision(s) may be severed and shall not impair the validity or enforceability of the balance of the Agreement. This Agreement shall be interpreted and enforced in accordance with the laws of the jurisdiction in which the property is situate.

15. **LEGAL REPRESENTATION:** Each of the parties acknowledges having received a copy of this Agreement and having been advised to seek independent legal advice prior to signing. Each of the parties further acknowledges that they have either obtained such independent legal advice, or have declined to seek such advice and have otherwise entered into this Agreement with the knowledge that it creates firm and binding legal relations and in full comprehension of the terms and consequences set out herein. Notwithstanding the source of this document, the doctrine of "Contra Preferentem" shall not apply and the Agreement shall be interpreted and construed equally among the parties.

The Buyer's lawyer is:	The Seller's solicitor, until further notification, is:
Name:	Name:
Address:	Address:
Phone:	Phone:
Fax:	Fax:

16. **OFFER:** This offer, or counter-offer, shall be open for acceptance and irrevocable until _______ [am or pm] on __________________________. and upon acceptance, and notification of same to the other party, there shall be a binding agreement of purchase and sale.

Dated: ________________________.

X ____________________ [Witness]	X ____________________ [Buyer]	[Seal]	____________ [Print Name]
X ____________________ [Witness]	X ____________________ [Buyer]	[Seal]	____________ [Print Name]

17. **ACCEPTANCE:** The Seller accepts this offer on the terms and conditions set out herein.

Dated: ________________________.

X ____________________ [Witness]	X ____________________ [Seller]	[Seal]	____________ [Print Name]
X ____________________ [Witness]	X ____________________ [Seller]	[Seal]	____________ [Print Name]

Chapter 21

Additional Forms

Telephone Profile

Date Called: ____________________

Name: ____

Telephone #: Day: ______________________________ Evening: ____________________

Where do you live now? ____

How did you hear about our home?

☐ Sign ☐ Ad ☐ Brochure ☐ Friend ☐ Other

How long have you been looking for a house? ________________________________

When would you like to move? ____

Do you own a home? ☐ Yes ☐ No

Is it currently for sale? ☐ Yes ☐ No

Are you coming by car? ☐ Yes ☐ No

Colour and make of car? ____

Will you coming alone? ☐ Yes ☐ No

If no, who will be with you? ____

Date of Appointment: ________________________________ Time: ____________________

Comments/Notes: ____

____

____

____

____

____

____

____

Visitor Comment Form

As you look through our home, please answer a few questions and make notes about any further information you need. Thank you

Name: ______________________________

Address: ______________________________

Telephone #______________________________

What features do you particularly like about our house?

____

____

____

What could be improved?

____

____

____

Would this home suit your needs? ☐ Yes ☐ No

If no, please explain: ______________________________

Is this house good value for the price? ☐ Yes ☐ No

If no, how do you think it should be priced? $ __________

Will you come back for a second visit? ☐ Yes ☐ No

Notes and Questions

____

____

____

____

____

____

4SBO Guest Register

Welcome to our home. Please fill out the following information in case we need to reach you. Thank you.

Name: ____________________

Address: ____________________

Telephone: ____________________

Car Make & Licence: ____________________

How did you hear about our home? Please check all that apply:

- ☐ Lawn sign
- ☐ Saw brochure
- ☐ Ad in paper
- ☐ A friend told us
- ☐ Internet
- ☐ Other (Specify) ____________

Signature: ____________________ Date: ____________

✂- -

4SBO Guest Register

Welcome to our home. Please fill out the following information in case we need to reach you. Thank you.

Name: ____________________

Address: ____________________

Telephone: ____________________

Car Make & Licence: ____________________

How did you hear about our home? Please check all that apply:

- ☐ Lawn sign
- ☐ Ad in paper
- ☐ Saw brochure
- ☐ A friend told us
- ☐ Internet
- ☐ Other (Specify) ____________

Signature: ____________________ Date: ____________

Score Sheet For Picking The Best Realtor

Agent's Name	Education	Experience	Creativity	Personality	Appearance	Integrity	Portfolio	Total Score

4SBO Membership

Thank you for purchasing the 4SBO kit. Your purchase has also made you eligible to become a private member of the 4SBO Club which entitles you to the following free benefits:

Free Website listing on canada.com (search word: 4sbo)

You can now sell your home, private business or vacation property on the web site. Write your ad (see sample below), using up to 200 words. You also have the option to increase the impact of your ad with four colour pictures for a nominal charge. Your ad will run until your home is sold.

REGAL ESTATES. $285,000 buys you a magnificent home that reflects your unique taste and lifestyle. This 5,600 sq. ft. home is nestled midst the trees on a ravine in this most exclusive area of Unionville, Ont. Floor-to-ceiling windows in the kitchen, living room, dining room and master suite overlook three acres of mature trees, a private pond, waterfall and rustic bridge Five bedrooms, four bathrooms, billiards room so large the walls never interfere with a good shot, large library/den. Huge atrium with fishpond creates impressive entrance. Two fireplaces, main floor laundry room, renovated kitchen If you are looking for an exceptional home, call and book an appointment to view this remarkable property. Private sale by owner. No agents please. 416-416-4166.

Extra 4SBO forms are available on the site including:

- Telephone Profile forms
- Visitor Comments forms
- Guest Register (for Open House)
- Pick the Best Realtor Score Sheets
- Purchase Agreement forms for each Province
- Free bulletin board and chat room to trade money making ideas and valuable solutions to your home selling challenges

PLUS Money saving offers from:

- Mortgage companies
- Appraisal firms
- Home Inspectors
- Movers
- Hardware Retailers
- Appliance Retailers
- PLUS a free Bimonthly Canadian Real Estate Update
- And more...

HOW TO TAKE ADVANTAGE OF YOUR FREE MEMBERSHIP

To register online,

- simply go to canada.com
- type in the searchword ("4sbomember")

✂---

To register by mail, fill out the form below and send it to: 4SBO C/O canada.com 333 King Street East, Toronto, Ontario, M5A 4R7

Name.____

Street____

City____________________Prov.__________Postal Code_________________

Tel: Include Area Code (   ) ______________

I Would like to receive addition information on a regular basis from 4sbo Inc. on topics related to selling or purchasing a home in Canada.
Yes_______ No_______

Attach to a separate sheet on which you have typed your ad for the property for sale(200 words or less). Remember to include the sale price.

(also include up to four photos if you would like to be contacted to add the photo option to your free listing.

Congratulations, you are now a private member of the 4SBO Club. Welcome!